Stalingrad

'This is the finest history of its type published to date.' David Glantz

'This book is a milestone; other accounts, such as Beevor's, describe well how people fought at Stalingrad, but Jones' treatment goes much deeper in assessing why they did, and incidentally corrects several errors found in the earlier works.' Geoffrey Jukes

'. . . full of insights; it will undoubtedly change the way we think about Stalingrad.' Gary Sheffield

'Of all the books written about Stalingrad, there have not been many like this one . . . Michael Jones probes the minds of men at the edge of the abyss, digging into the psychological factors that allowed them to withstand hopeless odds and untold horrors, and still emerge victorious.' *Stone & Stone*

'. . . a landmark account of the battle that gets under the skin of . . . the ordinary Soviet soldier. It bares the soul of the the fighting men whose victory this was and takes us beneath the radar of Soviet propaganda to present the "frontoviks" reality . . . Michael Jones has produced a book from which I not only learnt but which reawoke that emotional connection and admiration for the incredible resilience of the Red Army soldier.' *East-West Review*

'Michael K. Jones's outstanding new book uses memoirs, eyewitness accounts, and recently opened Soviet archival material to uncover how the soldiers of Gen. Vasily Chuikov's Sixty-second Army overcame incredible odds to save Stalin's namesake city from German invaders. . .The result is compelling, drawing us into a vivid, illuminating account of how much of a "near run thing" the legendary Red Army victory actually was.' *World War II*

'Although the epic quality of the battle has attracted many historians, Jones' contribution is special for two reasons. First, he seems to have been able to dig deeper into the Soviet archives than previous authors, and he got some extraordinary testimony from survivors. Second, he addresses the core question of just what it was that motivated these men to keep on fighting, given the low probability of survival and the terrible conditions. The order to hold every position until death was well known, but Jones demolishes the notion that the soldiers fought solely under duress . . . compelling and moving.' *Foreign Affairs*

'. . . an outstanding new book, important for two reasons: it provides a previously too-often ignored Soviet point of view of the battle; and the compelling eyewitness testimonies of the Red Army veterans who fought it cuts through much of the Communist-era mythmaking about how the battle actually unfolded . . . compelling reading.' *Armchair General*

'A compelling military history and analysis that lives up to its title.' *The Wisconsin Book Watch*

Stalingrad

How the Red Army Triumphed

Michael K Jones

Foreword by
David M Glantz

Pen & Sword
MILITARY

First published in Great Britain in 2007
and reprinted in this format in 2010, 2011, 2013, 2014 and 2016 by
PEN & SWORD MILITARY
An imprint of
Pen & Sword Books Ltd
47 Church Street
Barnsley, South Yorkshire
S70 2AS

Copyright © Michael K Jones, 2007, 2010, 2011, 2013, 2014, 2016

ISBN 978 1 84884 201 4

The right of Michael K Jones to be identified as
Author of this work has been asserted by him in accordance
with the Copyright, Designs and Patents Act 1988.

A CIP catalogue record for this book is
available from the British Library

Printed and bound in England
By CPI Group (UK) Ltd, Croydon, CR0 4YY

Pen & Sword Books Ltd incorporates the Imprints of Aviation, Atlas,
Family History, Fiction, Maritime, Military, Discovery, Politics, History,
Archaeology, Select, Wharncliffe Local History, Wharncliffe True Crime,
Military Classics, Wharncliffe Transport, Leo Cooper, The Praetorian Press,
Remember When, Seaforth Publishing and Frontline Publishing.

For a complete list of Pen & Sword titles please contact
PEN & SWORD BOOKS LIMITED
47 Church Street, Barnsley, South Yorkshire, S70 2AS, England
E-mail: enquiries@pen-and-sword.co.uk
Website: www.pen-and-sword.co.uk

The earth was belching out red-hot lava
A volcano, pouring fire and metal,
Enveloping the burning city with ash
As if it was poison.

And for those who clawed themselves out from this hell
And got used to the glow of whiteness,
The black ash of Stalingrad blows into their old men's dreams.

Alexander Rytov

Contents

Preface

On 27 September 1942 a recent arrival at Stalingrad, a Russian soldier named Josef Furman, wrote to his family in Irkutsk in Siberia: 'Today is my second day on the frontline, where the greatest battle in human history is taking place.' Every soldier felt a heady mixture of exhilaration and terror on entering this ghastly battlefield. But Furman had caught a real truth about the mighty clash of arms between Germany and the Soviet Union which became a defining moment of the Second World War. The battle of Stalingrad will always fascinate us.

This book concentrates on the Russian defenders of the city: the embattled 62nd Army. It attempts to recreate the spirit of a truly remarkable band of fighters. The life expectancy of one of these soldiers was less than two days. 'Not a second passes without the sound of artillery salvoes, the shriek of falling shells, the rattle of machine gun fire', Furman continued. 'Everywhere there are corpses. I do not know what will happen in the next hour.' Yet those who survived this terrible initiation developed an extraordinary will to survive. Red Army veterans believe it was this spirit – forged in the most horrifying conditions – which enabled them to withstand an annihilating enemy offensive.

Because Stalingrad was a catastrophic German defeat the story of this famous battle has usually been told in terms of the strategic blunders of Hitler and his High Command. But Stalin and his commanders also made serious mistakes. They had never intended to leave Stalingrad's defenders cut off in the city for so long. But in September 1942 poor military planning led to the failure of one Soviet relief effort after another, forcing the 62nd Army to fight the overwhelming might of the Germans entirely on its own.

How it managed to do so still mystifies surviving Russian veterans of the battle. On 11 November 1942, when the Germans launched their last major assault on Stalingrad, the 62nd Army's war diary recorded that the strength of some of its key divisions had shrunk to only a few hundred men. The battered remnants clung to a narrow strip of land along the Volga, and floating river ice impeded the arrival of desperately needed reinforcements. 'The army is in an exceptionally difficult situation', the war diary noted grimly. 'Only extraordinary heroism and steadfastness in combat have allowed us to hold our present positions and continue to resist the considerably superior forces of the enemy.'

I want to present the defenders' view of their incredible triumph. It is a point of view that has begun to emerge only recently, in the wake of the collapse of the Soviet communist state. Anatoly Kozlov, head of the Volgograd veterans' association, told me of a remarkable, spontaneous decision taken by these old fighters at a reunion held on the fiftieth anniversary of the battle: 'We decided to tell the truth about Stalingrad, giving a simple, direct account of the fighting, and avoiding all communist rhetoric and clichés.' Anatoly has been an invaluable source of guidance.

For the last five years I have led battle tours of Stalingrad, working closely with Russian veterans of the fighting. I am enormously grateful to Alan Rooney, of Midas and Holts Battlefield Tours, and Oleg Alexandrov, of our associated Russian travel company, who helped me create this tour. It was Oleg who set up our regular meeting with the Moscow Council of War Veterans – and their kindness and hospitality kindled my interest in the battle of Stalingrad. Some scattered landmarks of the fighting exist in the present city – renamed Volgograd in the Khrushchev era – but it is the testimonies of veterans which make these ruins come alive again. I have conducted many interviews with survivors of the 62nd Army in Moscow and Volgograd. For my meetings in Moscow I am particularly grateful to Maria Faustova, secretary of the 62nd Army veterans' council; for those in Volgograd, to Svetlana Orgasteva, deputy director of the Volgograd Defence Museum.

I am a battle psychologist – interested in the power of morale, motivation and inspirational leadership – and for this reason it has been vital to get grips with the leadership given to the defenders of Stalingrad. I have talked to many veterans about this but the insights shared by Anatoly Grigorevich Mereshko form the core of my account. Colonel-General Anatoly Mereshko rose after the war to become Deputy Commander of the Warsaw Pact. He has given weeks of his time to this project and travelled with me round Stalingrad's battle sites. Without his unstinting support and co-operation this book would never have happened.

Mereshko was on the 62nd Army staff, an 'officer for special tasks' reporting directly to Vasily Chuikov, the army commander. His forthright testimony has been enhanced by the considerable help of Alexander Chuikov, who shared with me his father's personal reminiscences of the battle and gave me access to his private papers and photographs, and Natalia Rodimtseva, who did the same for her father, Alexander Rodimtsev, commander of the 13th Guards Division. In September 1942 Chuikov brought Rodimstev onto the Army

Council and together they created a different style of leadership and the fighting tactics that allowed them to defy the German onslaught.

Chuikov and Rodimtsev led from the front, and by doing this began to create a new mood of self-belief amongst the Russian defenders. Rodimtsev's division had been badly mauled during the German advance into the Donbas in July 1942, and when it arrived in Stalingrad it had only a leavening of veterans: the majority of its men were recruits and conscripts, despatched to the burning city after only a few weeks training. Similarly Batyuk's 284th Division, which joined the Stalingrad battle in late September, had suffered serious casualties that summer in the fighting north-west of Voronezh and had been hurriedly recreated in the Ural Military District in August 1942. As David Glantz has emphasized to me, 'it is remarkable that both divisions performed as well as they did in the city fighting'.

Batyuk, like Rodimtsev, shared the dangers faced by his troops – and through this won their respect and unswerving loyalty. Military regulations stipulated that the commander should be a certain distance behind the frontline. But in the maelstrom of Stalingrad these regulations no longer held the same value. Batyuk wrote to his wife in matter-of-fact fashion on 11 October 1942: 'I was lucky today. A shell landed a metre in front of my feet, but did not explode. This is the third time this has happened.'

Stalingrad historian Jason Mark has worked closely with me, encouraging this project forward and providing a steady stream of advice. Jason's own work, *Island of Fire*, came out as this book was going to press. There is a passage in it which, for me, captures the essence of the Russian defence. Colonel Ivan Lyudnikov, the commander of the 138th Division, was visiting a regimental HQ. The regimental commander, Major Gunyaga, was unhappy about being so close to the Germans. 'I need normal conditions to work effectively – and I don't have them', he complained. 'I know', Lyudnikov commiserated. 'Here nothing is normal in terms of the usual practice of war. But we broke the rules ourselves. We forced the enemy to fight in a way he didn't want to.' Then Lyudnikov added: 'We are cut off from the rest of our people and have to be our own judges…The soldier sees your command post near his frontline trench. He knows how hard it is for you but you don't leave. And because you – the regimental commander – trust the ordinary soldier in this fashion, he won't give up. There's nothing dearer in the world to him than this trust.' The truth of this was proved time and again at Stalingrad

David Glantz has kindly read the text and contributed the foreword. David is compiling a detailed, day-by-day account of the first, 'defensive' phase of the battle. Geoffrey Roberts has also read the completed manuscript and Geoffrey Jukes provided a number of useful suggestions. Sergei Petrunin has located many of the combat records of the 62nd Army for me, and this important new material has been used to support the testimony of the veterans. Evgeny Kulichenko has shown me round the nooks and crannies of Stalingrad's battle sites and Russ Schulke has allowed me to quote from Furman's letter (in his own private collection) and given advice on topographical features of the battlefield. All have enhanced this work.

I have followed conventional practice in adopting the name 'Russia' in the book, except on occasions when it makes more sense to use 'Soviet'. But it is important to remember that the army at Stalingrad was drawn from all the Soviet republics. I have given Russian works under their English translation, and Peter Mezhiritsky has kindly advised me on the best form of spelling of some of the surnames. Jason Mark has sent me extracts from crucial new Russian scholarship on Stalingrad, in particular V. Beshanov's *The Year of 1942*, which contains (pp. 558–9) Chuikov's requests to evacuate the Army HQ to the eastern bank of the Volga at the crisis point of the battle on 14-15 October.

Laurence Rees and his producer Martina Balazova have encouraged my many interviews with veterans, and generously allowed me access to their own material, gathered for Laurence's BBC series *War of the Century*. My thanks go to Irina Cheremushnikova, who acted as my translator and interpreter in Volgograd, and Lena Yakovleva, who did the same for me in Moscow. I have worked closely with Lena on three separate trips to Russia, and witnessed her skill in bringing out the real stories that underlie the inevitable rhetoric present in veterans' conversations. The plight of the defenders was far worse than standard histories of the battle were able to acknowledge. On two critical days at Stalingrad, 14 September and 14 October 1942, the Red Army stood on the very brink of catastrophe. But once we grasp the truly desperate situation, we can better understand the heroism of these soldiers. I have sought to pay tribute to their astonishing courage.

Foreword

The name Stalingrad – Stalin's namesake city on the Volga River – evokes vivid images in the minds of Russians and Westerners alike. It was the most brutal clash of arms in the most terrible of twentieth-century wars. Russians, as well as many of the former Soviet Union's other ethnic minorities, saw the Red Army's victory at Stalingrad as a catharsis which saved Stalin's city and salvaged a nation's shattered pride. The horror, deprivation and pain of the disastrous first eighteen months of war was at last ameliorated and the army set on a course towards ultimate victory over Germany. Westerners, who tend nowadays to know little of the Soviet-German War, acknowledge, albeit often grudgingly, the contributions the Red Army's triumph made to the Allied victory over Hitler. Stalingrad was a pivotal moment in that titanic struggle.

Over the last sixty years a formidable array of Soviet, German, and other Western historians – together with many senior military commanders who fought at Stalingrad – have written hundreds of books, memoirs, and articles about the battle: a clear indication of the immensity and complexity of the topic. Soviet writers, understandably proud of the Red Army's achievements, led this effort. The best of these books include the magisterial history, *Stalingradskaia bitva* (The battle for Stalingrad), written in 1960 by A M Samsonov, the dean of Soviet military historians; the gripping and often surprisingly candid memoirs, *Nachalo puti* (The beginning of the road), *Stalingrad*, and *Stalingradskii rubezh* [The Stalingrad line] written in 1959, 1961, and 1979, respectively, by Generals V I Chuikov, N I Krylov, and A I Yeremenko, the commander and chief of staff of the Red Army's 62nd Army and the commander of the Stalingrad Front during the battle. In 1965 came the skillfully articulated military study of the battle, *Velikaia Bitva na Volge* (The great victory on the Volga), from General K K Rokossovsky, who served as commander of the Don Front during the most decisive stages of the struggle.[1]

As impressive as these books are, particularly in regard to the Red Army's performance and accomplishments, these Soviet authors present a propagandist version of the battle. It is vital for us, as Westerners, to understand that unless these accounts conformed to communist requirements, they would not have been published at all and their writers knew this. For political and ideological reasons, they frequently exaggerate the size and strength of opposing German forces to inflate the Red Army's feat of arms. To give a concrete example, all of these books include the 76th and 44th Infantry Divisions in the order of battle of German attack on Stalingrad – in truth, neither force took part in the city fighting. Soviet authors routinely emphasize the combat performance of some Red Army divisions at Stalingrad because they were 'Great Russian' in origin, while lessening the accomplishments of other 'non-Russian' divisions. They identify Rodimtsev's 13th Guards Rifle Division as an 'elite' formation, while playing down the role of Batyuk's 284th Rifle Division, which was raised in the Sumy region of the Ukraine. In fact, both divisions had lost many of their soldiers in the fighting during mid- and late July 1942 and, when they reached Stalingrad in early September, were largely manned by poorly equipped reservists and raw conscripts. Since the English translation of Chuikov's book is the primary source for most Western histories of the battle, these errors have tended to persist.

Although death or captivity denied many senior Wehrmacht commanders the opportunity to compile their own memoirs, other authors filled the void by presenting the German perspective on the fighting. The best of these books included the brief but poignant *Stalingrad*, written by the journalist Heinz Schröter in 1958; the superb study in command, *Paulus and Stalingrad*, written by the prominent German military historian Walter Goerlitz in 1963; and a soldiers' view of the battle, *Stalingrad: The Defeat of the German 6th Army*, written by Paul Carell in 1993, with the assistance of several German war veterans serving as his 'ghost-writer'. Until very recently, however, since the combat records of many German units that fought at Stalingrad were either destroyed in the war or captured by the Red Army, these accounts lacked a sound archival base.

Western historians began introducing the battle of Stalingrad to their audiences in the early 1970s, synthesizing materials from these and other Soviet and German sources. Leading the way were the seminal works, *Enemy at the Gates*, written by William Craig in 1973, and *The Road to Stalingrad*, an exhaustive history of the first half of the war by John Erickson in 1975. Following in succession were survey histories of the battle, *Stalingrad*, compiled by V E Tarrant in 1992, *Stalingrad 1942-1943: The Infernal Cauldron* by Stephen Walsh in 2000, and *Victory at Stalingrad* by Geoffrey Roberts in 2002, and the gripping, best-selling popular social history of the battle, *Stalingrad: The Fateful Siege, 1942-1943*, written by Antony Beevor in 1998. As successful as these books have been, however, they suffer from the same problems that marred the work of their predecessors, in particular, a lack of fresh military documentation and an over-reliance on Chuikov's flawed memoir. They maintain a context of 'old' history, repeating many of the same details and perpetuating the mistakes present in Chuikov's work.

As this important new book shows, this state of affairs has now drastically changed for the better. During the past few years, the Russian government has finally released the main archival records related to the battle for Stalingrad, specifically, the daily operational summaries of the Red Army General Staff and the war diaries of the 62nd Army and its subordinate divisions and brigades, all in unexpurgated form. At the same time, Russian historians such as Aleksei Isaev and V V Beshanov have penned candid and detailed histories of the fighting during this period based on these newly released materials.[2] Finally, thanks to the work of the Australian historian, Jason Mark, who has "trawled" German records to an unprecedented extent and produced magnificently detailed studies on Wehrmacht combat operations in Stalingrad, we now have accounts of the fighting from the German side comparable to those from the Soviet perspective.[3]

Michael Jones's book, *Stalingrad: How the Red Army Triumphed*, represents a milestone in the treatment of the battle. As in Beevor's well-received history, it strives to place a human face on those participating in the struggle, in this case by focusing on the experiences of the key command personnel as well as the rank-and-file soldiers in the 62nd Army. But to a far greater extent than Beevor, Jones is able to zero in on the psychological state of Red Army combatants and successfully determine just what motivated them to fight and endure as they did in such extreme circumstances. Unlike Beevor's work, which crafted a skilfully constructed mosaic onto a structure of 1970s vintage history, Jones – by using the military archive to underpin dramatic new veteran testimony - is able to correct the many persistent errors in the operational record of the battle. By focusing on the 62nd Army and its soldiers and giving powerful vignettes of the fighting in the city from mid-September through mid-November 1942, he captures a far more intimate view of Stalingrad: a distillation that reflects the essence of the struggle.

The result is highly effective and utterly captivating. Previous accounts have been unable to fully convey the desperate ferocity of the battle. Now we see it in all its horror – and better understand the courage of Stalingrad's defenders. This is the finest history of its type published to date.

David M Glantz
Carlisle, PA

Notes
1 See A M Samsonov, *Stalingradskaia bitva* (The Battle of Stalingrad) (Moscow: 'Nauka', 1960), V I Chuikov, *Nachalo puti* (The beginning of the road)

(Moscow: Voenizdat, 1959) (English translation as *The Battle for Stalingrad* in 1964), N I Krylov, *Stalingradskii rubezh* (The Stalingrad line) (Moscow: Voenizdat, 1979), A I Eremenko, *Stalingrad* (Moscow: Voenizdat, 1961), and K K Rokossovsky, (ed.), *Velikaia Bitva na Volge* (The great victory on the Volga) (Moscow: Voenizdat, 1965).

2 See Aleksei Isaev, *Kogda vnezapnosti uzhe ne bylo: Istoria VOV kotoruiu my ne znali* (When there was no surprise: The history of the Great Patriotic War we do not know) (Moscow: 'Yauza', 'Eksmo', 2005), and V V Beshanov, *God 1942 – 'Uchebyi'* (The year 1942 – 'Training') (Minsk: Harvest, 2002).

3 See Jason D. Mark, *Death of the Leaping Horseman: 24. Panzer-Division in Stalingrad, 12th August-20th November 1942* (Sydney, Australia: Leaping Horseman Books, 2003); Adelbert Holl, *An Infantryman in Stalingrad*, trans. Jason D Mark and Neil Page (Sydney: Leaping Horseman Books, 2005); and Jason D Mark, *Island of Fire: The Battle for the Barrikady Factory in Stalingrad, November 1942-February 1943* (Sydney: Leaping Horseman Books, 2006).

List of Plates

Pavlov, Rodimtsev, Chuikov and sculptor Evgeny Vuchetich (creator of the Mamaev Kurgan memorial complex, which was opened in 1967) return to 'Pavlov's House' on the 25th anniversary of the battle.

The entrance to the conduit pipe that served as Rodimtsev's HQ.

The 39th Regiment of the 13th Guards moves into a new defence line on the morning of 22 September 1942 – nicknamed the 'day of death'.

A storm group goes into action.

Chuikov and Gurov admire Vasily Zaitsev's sniper rifle.

General Stephan Guriev [foreground] and the staff of the 39th Guards Division.

The 'village on the Volga' – army dugouts along the river embankment.

Sokolov – the commander of the 45th Division – consults a map of the city's factory district.

Mikhail Panikakha's heroic deed.

The small boats that supplied Stalingrad's defenders after crossing 62 was lost.

Chuikov and Batyuk [far right] at an advanced observation post.

'The soldiers' fires are smoking': scenes from army life – preparing food, sharing cigarettes.

Music and singing lifted the morale of Stalingrad's defenders.

Shell and bullet holes in a telegraph pole opposite the central Railway Station – preserved as a memorial to the fighting there.

The bullet-pocked walls of the 'Nail Factory' in central Stalingrad.

This statue of Vasily Chuikov, the commander of the 62nd Army, fittingly stands defiant on the Volga embankment. It was made by his son Alexander.

The Mill – the stronghold seized by the 13th Guards on 14 September 1942 and held throughout the battle.

Relics of the 13th Guards' last defence line on the Volga embankment.

The Mamaev Kurgan – showing the Mother Victory statue and the modern church.

A monument to the fighting: the 'ruined walls' on the Mamaev Kurgan. The tableau shows soldiers swearing an oath before a military standard. Inscribed underneath are the words: 'There is no land for us beyond the Volga'.

This building – in the workers' settlement of the Tractor factory – was used for defence by the 37th Guards on 14 October 1942. The repairs to the brickwork in the centre show where the gun emplacement was situated.

The forecourt of the Tractor Factory, where units of the 112th Division made their last desperate stand on 14 October.

The 'Gully of Death' – which ran down to the Volga between the Red October and Barrikady Factories. In late October and November 1942 German snipers held the key vantage points overlooking the gully

A Stalingrad time capsule: the steel processing laboratory in the Red October Factory, preserved exactly as it was during the battle [four photos]. The plaque honours the men of the 253rd (Tarachansky) Regiment of the 45th Division, who defended the building.

The ruined command post of Lyudnikov's 138th Division, behind the Barrikady Factory.

This tank turret, mounted on a pedestal (one of seventeen throughout the city) marks the last defence line of Stalingrad's defenders.

Red Army weaponry on display at the Volgograd Defence Museum.

The HQ of the 64th Army at Beketovka – where Paulus formally surrendered to General Shumilov.

The author and Colonel-General Mereshko at the Museum of the Great Patriotic War, Moscow.

A Note on the Illustrations

I have tried to avoid the well-known – and frequently artificially posed – images of Stalingrad's defenders. I am especially grateful to Alexander Chuikov and Natalia Rodimtseva, who have provided me with many private family photographs, and to Svetlana Orgasteva, for permission to use the valuable illustrative material gathered in the Volgograd Panorama Museum's anthology, *Only a Moment* (Volgograd, 2004).

The photographs in section 1, pp. 1–4, have been supplied by Natalia Rodimtseva and Alexander Chuikov; those on pp. 5–8 are from the anthology *Only a Moment*. The modern photographs of the battlefield in section 2 have been taken by the author.

Maps and Documents

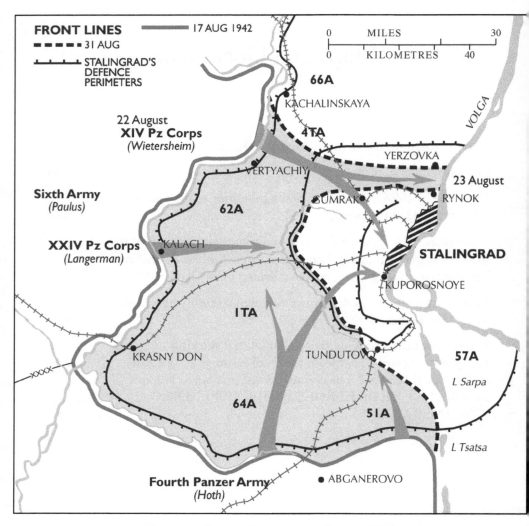

FRONT LINES ━━━ 17 AUG 1942
━ ━ ━ 31 AUG
⊢⊢⊢⊢ STALINGRAD'S
DEFENCE
PERIMETERS

MILES
0   30
0   30
KILOMETRES
0   40

66A

KACHALINSKAYA

22 August
XIV Pz Corps
(Wietersheim)

4TA

VOLGA

YERZOVKA

VERTYACHIY

23 August

Sixth Army
(Paulus)

GUMRAK

RYNOK

62A

XXIV Pz Corps
(Langerman)

KALACH

STALINGRAD

KUPOROSNOYE

1TA

KRASNY DON

TUNDUTOVO

57A

L Sarpa

64A

51A

L Tsatsa

Fourth Panzer Army
(Hoth)

ABGANEROVO

The campaign on the steppe – August 1942.

Opposite page: City of Stalingrad map

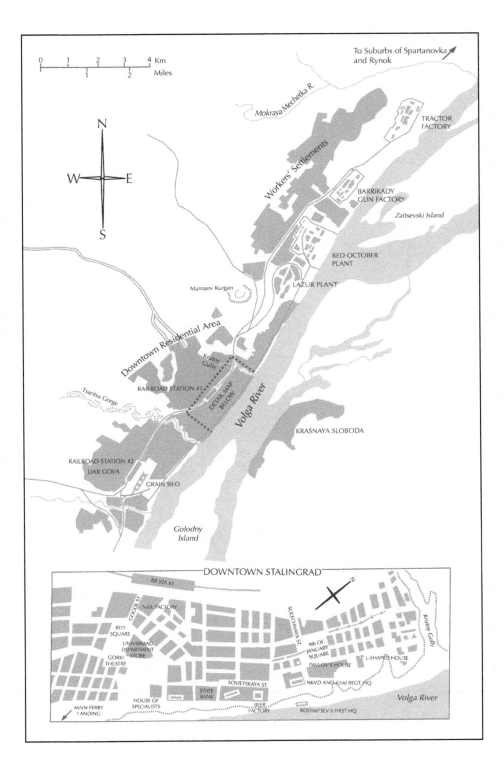

DOWNTOWN STALINGRAD

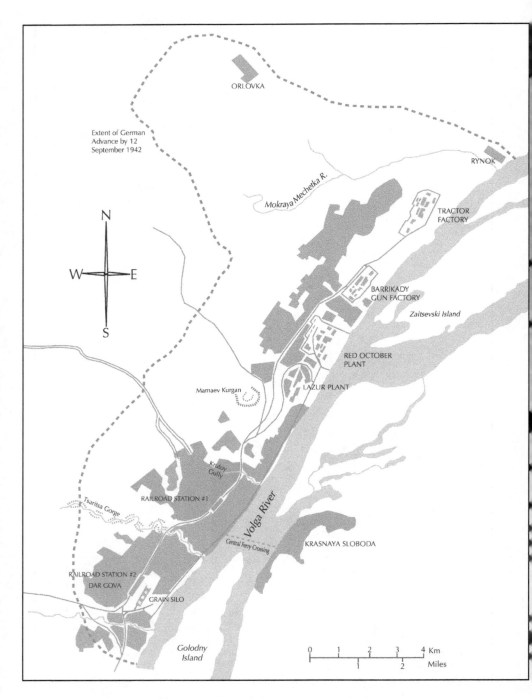

Line held by the 62nd Army at Stalingrad prior to the German offensive of
13–14 September 1942

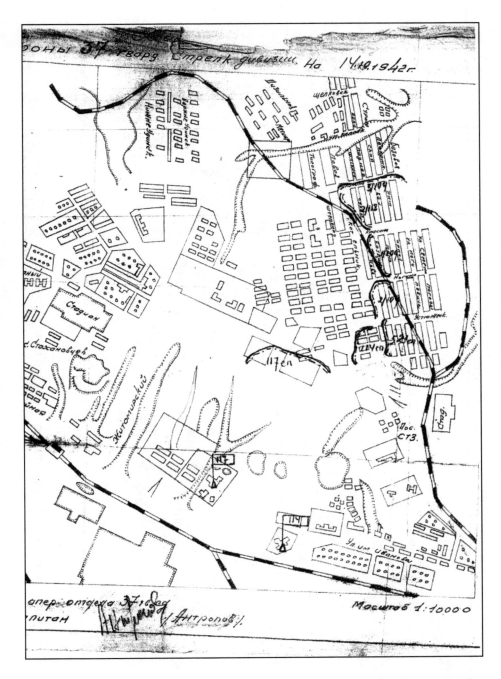

37th Guards sketched combat map showing their positions in the workers'
settlement of the Tractor Factory when the Sixth Army launched its greatest
attack on the morning of 14 October 1942.

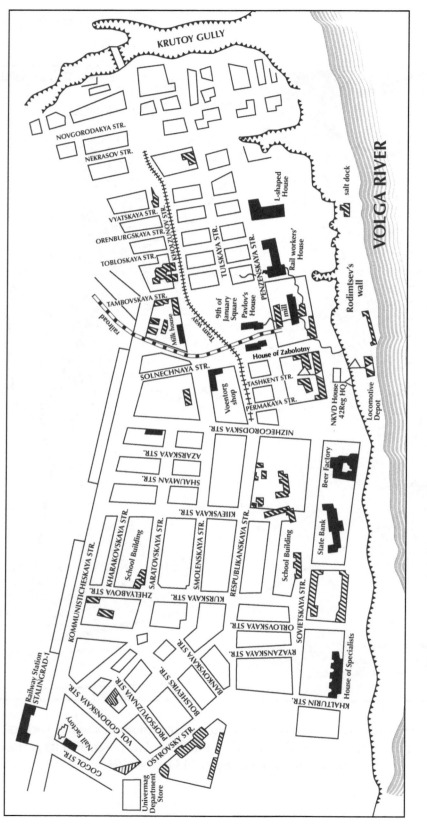

Fortress strongholds in downtown Stalingrad (kindly provided by Evgeny Kulichenko)

ДОНЕСЕНИЕ

Бр.11.30.

Гвардии Ст.Лейтенанту ФЕДОСЕЕВУ 20.9.42.

Доношу, обстановка сл: Противник старается всеми силами окружить всю роту, заслать в тыл моей роты автоматчиков, но все его попытки не увенчаются успехом. Несмотря на превосходящие силы противника, наши бойцы и командиры проявляют мужество и геройство над фашистскими шакалами. Пока через мой труп не пройдет не будет успеха у немцев.

Гвардейцы не отступают! Пусть падут смертью храбрых бойцы командиры, но противник не должен пройти нашу оборону.Пусть знает вся страна 13 Гв.дивизию,3 стр.роту. Пока командир роты жив, ни одна сволочь не пройдет. Тогда может пройти, когда командир роты будет убит или тяжело ранен.

Командир 3-й роты находится в напряженной обстановке и сам лично физически нездоров: на слух оглушен и слаб, происходит головокружение и падает с ног, происходит кровотечение из носа.

Несмотря на все трудности, гвардейцы и лично 3 рота и 2-я не отступят назад.Погибнем героями за город СТАЛИНА! Да будет ли могилой Советская земля. Лично убил командир 3 роты КОЛЕГАНОВ 1 и 2 мг пулеметчиков фрицев и забрал пулемет и документы, которые представлены в штаб батальона.

Надеюсь на своих бойцов и командиров. Пока через мой труп ни одна фашистская гадина не пройдет! Гвардейцы не жалеют за полную победу Советской власти.

БУДЕМ ГЕРОЯМИ ПРИ ЗАЩИТЕ СТАЛИНГРАДА.

Командир 3 стр.роты
Гвардии Мл.Лейтенант (КОЛЕГАНОВ)

Командир 2-й роты
Гвардии Лейтенант   (КРАВЦ В)

Extract from the 13th Guards combat journal showing Koleganov's report – sent from the 'Nail Factory' at 11.30am on 20 September 1942. His closing rejoinder is typed in block capitals: 'LET US BE HEROES WHILE DEFENDING STALINGRAD'

Timeline

17 JULY 1942: The battle of Stalingrad begins when units of the Russian 62nd Army meet the German Sixth Army on the river Chir, a tributary of the Don.

25 JULY: The 62nd Army is pushed back to the river Don.

27 JULY: The first commander of the 62nd Army, General Kolpakchi, is dismissed.

28 JULY: Stalin issues Order 227 – the 'Not a Step Back!' Order.

29 JULY: The military orders of Alexander Nevsky, Suvorov and Kutuzov are revived.

6 AUGUST: Lieutenant-General Chuikov, deputy commander of the 64th Army, repels a German advance on the Aksai river, south-west of Stalingrad

7-8 AUGUST: The Germans complete the encirclement of most of the 62nd Army on the western bank of the Don.

23 AUGUST: The Germans reach the Volga north of Stalingrad, at Rynok, isolating the 62nd Army from the Soviet forces north-west of Stalingrad. Repeated Russian attempts to breach this German 'land corridor' and link up with the 62nd Army fail. Massive bombing of the city begins.

25 AUGUST: Stalingrad is placed under martial law. Colonel Sarayev of the 10th NKVD division takes command. Fearing an imminent German capture of the city, all key installations and factories are mined to prevent them falling into the hands of the enemy.

28 AUGUST: Mass flight of civilians from Stalingrad – an event which is suppressed in post-war Soviet accounts of the battle.

29 AUGUST: Gorokhov's 'Northern group' is formed in a desperate attempt to stabilize the defence of the city.

6 SEPTEMBER: Faced with the combined advance of the German Sixth and Fourth Panzer Armies, the second commander of the 62nd Army, General Lopatin, withdraws the 23rd Tank Brigade from the designated defence line and pulls back towards the city. He is arrested for 'disobeying Order 227 and lying to the High Command'.

8 SEPTEMBER: The left flank of the 62nd Army disintegrates, allowing the Germans reach the Volga at Kuporosnoye, splitting it from the 64th Army. The battered remnants of the 62nd Army are now completely isolated from the northern and southern sections of the Front The staff of the Stalingrad Front are evacuated from the city to a new HQ on the eastern bank of the Volga. The decision to defend Stalingrad is to be reviewed on a day-to-day basis.

12 SEPTEMBER: Vasily Chuikov is appointed commander of 62nd Army.

13 SEPTEMBER: Paulus resumes the German offensive. Alexander Voronin, head of Stalingrad's NKVD, requests of Lavrenti Beria measures to be taken 'if the Red Army abandons the city'.

14 SEPTEMBER: German forces break into Stalingrad. At 1.00pm the Mamaev Kurgan is taken. The main railway station is captured and German machine gunners advance on the central ferry crossing. That afternoon units of the 62nd Army refuse to obey orders, believing the city is lost. The first detachments of Rodimstev's 13th Guards are forced to cross the Volga at 5.00 p.m. – in broad daylight – to stabilize the situation. Many soldiers die in the heavily bombed river crossing but the Mill – a vital stronghold on the Volga embankment, commanding the ferry crossing – is recaptured from the enemy. That night thousands more of Rodimtsev's Guards arrive in the city.

15 SEPTEMBER: A reinforced reconnaissance battalion from the 42nd Regiment of the 13th Guards recaptures the main railway station in a surprise attack in the early hours of the morning. A German incendiary attack forces it to withdraw later the same day. The heroic resistance of this force is later inflated, first to five, then to ten days.

16 SEPTEMBER: The 39th Regiment of 13th Guards retakes the Mamaev Kurgan, hoisting the red flag above the water towers on the hill's summit.

18 SEPTEMBER: A three-day siege of the Grain Elevator begins in southern Stalingrad. A storm group is used for the first time to capture the State Bank on the Volga embankment in the central part of the city, but the Germans counter-attack and regain it only hours later.

19 SEPTEMBER: Gorishny's 95th Division brought over in the early hours of the morning.

22 SEPTEMBER: The 'day of death'. A major German offensive pushes the

13th Guards back to the Volga embankment but is unable to break their defence line.

24 SEPTEMBER: Batyuk's 284th Division crosses to Stalingrad.

26 SEPTEMBER: Chuikov encourages the use of storm groups within the 62nd Army.

27 SEPTEMBER: The Germans attack Stalingrad's northern Factory District. That night Smekhotvorov's 193rd Division crosses the Volga. Sergeant Jacob Pavlov's six-man reconnaissance group captures 'Pavlov's House'.

1 OCTOBER: Mikhail Panikakha, on fire from a Molotov cocktail, dies in the workers' settlement of the Red October Factory flinging himself upon an enemy tank. Colonel Andryushenko's 115th Brigade continues to fight on, in encirclement, in the Orlovka salient. A German night attack on Rodimtsev's 13th Guards is beaten back.

1-3 OCTOBER: Guriev's 39th Guards take up positions in the Red October Factory, Gurtiev's 308th Division in the barrikady and Zholudev's 37th Guards in the Tractor Factory.

8 OCTOBER: The first fully successful night attack undertaken by storm groups. The 37th Guards capture house 1 in the hexagonal housing block in the Tractor Factory workers' settlement. The intrepid house garrison of 6/1 is later immortalized in Vasily Grossman's *Life and Fate*.

14 OCTOBER: A German onslaught breaks through the Tractor Factory and reaches the Volga, splitting the 62nd Army in two. At 9.40 p.m. Chuikov requests permission to move his HQ to the far [eastern] bank of the Volga.

15 OCTOBER: At 1.00 a.m. Military Order 205 shows Chuikov has been replaced by Krylov as 62nd Army commander. Chuikov is quickly reinstated – probably on the direct intervention of Stavka, Stalin's High Command. A second request by Chuikov to evacuate his HQ is turned down. Lyudnikov's 138th Division is made available to reinforce 62nd Army. Chuikov prepares to direct artillery fire on to his own HQ if the Germans break through.

16 OCTOBER: The slogan 'There is no land for us beyond the Volga' is coined by Vasily Zaitsev and circulated by Chuikov. It becomes a sacred oath for Stalingrad's defenders.

16–17 OCTOBER: Lyudnikov's Division shores up the Russian defence line.

17 OCTOBER: Paulus belatedly prepares to move his last fresh division – the

79th Infantry – into the city. Chuikov feared it would be brought in several days earlier, with calamitous consequences.

19 OCTOBER: German forces moving into the Barrikady Factory are briefly beaten back in a surprise counter-attack by the 339th Regiment of Gurtiev's 308th Division.

23 OCTOBER: The Germans launch their attack on the Red October Factory.

26 OCTOBER: The last Russian ferry crossing – crossing 62 – comes under fire from German units.

27 OCTOBER: German machine gunners reach the HQ of Guriev's 39th Guards. They are beaten back by a rescue unit drawn from Chuikov's own staff.

31 OCTOBER: Sokolov's 45th Division crosses to Stalingrad and launches a counter-attack, regaining several workshops in the Red October Factory.

11 NOVEMBER: Paulus's last major offensive. The Germans reach the Volga behind the Barrikady Factory, surrounding the 138th Division – creating Lyudnikov's Island – and splitting the 62nd Army into three groups, holding a line often less than 200 metres from the river.

19 NOVEMBER: The Soviet forces launch Operation Uranus, attacking the Romanian forces north-west of the German Sixth Army on the Don. The southern Soviet group strikes at Romanian forces on the Kalmyk steppe a day later.

23 NOVEMBER: The two Red Army pincers link up near Kalach, encircling the German Sixth Army.

3 DECEMBER: Russian storm groups capture a series of German strongholds along the Volga embankment – including the House of Railway Workers and the L-Shaped House.

18 DECEMBER: Lyudnikov – attempting to reach the rest of the 62nd Army – uses a new tactical formation of storming, consolidation and reserve groups. It subsequently becomes standard practice in storm group fighting.

24 DECEMBER: Manstein's relief army is forced to withdraw – sealing the fate of the German Sixth Army.

31 DECEMBER: Lyudnikov's 138th Division is reunited with the main group of the 62nd Army.

10 JANUARY 1943: The Soviet armies surrounding the Stalingrad pocket or 'cauldron' launch Operation Ring to annihilate the encircled Germans.

11 JANUARY: Batyuk's 284th Division recaptures all of the Mamaev Kurgan; Sokolov's 45th regains the remainder of the Red October Factory.

26 JANUARY: Advancing Soviet forces link up with the 13th Guards and 284th Divisions of the 62nd Army, ending its five month period of isolation.

31 JANUARY: Paulus surrenders to General Shumilov's 64th Army, which has advanced into downtown Stalingrad from the south.

2 FEBRUARY: German forces in the north of Stalingrad surrender, marking the end of the battle.

Introduction

The Last of the Mohicans

'There are fewer and fewer of us', Anatoly Mereshko said, downing a glass of vodka, 'it sometimes feels like we are the last of the Mohicans'. Mereshko was with Russia's 62nd Army throughout the battle of Stalingrad, and subsequently fought his way to Berlin and to the Reichstag, the central symbol of Hitler's regime. After the war he rose to Deputy Commander of the Warsaw Pact, finishing his career teaching at a military academy. But the battle of Stalingrad remains the abiding memory of his life. 'It is impossible to understand if you were not there', he remarked,

> for when you looked at the city from the far bank it seemed un-believable that anybody could survive in that inferno. But at the crisis point of the battle the spirit of our army was extraordinary. Even when we were pressed back within 200 metres of the Volga, we came to believe we could hold out. It was an incredible feeling. Even raw recruits got it – those who survived the first couple of days fighting were often totally transformed.

Anatoly Grigorevich Mereshko is well-qualified to talk about the battle – a turning point of the Second World War and one of the most decisive in military history. He learnt to fight in the terrible summer of 1942 when German armies tore a 400 kilometre hole in Russia's southern front and raced towards the Caucasus, with its vital oil reserves, and the city of Stalingrad, a centre of the country's armament industry and a vital hub of communications and trade. In the ferocious fighting in the city he was promoted – although only 20 years of age – onto the staff of the 62nd Army, the beleaguered force defending Stalingrad. He fought at many of the battle's key locations, and also gained an exceptional understanding of what was happening at the army HQ.

The testimony of Mereshko, along with that of other Red Army veterans, and fresh documentary evidence, will underpin my account of this famous battle. It focuses on Russia's 62nd Army, the army that held the city against the Germans, and looks at its leadership, morale and motivation: how its

1

soldiers bonded together in the most desperate of circumstances. An extraordinary sense of comradeship existed amongst these fighters, and it was this comradeship which helped them hold out for so long, in the direst of battle conditions.

Veteran Testimony

Many of the veterans of this remarkable army have passed away. Others are fading fast, with hospital check-ups becoming more and more frequent. Streetfighter Suren Mirzoyan is one of them. He created a stir when he suddenly appeared at the Defence of Stalingrad museum in Volgograd with a large suitcase, looking for accommodation in the present-day city. He and his younger wife left their spacious house in Armenia because Suren wanted to return to Stalingrad – now renamed Volgograd – before he died. He had a plot on the city's Mamaev Kurgan, the hill which bore some of the fiercest fighting, in mind as the place he wanted to be buried.

The magnetic power of the city and the awful battle for which it will always be remembered will come as a surprise to most Westerners. They have learnt to regard it simply as a hell on earth, where Russian and German soldiers suffered terribly. Who in their right mind would want to return there?

Yet this 'hell-hole' created a remarkable sense of affection – seen in the veterans' stories, with their astonishing pride in the battle and love for the city that suffered so much. Vladimir Turov was an infantry lieutenant from a village near Smolensk. He fought at the battles for Tula and Moscow in 1941, and carried on fighting to the very end of the war. But it was Stalingrad that he always remembered. He fought in the Orlovka salient, to the north-west of the city, in August and September 1942. Later in the war, in July 1943, Turov's unit was transported through Stalingrad on its way to the Ukraine. They had a couple of hours before moving on – and went out to explore. The city was still littered with wreckage, and the shattered hulks of German planes and military equipment lay everywhere. The terrain had a lunar quality, pockmarked with shell-holes, and criss-crossed with tunnels, dug out by the city's Red Army defenders.

Turov and his comrades wandered around, moved and intrigued by what they saw. One shell-hole was covered by a piece of fabric. They lifted it up and found a group of young women inside. They were working in Stalingrad – helping to restore the city – and were living there. 'What on earth are you doing?' Turov asked. Then he realized the war damage was so great there was nowhere else for them to go. 'We have tried to live in the fuselage of broken planes', they answered cheerily, 'but the metal was too jagged and sharp.' Suddenly Turov was overcome with emotion, feeling extraordinary love for the city that had suffered so much. 'I swore to myself that if I stayed alive for the rest of the war I would return and live here.' Turov kept his promise. After leaving the army he travelled to Stalingrad and found work in one of its factories. He has remained in the city ever since.

The depth of identification felt by Russian veterans for this place is quite remarkable. Feodor Shatravko was a tank brigade commander from Kharkov. He fought in the battle for Moscow in 1941 and had been in Stalingrad since April 1942 setting up a training school for tank men. Shatravko helped defend the city against the first Nazi attacks. In late September 1942 he and his unit were ambushed by the Germans in the city's northern suburb of Spartanovka and his tank blown up. Shatravko still has a piece of tank fragment clearly visible under his skin. It was too close to the nerve to operate on, and he has carried it around with him ever since. Shatravko was hauled out of his burning tank by two comrades, but these men were subsequently killed. No other Russian soldier in his unit survived the fight.

As he recovered in hospital, Shatravko heard about the fate of his men. He felt a terrible sense of grief and remorse that he had survived and they hadn't. He also wondered how on earth he had got to the pick-up point on the Volga where the wounded were evacuated. He was told that the Red Army had employed a special team of dogs to recover the wounded. They had been trained by smell, recognizing the difference between a dead body and a man who was still alive. They worked in a pack, with some harnessed to a sledge and others running ahead to seek out the wounded. With no human being able to help, a team of these strong dogs had found Shatravko, hauled him onto the sledge, and escorted him down to the river. As he reflected on such desperate ingenuity, it began, over time, to hold a deeper, primal meaning. It seemed to him that the struggle at Stalingrad was utterly different from anything else he had experienced in the war.

At the end of April 1945 Shatravko fought his way into Berlin. He and his fellow soldiers made their way to the Reichstag where a huge throng of Red Army fighters was carving graffiti on the ruined walls. There were so many of them that the area had been cordoned off, and fresh troops were only allowed into the area in small groups of eight or nine men. Eventually Shatravko got in. He was passed some tools and hoisted up to an unmarked section of the Reichstag. But what to write? Many of his fellows were inscribing the place they came from. Shatravko was born in the city of Kharkov, but some other instinct suddenly overcame him. Quite spontaneously he carved 'I am from Stalingrad.'

The battle was an incredibly powerful emotional experience for many

Russian survivors, but it is a story that has struggled hard to breathe and come to life. The Red Army was part of a Communist regime that constantly distorted and edited the reality of the war. Stalingrad became an icon of that system and tales of the city's endurance and heroism were refashioned, and sometimes mangled almost beyond recognition, to reflect the glory of the state. Even committed Communists in the army were left cynical by the rendition of the battle that everyone was forced to parrot.

Gamlet Dallakian was a staff officer to Yeremenko and Khrushchev as they first tried to organize Stalingrad's defence, in the late summer of 1942. He confessed:

> We could not describe what it was like for a very long time. We were afraid to do so. Of course we did not think the city could hold out in the early stages of the battle. We had so few regular troops and were forced to rely on poorly trained recruits from the civilian population. There was virtually nobody to defend the city. But it was forbidden to admit that Stalingrad could have fallen – I would have been arrested. However there were a lot of people with the same opinion as me.

Dallakian continued:

> During the defensive period of the battle, the idea that our soldiers never lost faith in an eventual victory was a propaganda myth. No one talked about victory at the time. We were preoccupied with one thought – simply to hold out. Only when we encircled the Germans did the mood change – and it happened very quickly. For the first time there emerged a belief that we would win the battle, and eventually the war itself.

In private, things were very different. 'Honesty was an absolute rule among the veterans', Alexander Chuikov recalled, when his father Vasily, commander of the 62nd Army, met with fellow Red Army soldiers. 'Their stories made my hair stand on end – and they were totally different from anything I read in the official accounts.' All knew that public utterances must carefully toe the accepted line. Vasily Chuikov remembered a photograph issued during the course of the battle, showing him with a group of fellow officers and soldiers, by the bank of the Volga. The men were laughing together and the object of their attention was a young soldier's hand-held machine gun. The message was clear enough – the young soldier had just returned from a combat mission, and had successfully dispatched more of the hated enemy. However, the reality was more homely and touching: the young soldier was in fact holding aloft a little puppy dog he kept as a mascot – the shared laughter was the men's delight this little creature had survived the day's fighting. The Soviet censors found the moment was too frivolous for their taste: the puppy was airbrushed out of the picture and the machine gun put in instead.

Layers of revisionism cover the terrain of battle – and are still with us today. In the Communist era, it was not possible to write anything deemed 'negative' about Stalingrad. But in the attempt to remove horror and doubt and paint a picture of triumphal certainty, much more was lost than gained.

How the Battle was Seen by Others

Stalingrad represented a crushing defeat for Nazi Germany and a turning point in the Second World War. It was unprecedented for an entire German army to be destroyed and so many prisoners taken. Not surprisingly, Russians praised the achievement highly, but the tribute of Marshal Konstantin Rokossovsky, written on the twenty-fifth anniversary of the battle, stands out:

> There have probably been hundreds of books written about this battle. And I think that for as long as people will be living on this Earth, they will remember it. And this is not surprising, for it was the largest battle in military history, in which socialism and fascism came face to face. For us, it was life and death which met on the Volga. And it was life which won the fight.

From the opposing side, General Hans Doerr fought at Stalingrad and subsequently wrote the first major German study of the battle. He saw it as: 'the turning point of the Second World War. For Germany the battle of Stalingrad was the worst defeat in its history, and for Russia, its greatest victory.'

These were retrospective comments, but they were matched by an exceptional interest felt at the time. In early October 1942 British Home Office intelligence reports indicated that Stalingrad had 'almost become an obsession', dominating public interest to the virtual exclusion of other war news. Perhaps the most interesting contemporary comment was an editorial by the Chinese communist leader Mao Tse-Tung for *Liberation Daily* on 12 October 1942, at a time when the fighting was reaching its peak:

During these days, the news of each setback or triumph from the city gripped the hearts of countless millions of people, now bringing them anxiety, now stirring them to elation.

At about the same time the German newspaper *Berliner Borsenzeitung* wrote:

The struggle of world importance now in progress at Stalingrad has become an enormous, decisive battle. Its participants are able to grasp only some of its horrible details, without being able to realize its significance or foresee its end . . . Those who, in straining every nerve and muscle, will have survived this battle, will have this inferno impressed upon their minds, as though their consciousness had been branded with a red-hot iron . . . Only later will all the details of this unprecedented battle, with its street fighting, be properly registered. Never in all the history of wars has there been such a concentration of weapons in such a small space and for such a long time. Never before has a city fought till the collapse of its last wall . . . In this battle, despite our numerical superiority, we are not achieving the necessary result.

Vladimir Turov described the progressive impact of all this attention on the ordinary Red Army soldier:

During the battle for Stalingrad we came to feel that everybody in the world was watching us – and hoping for something heroic, a turning point. It became absolutely clear that the destiny of fascism and the world would be decided at Stalingrad – and we realized this.

Artilleryman Nikolai Danilov, a soldier of the 62nd Army, was defending Stalingrad's factory district. He felt this same sense of destiny. On 12 October 1942, the exact day that Mao penned his editorial in *Liberation Daily*, he wrote: 'This part of the battle is harder than all previous ones. But the complete defeat of the Germans will be here.'

Stalingrad: A Brief Overview

How can this extraordinary battle be understood? It is normally divided into three phases:

- The first, the so-called 'defensive phase', lasted from 17 July to 19 November 1942. It saw the German 6th Army advancing towards Stalingrad, first fighting its Russian opponents on the steppe and then in ferocious clashes in the city itself.
- The second phase, the 'encirclement', from 19 November 1942 to 10 January 1943, witnessed a secretly prepared Soviet counter-attack on the northern and southern flanks of the 6th Army's position. Its two pincers closed behind the German troops at Stalingrad, leaving them trapped and surrounded. In December fresh German forces attempted to break through the Russian lines and relieve them, but they failed.
- Finally, in the third phase, from 10 January to 2 February 1943, the Soviet forces surrounding Stalingrad launched a battle of annihilation, destroying the Germans and their Romanian allies inside the Stalingrad 'pocket' or 'cauldron', as it was grimly named. On 2 February 1943 the remnants of the Wehrmacht's once-proud 6th Army surrendered in the northern part of the city, and the battle of Stalingrad was over.

The first, 'defensive phase', lies at the heart of any Russian veteran's experience of the battle. In private, Chuikov would say simply:

The story of the 62nd Army *is* the battle of Stalingrad. If the Germans had wiped us out and crossed the Volga everything would have been different – the psychological effect of capturing Stalingrad would have been enormous. The counter-offensive would not have worked.

He described the 62nd Army as 'the army of the city battle':

Even Soviet soldiers who had fought all the way through to Berlin could not imagine the sheer horror of Stalingrad. We were impaled upon a line of burning fire – it was utter, indescribable hell. No one else was able to understand what we went through. We would say to each other afterwards – are you a veteran of the western bank, the fighting in the city?

When asked how they had managed to hold out Chuikov was brutally honest: 'It was beyond the understanding of any of us.'

Stalingrad was undoubtedly a battle of attrition, and the Germans were drawn into increasingly costly street fighting in the ruined city landscape. This wasteful combat drained their manpower and resources while allowing the Russians time to build up their forces and strike on the weaker flanks of their enemy. The Wehrmacht became bogged down in the kind of battle that did not suit its strengths, as Basil Liddell Hart made clear:

> The struggle became a battle of battering-ram tactics on the Germans' side . . . The more deeply they penetrated into the densely built-up area of the city, the slower their progress became. In the last stages of the siege the front line was barely half a mile from the west bank of the Volga, but by then the strength of their efforts was fading, as a result of very heavy losses. Each step forward cost more and gained less.

The battle for Stalingrad was an entirely new experience for both sides. General Hans Doerr described the very different nature of fighting within a city:

> The time for conducting large-scale operations was gone for ever. The mile as a measure of distance was replaced by the yard . . . For every house, workshop, water-tower, railway embankment, wall, cellar and every pile of ruins a bitter battle was waged.

Colonel Herbert Selle, who commanded the engineers' detachment of the German 6th Army, recalled the horror of this kind of combat:

> Attack and defence, assault and counter assault, constant burning, excited yelling, mortar and artillery fire, and flamethrowers – Stalingrad became the living hell for which it is remembered. Rubble became fortresses, destroyed factories harboured deadly sharpshooters, behind every lathe and every machine tool lurked sudden death. Every corner and every cranny threatened a sudden burst of automatic rifle fire. Every foot of ground had to be literally torn from the defenders.

Selle emphasized the awful ferocity of the struggle:

> The city itself was never quiet. Time and time again bitter fighting broke out. Entire rows of houses disappeared in dust and ashes when

screaming bombs and shells tore into them. Fires raged incessantly, creating a deathly shroud of smoke around the doomed city. Giant construction girders were torn and bent into strange shapes and forms. Only in cellars and bunkers was there life. There, troops and command posts huddled precariously, often in a state of near-asphyxiation as shells ricocheted into entrances, sending down showers of debris and searing, fiery blasts into the air.

Tactical Innovation

Vasily Chuikov realized that different tactics would have to be employed for his men to hold out at Stalingrad against a mighty German offensive:

> City fighting is a special kind of fighting. Things are settled here not by strength, but by skill, resourcefulness and swiftness. The buildings in the city are like breakwaters. They broke up enemy formations and made their forces go along the street. We therefore held on firmly to strong buildings, and established small garrisons in them, capable of all-round fire if they were encircled . . . In our counter-attacks, we abandoned attacks by units and even sections of units. Towards the end of September [1942] storm groups appeared in all regiments – these were small but strong groups . . . Fighting went on for buildings and in buildings, for a cellar, for a room.

Chuikov was proud of the creation of storm groups – the new, mobile combat formations that took on the Germans in the city's ruins. One of his favourite photos from the battle showed a young storm group member, in torn uniform, shredded by bullet holes, standing in the ruins of the Tractor Factory. The picture was taken in early October 1942. Storm group tactics needed time and extensive training to be effective, and were only fully perfected several months later, after the German forces had been encircled and thrown on the defensive. However, this new way of fighting encouraged ordinary Red Army soldiers from the outset. At last the Germans were not having it their own way. Anatoly Mereshko expanded on a simple metaphor, typical of the down-to-earth way Chuikov communicated with his men:

> Imagine a strong wave from the sea. It hits the coast with tremen-dous force. But when you have breakers in the sea, the wave gets

broken. The same was true in the steppe. There the Germans had the power of the whole wave. In the city, they were broken into smaller streams. Houses, especially stone houses, became obstacles. And the further the Germans went into the city, the more resistance they received from the flanks. The Germans did not change their tactics at all. The same tactics they used in the steppe they used in the city. But a town gives a completely different war arena – especially ruins. We would split into small groups and occupy strongholds – to split their river into tributaries. We were very successful in achieving this.

But Mereshko did not attempt to explain the battle solely through tactical factors. Instead he said something rather different, echoing the private comments of Chuikov that the outcome of the struggle 'was beyond the understanding of any of us':

The defence of Stalingrad is a paradox of military science. The encirclement and our final offensive at Stalingrad can be understood in terms of military science – but our defence is impossible to comprehend through any system of rational analysis. It remains an utter paradox. The odds against us were so great – from October and November 1942 we had so little left. The Germans had an overwhelming superiority: the ratio of attackers to defenders was so disproportionate – you can hardly find another example of this in history.

To back up his point, Mereshko described the dwindling troop strength of the 62nd Army, which by December 1942 amounted to scarcely 6,000 combatants, less than the complement of a regular division. 'Our line was reduced to a strip of land between 500 and 100 metres from the Volga – and yet, somehow, we still managed to hold on.'

Vladimir Turov was keen to make the same point: 'In terms of our military understanding, how we held out at Stalingrad is still a complete mystery to us.' Mikhail Serebryakov, a reconnaissance officer with the Russian 57th Army, who fought his way into Stalingrad in January 1943, warned: 'A lot of these so-called "definitions" were devised well after the fighting had finished. At the time, men didn't have much opportunity to think about what was happening.'

The Psychological Dimension

Serebryakov emphasized that the psychology of the battle was all-important:

> It was a struggle for survival – and both sides learnt from each other along the way. There was one vital factor which coexisted alongside the terrible exhaustion caused by combat at close quarters: in this extreme situation, extraordinary inner resources were released within people. I witnessed a mother lifting up the entire side of a German truck to free her trapped child and saw small nurses carrying wounded paratroopers twice their size back to the trenches. Such things seemed physically impossible, but something was happening to people, both physiologically and psychologically. Some sunk under the stress of the fighting; others found something greater to draw upon. One such guiding principle was to always look out for others. We would put it like this: help your comrade first, then worry about your own survival. It was an attitude that really sustained our soldiers.

Many veterans agree: 'We remembered the saying of Suvorov [the founder of Russia's professional army in the eighteenth century]', said Ivan Burlakov, a defender of Stalingrad's Barrikady Factory: ' "Though you may perish in the attempt, come to the aid of your comrade-in-arms!" '

To understand, we need to recreate the spirit of Stalingrad's defenders. Mereshko put it like this:

> There was a special mood amongst our troops which came into being during the battle itself. Courage was the watchword under the command of Chuikov. Men were proud to be part of this army and their devotion led ordinary soldiers to perform extraordinary deeds. They were not pushed into them by commissars or anybody else. It was the call of their pride.

Mereshko stressed one particular point:

> Despite the ferocious fighting, nearly all the wounded who got to the far bank of the Volga and received medical treatment asked to return as quickly as possible, even though the chances of survival were incredibly low. This was the real spirit of Stalingrad – one of unity and friendship. It is difficult to convey what Stalingrad was like. It

was a firestorm for 50 kilometres along the Volga river. Flames, smoke, the permanent roar of explosions, huge bombs being dropped on the Mamaev Kurgan, the constant artillery attacks. It was so terrible. People did not believe that we could hold out. But when only a few hundred were left out of a division that once had more than 7,000 soldiers, they would hold the ground for their dead friends.

It was a powerful bond of friendship between fellow soldiers – not endlessly recycled eulogies to the communist system – that Mereshko remembered so vividly: 'I want to speak about what I saw, what influenced me, in simple words – the way it was at Stalingrad. I realize my personal recollections do not coincide with the official history.'

Anatoly Mereshko – a Key Witness

Mereshko was only 20 when he fought at Stalingrad – a young lieutenant with relatively little combat experience. How did his rapid promotion come about? In his memoirs Marshal Krylov, chief of staff of the 62nd Army, whose partnership with Chuikov was a key ingredient in creating the conditions for victory, paid tribute to Mereshko. Many years after the war he returned to Stalingrad, and climbed the Mamaev Kurgan, the hill so fiercely fought over that dominated the battlefield:

> For a long while I stood there on the grass covered mound, remembering my dear fighting comrades, both dead and alive. And again I was pleased to have had the luck to have travelled the road from the Volga to Berlin. I was pleased for our army commander Vasily Ivanovich Chuikov, for the courageous Stalingrad divisional commanders Lyudnikov, Rodimtsev and Smekhotvorov, for our brave tank commander Weinrub, for our sniper Zaitsev – who lost none of his accuracy when on German soil – for my self-sacrificing assistants on army staff Kalyakin, Velkin and Mereshko.

Krylov recalled Mereshko joining the staff of the 62nd Army:

> Reporting to me one difficult day was Lieutenant Anatoly Mereshko – small in stature, lean, with a 'For Courage' medal pinned to his

dirt-covered and sweat-soaked uniform. He had earned this medal during combat on the Don while leading the machine gun company of an officer cadet regiment. We had more recently taken him on the army staff. ('Has almost no staff education, but is well-trained as an army officer and is a developed and clever man', was how Brigade Commander Nikolai Yeliseyev had recommended him to me.) He now repaid me with his initial report. I no longer remember to which defensive sector and division we had sent him. All I recollect is the confidence with which he stated the facts, the details of the situation.

This was an army which, in the direst of military situations, promoted rapidly and on merit, as Krylov now made clear:

> It was felt that this 20–year-old lieutenant was ready to put his hand into the fire for the sake of accuracy in his reports. I knew it was vital for us to ascertain in detail, every day, the state of affairs on almost all sectors and get the gathered information to our command post. And I was somehow immediately certain that the newest and youngest worker of the operations section could be relied upon, and because of that, he would not be inferior to the other, more experienced officers. Still, there was no time to give vent to feelings. And I did not embrace this brave young lad. I simply shook his hand, poured him some vodka from a bottle I'd put aside for special occasions, and gave him a sandwich from my breakfast. 'Brace yourself, and try and get a couple of hours sleep. We will probably need you again soon.' Anatoly Grigorevich Mereshko would later become one of the best officers of our staff. After less than a year he was already a liaison officer for an entire rifle corps, and nowadays he is a high-level staff officer and already a long-standing general.

Krylov soon had a nickname for his young officer. As Mereshko returned to deliver a reconnaissance report a bomb exploded, leaving him slightly wounded and sick through sheer shock. He stumbled to the command post, flecked in blood and vomit, stood to attention and began to give his report. But each time he started his voice broke into a shrill, incomprehensible bray. Battle was raging all around and the military situation critical, but Krylov gestured to Mereshko to stop: 'Lieutenant', he said sombrely, 'I see the problem. You shouldn't be trying to speak. You should sing!' There was a surprised pause amongst the assembled 62nd Army staff, and then a guffaw of delighted laughter. 'From then on', Mereshko recalled, 'I was known as "the singer"'.

Leadership – the Vital Factor

The conditions in Stalingrad were chaotic, and some of the battle's famous episodes were only reconstructed years after the event. But Mereshko was well placed to see the functioning of the army's command, both at HQ and divisional level, and how it affected the soldiers on the frontline. He felt that the morale of the defenders grew as the battle progressed and become the driving force behind their improbable victory. And he believed that it stemmed from the exceptional bravery and self-belief of their leaders.

There is no substitute for the testimony of Stalingrad's defenders. The war journalist Vasily Grossman was a perceptive commentator and he was in the city for much of the fighting. But Grossman, increasingly disillusioned with the Soviet system, distanced ordinary soldiers from their commanders, believing they had discovered a will to resist entirely on their own. As a result, he completely misunderstood one of the battle's most dramatic incidents, when at the beginning of October 1942 the Germans targeted the oil storage tanks above Chuikov's HQ. The Russians had thought they were empty. They were mistaken. When Grossman wrote his epic novel *Life and Fate* he recreated this moment:

> It seemed impossible to escape from the liquid fire. It leaped up, humming and cracking, from the streams of oil that were filling the hollows and craters and rushing down the communication trenches . . . The life that had reigned hundreds of years before, the terrible life of the primeval monsters, had broken out of its deep tombs; howling and roaring, stamping its huge feet, it was devouring everything round about.

The effect of such writing is utterly hypnotic and Grossman's portrayal has strongly influenced Western views of the battle. He used the terrible fire above the Army HQ to reduce the Russian leaders to helpless bystanders: Chuikov and Krylov were hauled out of the flames in a state of bewilderment and shock; the staff officers of the 62nd Army then stood forlornly upon a small promontory until the morning, when they were evacuated to safety. The scenario fitted with Grossman's belief that ordinary Russian soldiers, not the army's commanders, were the real heroes of Stalingrad. But it was not what actually happened.

Anatoly Mereshko was in the HQ at the time and his account of what took place was the complete opposite of Grossman's version:

> We were saved by Krylov's calmness and quick-thinking. When the oil went up in flames above our HQ, Krylov came out from his dug-out and cried 'Stay where you are!' A lot of people got back into their shelters and this saved them. You see, it was fatal to try and stay outside – the trenches were quickly flooding with oil, and this fresh burning oil was the lethal danger. Over thirty of our staff were killed because they didn't heed Krylov's instructions and remained outside. When the rest of us reconvened in the surviving dug-outs, still surrounded by fire, we looked entirely Afro-Caribbean – but we were still alive!

Morale and Motivation

It was both a surprising and exceptionally courageous act to stay put in such frightening conditions. The bravery of the army's commander and his staff had an enormous impact on the soldiers, for in this terrible battle people were judged by their actions, not their words. Sergei Kozyakin, the editor of a divisional newspaper, wrote:

> War is like a mirror – it reflects the whole nature of the soul and of human behaviour. In everyday life you don't notice very much. People mind their own business. But in Stalingrad the fighting was so severe – with death everywhere – and people would change before your eyes.

No one could predict whether these changes would be for better or worse. Mark Slavin, who fought with the 45th Division, recalled one harrowing example:

> I was at the Volga crossing point, helping with the evacuation of the wounded. It was terrible there – we were under fire all the time. Suddenly I saw my junior commander. His head was bandaged and he was pushing his way through the queue, without any concern for others, so he could get on the boat first. I remembered what he had

taught us as students: then he was brimming with patriotic senti-
ments and uplifting examples of human behaviour. Well, he got on
the boat. There was a young nurse on it – her name was Katya
Shustova – an ordinary Russian girl in a sheepskin coat, but already
an experienced medical orderly. She went up to him and lifted the
bandage off his head. There was no wound at all. She reached down
inside her boot, pulled out a gun and shot him dead. We all saw it. I
went up to the boat and said 'Katya, you did the right thing –
bastard!'

Yet for every act of selfishness there was another of genuine heroism.
Kozyakin remembered composing a short piece on a young commissar named
Jacob Derganov. He was quiet and reserved – too reserved. He had not been
sent to address any meetings; it was felt that he was an uninspiring speaker. But
in the hell of the Red October Factory Derganov found his voice. It was not the
jargon of communist exhortation but something real and deeply authentic.
German tanks had suddenly broken through the factory walls and were accelerating towards the regiment's observation post, with their infantry following
behind. The commander yelled 'Man the machine gun – open fire on the
enemy.' But the young machine gunner was disorientated by the sudden attack
and froze in terror. Derganov ran up, shook him, and manhandled the gun into
its firing position. 'What are you looking around for?' he yelled. Between bursts
of fire he repeated: 'Remember this for the rest of your life. Here, on this
narrow stretch of land, this is our motherland – right here, where we are now.
There is no land for us beyond the Volga.'
     In a brief interval in the fighting Derganov spoke powerfully and from the
heart:

> Don't think about death. All your self-belief will drain away. You
> will lose all your strength. Gather yourself into a fist. Use all your
> concentration. Don't dwell on your fears or nightmares. Focus on
> the enemy. Summon all your anger against him. You are stronger
> than these fucking Fritzes. You stand on your own land.

Derganov seemed utterly withdrawn, but Stalingrad uncovered an exceptionally strong spirit. When enemy tanks crashed through he was ready to
sacrifice his life to save the situation. The young machine gunner was inspired
by his fierce resilience and tried to keep up; he recovered his own strength and
initiative. 'Great man – you are doing great!', Derganov encouraged him. Other
machine gunners followed his example and the German attack was blocked.

That evening Derganov was found unconscious by the observation point. He had given everything he had. The young recruits reverently covered him in a greatcoat and carried him to the medical post. They were now different men. Three days of incessant German attacks would follow but they did not yield their ground.

A Daunting Opponent

This is the power of authentic leadership. Such acts of exceptional courage were vital if the Red Army was to hold out at Stalingrad, for by their own admission they were up against an utterly terrifying foe. Mikhail Borisov fought against the Germans in three terrible retreats in 1942: the Crimea, Kharkov and the Don: 'I think the German army at that time was the best in the world', he acknowledged. 'Anybody would have been in trouble against them.' Anatoly Mereshko agreed:

> We really rated the German soldiers. Of course, we did not publicly admit this – but our soldiers did not think they had any major weaknesses. Even when they were encircled, without proper winter clothes and adequate food and ammunition, they continued to fight well for a very long time.

Vasily Chuikov summed up the enemy that he faced at Stalingrad with brutal simplicity: 'The Germans were smart, they were tough and there were a lot of them!'

Facing them was a Russian force that had only just come into being. The 62nd was one of Russia's youngest armies. In the summer of 1942 it was poorly trained, badly equipped and largely demoralized. On the approaches to Stalingrad it was hammered by the Germans and many of its divisions were smashed to pieces. But yet, in the ruins of the city, the battered remnants found the will and courage to confront their assailants and turn the tables on them.

Something remarkable happened at Stalingrad. At the outset of the battle the Germans held all the military advantages. But as one British newspaper, the *Daily Telegraph*, noted at the end of September 1942:

> It is, indeed, something more than material conditions, something that transcends the pure mechanics of war, that is involved at Stalingrad. It is the great imponderable morale that has turned a defensive with so many handicaps, a defensive, moreover, that

seemed spent, into this astounding episode that is clearly baffling the German Command.

The tale of the Russian defenders at Stalingrad transcends time and place. It tells of astonishing resilience and a triumph in the face of overwhelming odds. Morale and motivation transformed the 62nd Army into a fighting force of stupendous power. In private conversation, Vasily Chuikov discarded communist rhetoric to express a truth every soldier at Stalingrad would have understood: 'When a man is pushed to his very limits, and he realizes there is absolutely nowhere else to go – then he really has to start fighting!'

Chapter One

Not a Step Back!

It was the summer of 1942 and the German 6th Army was on the move. An elite formation, undefeated in battle, it had conquered Belgium and France in the summer of 1940, and Yugoslavia, Greece, southern Russia and the Ukraine in the summer of 1941. Now it had annihilated a Russian counter-offensive at Kharkov and was accelerating towards the city of Stalingrad, on the river Volga, to sever the country's grain and oil reserves and destroy a significant part of her industrial output.

Russia's southern front had been blasted wide open. The encirclement of Russian armies at Kharkov tore a massive gap in the country's defences and through it the Germans were advancing at the alarming rate of 40–50 kilo-metres a day. The troops thrown in to oppose them came from hurriedly formed reserve armies; they were poorly trained, ill-equipped and badly co-ordinated. It was an entirely unequal contest: the Germans overwhelmed and humiliated their opponents, creating a mood of deep despair.

The German summer offensive of 1942, codenamed Operation Blue, had two major objectives. The first was to reach Stalingrad and the Volga, cutting the transport of vital raw materials up the Volga river. Once this had been accom-plished, the second was to strike south into the Caucasus and capture its oilfields. Economic factors were the driving force behind Hitler's strategy and the full occupation of Stalingrad was not specified in the original operational directive. It was deemed sufficient to destroy the industrial capacity of the city and block the passage of the Volga. Events were to develop a terrible momentum of their own.

The official Soviet view was straightforward: Stalingrad would always have been held, regardless of the strength of the enemy offensive. In truth, as Anatoly Mereshko freely admitted, if the original order of Operation Blue had been kept to, Stalingrad's position would have quickly become hopeless. But the rapid collapse of Russian armies at Kharkov made Hitler over-ambitious and he now committed a fundamental error in strategy, insisting that Stalingrad and the Caucasus oilfields be captured simultaneously. On 23 July the two army groups on his southern front, A and B, were directed to move forward at the same time: A to capture the Caucasus, B to advance on Stalingrad.

The German Plan

Hitler's directive of 23 July 1942 defined the shape of the Stalingrad campaign. Herbert Selle, head of the German 6th Army's engineering section, described the situation:

> On 30 June 1942 the 6th Army had left its jumping off point, east of Belgorod, and began to take the offensive. After two days of hard defensive fighting Russian resistance seemed to be broken and the German units went into an all-out pursuit . . . By 23 July the main body of the 6th Army was astride the upper course of the river Chir.

This was the crucial moment. Selle continued:

> The original German plan of operation had called for the conquest of Southern Russia in chronological phases. First, Army Group B, with its 6th Army and 1st and 4th Panzer Armies, was to seize Stalingrad and establish a defence front between the Don and the Volga. After this, Army Group A was to advance in to the Caucasus further south. It was fairly certain that the strategic objectives of this plan could be achieved before winter. However, in view of the successful advance of the 6th Army, Hitler and the High Command decided that the Soviets were so shattered that only a fraction of these forces were now necessary to bring about the collapse of the Don–Volga front.

'Under the impulse of this wishful thinking', Selle concluded,

> the original operational plan was discarded and a new directive issued, which allotted to Army Group B the Don–Volga objective while, at the same time, Army Group A was assigned the mission of conquest of the Caucasus area. The idea of any point of main effort was dissipated by this dispersal of forces.

This undoubtedly led to a dilution of the German offensive, as one of their strongest mobile formations, pointing directly at Stalingrad, was diverted south. Herbert Selle caught the mood of frustration:

> On the basis of how our operations had proceeded up to that point, and with all the forces available to us, it had seemed logical, in July

1942, that the 6th Army would reach the crown of the great Don bend at Kalach in a few days. But many of our rapid, hard-hitting units, and a large quantity of transport material were transferred to Army Group A with the change in plans, at the very moment when everything depended on rapid action and concentrated effort.

Anatoly Mereshko agreed:

> After the Kharkov disaster there was a 300 kilometre hole in our front. But, to use one of our proverbs, the Germans 'wanted to catch two rabbits'. The 6th Army was so strong Hitler believed it could capture Stalingrad on its own. The 4th Panzer Army, one of their best mobile formations, had originally been on the left flank of the advance; it was now dispatched to Rostov. If it had been kept where it was, supporting a direct attack on Stalingrad, I think the city would have fallen to the Germans in July 1942. We would not have had the strength to oppose such a strong concentration of forces. Instead, the Panzers were pushed south, cutting across the communication lines of the 6th Army and impeding their advance. Diverting the 4th Panzer Army was their main strategic mistake.

So there was nothing preordained about the successful defence of Stalingrad. With hindsight, the Germans should have stuck to their original plan, and concentrated a quicker and stronger attack on the city. Hitler's directive of 23 July had another consequence for the course of the campaign. The original strategic plan, Operation Blue, had recognized the Germans were only strong enough to launch an offensive on one front, their southern one. Now Hitler decided to reopen a northern offensive as well, with an attack on Leningrad, codenamed 'Northern Lights'. After the German capture of Sevastopol, Manstein's 11th Army could either have been deployed in the Caucasus or to buttress the 6th Army's advance on Stalingrad. Instead, it was withdrawn from the southern theatre and transferred to the outskirts of Leningrad, effectively depriving the offensive of all substantial reserves.

Manstein, one of Hitler's best generals, was rightly critical of this decision:

> Could there be any justification for taking the 11th Army away from the southern wing of the Eastern Front, now that it was free in the Crimea, and employing it on a task which was palpably less important – the conquest of Leningrad? On the German side, after all, the decisive results in that summer of 1942 were being sought in the

south. This was a task for which we could never be too strong, particularly as it was obvious, even now, that the duality of Hitler's objective – Stalingrad and the Caucasus – would split the offensive in two directions.

Manstein believed the right strategy was for his force to follow the attacking army groups as an operational reserve.

It is worth stressing Manstein's objection: 'this was a task for which we could never be too strong'. The plan for Army Group B to occupy the Don–Volga line took a strategic risk, for its forces were not numerous enough to occupy a coherent front along the Volga, and instead, its main front would be drawn up a hundred kilometres further west, along the river Don. The bend of that river would be used as a jumping-off point for an assault on Stalingrad. All would still be well if Stalingrad fell quickly, but the longer term danger was obvious. The Germans were putting their heads in a noose – as crude Russian cartoons later depicted – and almost inviting a counter-attack on their flanks. Of course, the Russians had to hold out at Stalingrad first. But were they to do so, and if the siege became a protracted one, the German position would be increasingly vulnerable.

The danger was compounded as more and more German troops were funnelled into Stalingrad. The armies on their flanks, composed of the forces of their allies, the Romanians, Italians and Hungarians, were of unreliable quality. They made a tempting target. It was vital to back these armies up with a strong German reserve.

Finally, but particularly galling, Manstein's army was equipped with heavy siege guns. As Russian resistance in Stalingrad stiffened, these would have been devastating against their defensive positions within the city. Instead, they were moved north to Leningrad.

Manstein summarized the long-term risks for the Germans. The attempt to gain control of the Volga by taking Stalingrad was admissible on a short-term basis, only if the assault on the city was quickly successful. 'To leave the main body of the Army Group at Stalingrad for weeks on end, with inadequately protected flanks, was the cardinal error.' If Stalingrad continued to hold out, the most hard-hitting formations of Army Group B would be tied down in a battle within the city, leaving the Don front covered by the weaker forces of their allies.

But it is easy to be wise in hindsight. The mood of confidence was not confined to Hitler – it had infected the whole German High Command. They did not believe the Russians had any significant reserves left – and were thus incapable of holding Stalingrad or threatening them with a major counter-offensive. And both sides were to make major mistakes that summer.

The Russian Experience

The immediate Russian experience was traumatic. German strength appeared overwhelming and their own position hopeless. Anatoly Kozlov described what it felt like:

> It was very difficult to stop the German army – it was as if we had been ordered to stop a hurricane. We had hoped that our allies would open a second front in the summer of 1942 and there was a terrible sense of despair when we were left to face the Nazis alone and things went so wrong for us. There was this huge mass of retreating people: the structure of whole armies had disintegrated and it was impossible to find your division. When the Germans reached the Caucasus most of us had lost all hope of victory.

Gamlet Dallakian emphasized the feeling of desolation:

> Smashed at Kharkov, bled white and forced to retreat to the Don, we thought that the war was lost and we could never withstand such a strong enemy. There seemed no way of stopping the Germans – they were breathing down our necks the whole time we were retreating towards the Don.

The crisis began at Kharkov. Here Timoshenko's ambitious early summer offensive had been destroyed by a classic German battle of encirclement. This failure, and its terrible consequences, undermined the faith of even the most ardent Bolshevik. Praskovja Graschenkova had been taken onto the divisional staff of one of the newly formed Russian armies.

'The retreat from Kharkov was the most terrible time of my life', Graschenkova admitted frankly. 'It was an absolutely desperate situation. The Germans were so well-equipped. They had motorized divisions. We tried to fight them in the field but they spotted us from the air.' Her voice began to trail away and she looked down at the ground. 'I felt it was all so hopeless. Yes, I was a convinced communist but for the first time in my life I started praying, crying out to God to help me. I tried to remember my grandmother's prayers.'

Graschenkova's cry expressed the profound despair of many. The fighting in the summer of 1942 was an unequal contest between a highly professional, well-trained German army – whose morale was sky high – and a demoralized Soviet force flung in against them. Evgeny Kurapatov – who fought in one of the new makeshift Russian divisions – put it like this:

> We desperately needed better equipment and training. The commander might give an order but the tail of the division would still be waiting for it hours later. Instructions would reach our troops when it was too late to enact them. We made mistake after mistake.

Mikhail Borisov was the sole survivor of five different artillery crews during the retreat from Kharkov.

> Our failings included poor equipment and a chronic shortage of ammunition. We were stuck with an inadequate 45mm battalion gun, which was only able to penetrate enemy tank armour at a range of less than 100 metres. We had little confidence in the effectiveness of such a weapon – which we nicknamed 'Goodbye to the Motherland!', and it hardly helped when we were only issued with a pitiful two shells a day.

The situation in the skies above was little better. 'On one occasion our retreating infantry was strung out along the steppe', Borisov recalled.

> Above us were six of our I-16s [Polikarpov single-engine fighters]. These aircraft were ponderous and slow – the troops called them 'donkeys'. Suddenly one German Messerschmidt appeared. We watched the combat above but it proved to be a very short fight. The German plane shot them down, one by one. We were all at his mercy, for there was nowhere to take cover – and we waited help-lessly for him to open up on us with his machine guns. Instead, after flying over us several times at low level, he tipped his wings at us in a derisory, mock-salute, and flew off. You cannot imagine what that felt like! We were left so humiliated – left with such a hopeless anger in our hearts. I remember shaking my fist at that departing plane and thinking 'We cannot fight like this!'

The enemy relished any chance to humiliate the retreating soldiers. 'Two of us were sent out on reconnaissance', Mereshko remembered.

We took horses and rode out on the steppe to look for the Germans. Finally, we found them: line upon line of marching infantry. We galloped off as fast as we could, then two Messerschmidts appeared. One circled us, the other opened fire with his machine gun. They could have easily finished us off. Instead, they chased us for thirty minutes for the sheer enjoyment of it. I was yelling riding instructions to my mate, as we turned our horses this way and that, desperately trying to avoid the bullets. The machine gun fire got closer and closer. Then, suddenly, they tired of their sport and flew off.

Another witness to the terrible retreat was Viktor Nekrasov, who conveyed his impressions in his novel, *Frontline Stalingrad*. He recalled stupefying heat, the burning sun, all-pervasive dust and, always, the overwhelming speed of the German advance. 'The general mood was frightful. The Germans were deep inside Russia, descending like an avalanche on the Don – and where was our front – did it exist at all?' Nekrasov remembered the all-pervasive feeling of despair only too vividly: 'When civilians asked our retreating troops where they were going, we could not look them in the eye.'

The snippets of soldiers' conversations Nekrasov recorded carry an unmistakable sense of inferiority. 'What's the use in trying to fight the Germans. They are travelling from Berlin to Stalingrad in motor vehicles and here we are with 1890s rifles.' 'We cannot sustain such a loss in territory. Our evacuated factories are not able to work for us. The Ukraine and the Kuban have gone, so there's no grain. The Donbas has gone, so there's no coal . . . when the Volga line of communication is cut we will lose our oil from Baku.' 'Even if we fight to the last man, heroism is not enough. They will flatten us with superior organization and masses of tanks. *Only a miracle can save us now*' (emphasis added). In such desperate times, a rough-hewn yet almost spiritual language began to emerge 'Faith', Nekrasov recalled, 'that was all that was left to us then – faith'.

The body language of the rival armies said everything. Mereshko recalled:

The Germans were so confident, which was natural – because they had come all the way from Kharkov to the Don. It would make anybody confident. They marched forward purposefully in the summer heat, sleeves rolled up, wearing shorts, and singing their songs.

In awful contrast, Mereshko remembered seeing the retreating Russian army, and wondering if its troops were sleep-walking. Groups of men passed him in some kind of terrible trance: 'They were really desperate people, almost prostrate with exhaustion, absolutely numb, unable to react to anything. We realized that they were no use to us in that condition and we just took their weapons off them.'

In public, propagandist rhetoric was still served up. A letter from Red Army Private Bogolubov, who had joined the 62nd Army, declared emphatically: 'We are sure that our enemy will suffer bitter defeat, just like at the battle of Moscow. We are ready to die in such a place of honour. We won't let the enemy take another step forward.' Recently released NKVD reports convey a rather different mood amongst many ordinary soldiers. On 20 July 1942 regimental clerk Kolesnikov declared:

> The German army is far smarter and more capable than ours. Look at their equipment. And what do we have? A few ancient aeroplanes. The newspapers say we are holding the Germans, but it's not so. Our press is lying to us.

A letter from Private Ivan Chechkov to his wife Katya reiterated the same, dismal theme:

> We undertook an assault, but the enemy surrounded us. They dropped paratroopers ahead of our position and started to drop bombs. These killed many of our soldiers; others drowned attempting to cross the river Don. Those that didn't make it to the river were captured anyway. But they say it's not at the Don where Russians will suffer the most, but the Volga. The Germans promise to drown us all in the Volga. My dear Katya, my dear children, it's hard to stay alive here. It seems we are all sentenced to death. There's nowhere else to go – we will either drown, or be killed or taken prisoner by the enemy. It will be a massacre at Stalingrad.

'It was a time of terrible panic', Tamara Kalmykova recalled. 'Everyone was frightened out of their wits. The commanders ran off first, the rest followed.'

The battle of Stalingrad started on the 17 July 1942, when units of the recently formed 62nd Army first met their German opponents on the river Chir, a tributary of the Don. The new army had been hurriedly formed up from the reserves a few days earlier and moved to the region of the Don, covering the central part of the Russian front. It was here that the main weight of the German attack would fall. The force was short of men and weapons, had not been properly 'knocked together' as an army unit, and had no actual experience of fighting. It was to suffer a baptism of fire.

Things went wrong from the beginning. The new commander, Major-General Kolpakchi, overcommitted his forces and, while soldiers and equipment were still being unloaded from trains in his rear, put five divisions in the first line of defence, and only one in the second. There had been insufficient time to dig a proper system of trenches and the ground was baked hard in the summer heat. Soon the German aviation appeared. 'Their Junker 87s put their sirens on, and bombed everything to smithereens,' recalled Mereshko. 'Then the German panzers and infantry rolled into the attack.'

The Battle on the Don

By early August 1942 the Germans had pushed the 62nd Army back to its main line of defence on the Don and the opportunity now arose to fight a classic battle of encirclement, breaking the main strength of the Russians on the Don river. Herbert Selle of the 6th Army described the moment: 'We now saw a decisive chance, not only of beating the enemy, installed in a broad, risky semi-circle about Kalach, but of annihilating him in a double pincer action along the Don.' If successful, this operation would open up the possibility of a rapid attack on Stalingrad.

Alexander Fortov, who commanded an artillery unit of the 112th Division, remembered those terrible July days as they were pushed back towards the Don:

> There was constant bombing by the Germans and in the chaotic conditions no food got through to us – we were trying to survive on emergency rations. And the heat was terrible: I had a constant desire to drink. We found most of the wells dried out – passing through a succession of semi-deserted villages, and occasionally, finding bitter, brackish water at the bottom of a well.

For Fortov and his comrades the tension was palpable. They knew a big German attack was in the offing as they fell back to the high, western bank of the Don. Paulus, the commander of the German 6th Army, had made his preparations thoroughly, adopting the usual German tactic of attacking on the flanks, with the aim of encircling and destroying his opponents. Two groups were created, each consisting of a panzer and two army corps: their objective was to break through to the right bank of the Don, and then drive behind the encircled Russians, meeting at Kalach, and destroying most of the 62nd Army. Then the attack on Stalingrad could be made in the most advantageous of circumstances.

On the morning of 24 July the Germans launched a massive attack on the right flank of the 62nd Army, with strong aviation support, and soon secured a devastating success. They broke through the Russian defence line, surrounded two infantry divisions and quickly reached the Don. In a most unusual response, the operational head of the 62nd Army HQ, Colonel Zhuravlev, was flown into the encircled area to take command of the troops. This nervous measure achieved little. On 25 July the Germans struck in the south, smashing through the left flank of the 62nd Army.

In the heat of battle Kolpakchi was dismissed, and a representative of Stavka – the Soviet supreme command – intervened. Colonel-General Vasilevsky launched an armoured counter-attack with forces drawn from the 1st and 4th tank armies in an attempt to prevent the total destruction of the fledgling army. But the Germans destroyed the majority of the tanks from the air and then surrounded all six divisions of the 62nd Army on the right bank of the Don. It was a classic battle of encirclement and it created the conditions for a successful assault on Stalingrad.

Anatoly Kozlov was a liaison officer in the First Tank Army. He commented frankly:

> It is often said during the retreat that we traded space for time. Well, if we bought a little time with this brief counter-attack it was at enormous cost. My own brigade advanced with 75 tanks – only three of them survived, and those had to be ditched in the river Don. In all, we lost more than 700 tanks: German air superiority ripped us apart. They were so confident – one plane even flew so low that we shot it down with a tank!

Kozlov was scathing about the plan of campaign: 'The decision to try to stop the Germans reaching Stalingrad at such a distance – about 100 km from the city – was a terrible mistake. The enemy's strength was utterly overpowering.'

The fate of individual divisions within the 62nd Army bears out Kozlov's comments. The 192nd, covering the army's right flank, disappeared completely; most of the 184th perished, including their commander. The 181st eventually surrendered – and the 33rd Guards Division – one of the army's best – was reduced to a scratch force of a few hundred men. The 196th fought its way out of the encirclement, but suffered terrible casualties in the process. 'This was the crucial moment', Kozlov emphasized, 'the destiny of our county, our motherland, was now dependent on events at Stalingrad – and everybody realized this.'

Evgeny Kurapatov fought with the 196th Division. He recalled:

> Our divisional commander was Dmitri Averin. We respected him – he had good military experience: he had fought in the Civil War, and then at the battle for Kiev in September 1941. He was tall, serious looking – and he had plenty of reason to look serious. We were surrounded by the Germans – became part of Zhuravlev's northern group – and on 7 August 1942 the enemy launched an all-out offensive. They easily overran our defence lines and columns of tanks broke through our position and headed towards our HQ.

For years Kurapatov had no idea what subsequently happened.

> I even studied the records of the Ministry of Defence on the 62nd Army, but they simply said that on the morning of 7 August the 196th Division ceased to exist. Then in 1982, on the fortieth anniversary of the battle, I met up again with our political officer and he told me about the tragedy that followed. Enemy tanks scythed through our defences and a group of them made for our command post. Averin made a last stand there – he just had his personal weapons, some grenades, one machine gun, and a small guards unit. Well – you can't fight tanks like that. Averin gave the order 'Save our banner!' and his commissar wrapped it around his body. Averin gave him a five-man bodyguard and ordered him to get across the Don with it. That was the last anybody saw of our commander. It was all so desperate – the whole of our front was disintegrating. I couldn't make any sense of what was going on. I felt so ineffectual, so completely and utterly lost.

'The Russians had been beaten in a battle of annihilation', Herbert Selle observed with grim satisfaction. 'The enemy, in addition to suffering many casualties, have lost over 1,000 tanks and 750 guns. Over 50,000 have been taken prisoner.' Selle recalled a meeting with Paulus, the 6th Army commander, shortly after this success. Stalingrad seemed within their grasp. 'The army was full of hope . . . my eyes met those of Paulus, questioning, almost unbelieving . . . were the Russians finally at the end of their tether?'

The traumatic Russian retreat shaped the battle in Stalingrad. The two experiences seemed poles apart, as a war of mobility, space and speed on the Russian steppe, which had ideally suited the German motorized formations, was replaced by one of close combat in the debris and rubble of Stalingrad. Yet it was a fight the Germans expected to win. When a Wehrmacht staff officer visited frontline divisions in the city in September 1942, officers told him that they were in a battle of attrition with the Russians, but they believed they would capture Stalingrad shortly.

Both sides learnt a lot about each other on the steppe that summer. The Germans held five trumps in the battle for Stalingrad.

Professionalism

The 6th Army had reached an exceptional height of professional organization in 1942. The Red Army at Stalingrad could not hope to match it. Instead, it had to find an answer of its own – devising tactics that would suit its own strengths, rather than compete with those of the Germans.

The Germans were well trained and had over two years of solid combat experience. Tamara Kalmykova, a communications officer with the 64th Army, described the background of those flung in to face them:

> What was a reserve army in 1942 – the armies that were desperately thrown in against the Germans? Our regular army was already in battle – and many of them had died or been taken prisoner. And in the reserve army were volunteers: young communists and older people, who had not been called up at the beginning of the war. These were not armies or divisions in any real sense – the military training just wasn't there.

Shortage of equipment reinforced the sense of inadequacy. Kalmykova continued:

> How long will an anti-tank rifle last if it only has six boxes of cartridges? It's no good against two or three hundred tanks. That's why many of our soldiers threw themselves under tanks with grenades – it was sheer desperation. And many of our troops had no proper weapons at all – just a spade and a knife.

The contrast between the two sides was striking. 'The German troops acted with such incredible efficiency', Kalmykova added.

The way they deployed their forces amazed us. I have to admit it – they taught us how to fight. We learnt so much from them: the co-ordination of different units, their communication system, their reconnaissance and cartography. We began to use all their things, the 'trophies' we could capture from them – we were even using their maps!

Anatoly Mereshko described the clockwork professionalism of their opponents:

The Germans did everything according to a schedule. At dawn their reconnaissance plane usually arrived. After a short gap the bombers would turn up, then came the shelling, and then infantry and tanks attacked. We had not the strength or the organization to stop them. There were no tanks, no support batteries, no support whatsoever – only the people you had with you and the weapons you held in your hand. We seemed so powerless to do anything against the Germans.

Our counter-attacks were hopeless. We would be told to attack after fifty minutes of shelling and an air strike. But there wouldn't be any shelling and, no matter how long we waited, our aviation never appeared. The red flare rocket would go up – the signal for our attack – but there had been no preparation and the enemy positions were completely intact. We would fix bayonets, run 300 metres, then the Germans would open fire with everything they had got and we would be forced back to our starting positions. We felt such desperation and anger – we were so disorganized. Time and time again we wondered of our High Command 'Why don't they help us fight the enemy properly?'

NKVD reports on the July fighting confirm the substance of Mereshko's complaint. In one of the battles on the steppe it was noted:

Tank forces from the 23rd Brigade commenced their assault without any information on the number of enemy opposing them and lacking any effective interaction with infantry, artillery and aviation. As a result our tanks were easily ambushed – and subjected to heavy artillery fire and attacks from the air. Our formations were completely broken up. Meanwhile, the enemy kept advancing.

This sense of frustration became even more heartfelt in the close combat of Stalingrad. Alexander Voronov, an artilleryman with the 13th Guards Division, said of the Germans:

> when we met them in city fighting, their discipline and organization stunned us. We manhandled our artillery shells into position – exhausting and difficult work, for they were heavy – and we piled them next to the gun, which was really dangerous, because if the gun was hit the shells would explode as well. With the Germans every-thing was well-planned and smoothly efficient – their shells were not hand delivered but properly transported by motor vehicles, to make the life of their soldiers easier. The bulk of them were stored away from the gun emplacement, neatly stacked by calibre. I was amazed and depressed at the difference between us.

Voronov emphasized the effect this had on morale: 'In September 1942, with such a superb system of supply, the Germans were naturally confident of victory. Our army was struggling to function at all – we were constantly short of ammunition, and this naturally undermined the spirit of our soldiers.'

The Russians had to devise a way of fighting that would disrupt the smooth professionalism of their assailants. Mereshko recalled:

> We noticed occasional moments of vulnerability when we faced the Germans on the steppe. Their infantry disliked man-to-man combat and also seemed uncomfortable in night fighting. So we employed both methods at Stalingrad in an attempt to unsettle the enemy.

This is why street-fighting tactics were so important: the Red Army found a different system from the Germans, and in using it, recovered its own *esprit de corps*. It drew upon different attributes, primal Russian qualities of resilience and courage under conditions of terrible hardship. It took time for these tactics to become militarily effective. But, even when initially unsuccessful, this new way of fighting was a source of tremendous pride to Stalingrad's defenders. It transformed the psychological atmosphere of the battle, as ordinary Russian soldiers regained a sense of hope and self-belief.

Logistics

The issue of logistics was all-important at Stalingrad. The Germans noticed on the steppe that the Russians struggled to supply their troops properly and this influenced their evolving campaign strategy. They knew city fighting demanded vast quantities of ammunition – and Russian supplies would have to be brought in to Stalingrad across the Volga. Their operational plan had a surgical simplicity – cutting the defenders off from their fellow armies to the north and south and subjecting the river crossings to constant air and artillery attack. Once the Russians ran short of supplies they would no longer be able to maintain an effective defence.

The abiding fear of Stalingrad's defenders was that they might completely run out of ammunition and this fear hung over the entire course of the battle like a ghastly spectre. An NKVD report shows that during 13–15 September 1942, when the Germans first broke into the city, there was a 'catastrophic shortage of ammunition'. The defending 62nd Army had only enough grenades and mortar shells for one day of street fighting. There was a massive shortage of bullets – no less than 500,000 were urgently needed for the army's machine guns. The Volga river crossing was poorly organized and subject to constant German air bombardment.

Feodor Shatravko remembers meeting the newly appointed commander of the 62nd Army, Vasily Chuikov, at this time. He was part of the so-called 'northern group', based around the Stalingrad suburb of Spartanovka, and he accompanied his own commander to Chuikov's HQ on the Mamaev Kurgan on 13 September: 'Chuikov asked us how things were,' he related. 'Well, we were honest with him – the mood of the men was terrible because of the drastic shortages in equipment and ammunition. The atmosphere was really ugly.'

Anatoly Mereshko spoke of the 'huge supply difficulties' that continued to plague the 62nd Army, difficulties which, he acknowledged frankly, were never fully overcome.

> However well we organized things during the battle there was always a desperate shortage of ammunition and food. Things were always difficult – but by late October 1942 we reached our moment of greatest crisis. We knew that the Volga would soon be partially blocked by ice – rendering river transport impossible. Our reconnaissance reports told us that fresh Nazi troops were still entering Stalingrad – and we would soon be cut off from any further reinforcement and ammunition. Our commander, Chuikov, was stockpiling an emergency reserve to keep us going a few more days – but the general outlook was terrible.

For the defending 62nd Army the shortage of supplies was a fearful handicap. A different spirit of leadership was needed to counter it, and to maintain the will to resist. Shatravko recalled Chuikov's personal assurance on the slopes of the Mamaev Kurgan.

> He spoke to us frankly, in man-to-man fashion. He told us that the present supply situation was completely unacceptable and promised us he would do everything in his power to improve it. We believed him and we felt for the first time that we had a commander who really cared about his soldiers.

Communications

It is often said that communications are the nerve centre of an army. The German communication system was excellent; the Russians struggled with one that was outmoded and poor. This was noticed on the steppe and fully exploited at Stalingrad.

Vasily Chuikov, who more than anyone else was to turn the situation around at Stalingrad, later wrote:

> Communication was still our weak point in the second year of the war. The Hitlerites were using radio devices in all their units and we were mostly relying on cable communication – and it was constantly falling out of use. All the time we had to send officers away to learn what was going on – and it complicated the management of our troops to an incredible degree. And often orders with the words 'immediately' in them were arriving at an army detachment when the settlements mentioned in those orders had already been abandoned, or the units which were supposed to fulfil the orders did not exist any more.

In July 1942, Colonel-General Vasilevsky confessed:

> Our combat experience is showing us that control of troops in the Red Army is at an unacceptable level. Unfortunately, I have to note that the main means of communication within the army remains the copper-wire telephone. Commanders are able to control their personnel when the wire is intact, but when it is disrupted all control is lost.

Anatoly Mereshko is open about the communications problems the defenders faced:

The Germans first realized our weakness out on the steppe. All their tanks had radios whereas with us only the commander of the unit had one – and the remaining tanks had to follow him. Communication was by hand signals and flags. The enemy quickly exploited this and as soon as the tank commander got up to direct the others he became a German sniper target.

Nikolai Orlov was the commander of one such tank company. His battalion was deployed in the north of Stalingrad to stop the Germans entering the city:

The enemy had reached the Volga at Rynok and we were ordered to dislodge them. We launched a counter-attack and I was supposed to signal to my other tanks to direct the fighting, but as soon as I rose above the hatch a German sniper caught me in his telescopic sight. His first bullet hit my radio headset, and the blow was so strong it sent me sprawling to the ground. I felt as if someone had hit me with a club. I leapt to my feet but a second bullet cut through my waist-belt and a third pierced my lung. Somehow I was carried back to a field hospital – I think it was a miracle that I survived at all.

Mereshko outlined the wider problem:

Our radio communication was very poor, and our officers were reluctant to use it, as the Germans intercepted our signals. Their equipment was so much better than ours. They could create radio interference to stop us communicating – or actually break in to our conversations and speak to us directly, mocking us with their tech-nological superiority, suddenly declaring: 'Russ – stop talking now!'

Radio operator Maria Faustova confirmed this depressing state of affairs: 'I was in a communication battalion situated on the Volga embankment. The Germans interfered with our radio transmission all the time. They were able to intercept our signals with relative ease – and this caused serious problems for us.'

This is an area where Paulus – who came to be derided for his role in the Stalingrad battle – deserves serious credit, for he built up a radio intercept unit of impressive skill within the German 6th Army. It performed wonders during the encirclement – and its importance in the German offensive, particularly the all-out assault of 14 October, has not received the attention it deserves.

The Russian weakness in radio equipment and training forced an over-reliance on the field telephone, as Mereshko made clear:

Our main method of communication was still telephone cable. This was particularly vulnerable in the fighting at Stalingrad. We tried to use underground routes – sometimes the sewers – but mostly this was not possible. So we had to lay the cables overland – and these wires on the surface were easily broken.

Leonid Gurevitz, a communication officers with the 13th Guards Division at Stalingrad, remembered: 'We were carrying these cables and telephone machines hundreds of metres through the desolate and dangerous landscape of the ruined city, but we had to keep going, because our infantry could not do without it.' The vulnerability of the Russian communication system at Stalingrad was exploited again and again by their opponents.

Army unity

The soldiers of the German 6th Army had been fighting together for two years, while their opponents were thrown together in a few weeks in an atmosphere of crisis. I have used the word 'Russian' as accepted shorthand for the Stalingrad defenders, but in fact the Soviet Union, of which Russia was the largest part, comprised a large mix of nationalities. Richard Overy, in *Russia's War*, put it like this:

It was not of course just 'Russia's War'. The Russian Empire, and after it the Soviet Union, embraced a complex ethnic geography. In 1940 Russians made up only 58% of the population. There were at least twenty other nationalities, most prominent among them the Ukrainians and Belorussians, on whose territories in the western Soviet Union most of the war was fought out.

As Overy points out, the Soviet Union also spanned the whole of northern and central Asia – and it was often untrained recruits from the central Asian republics who were hurriedly pushed into service in the military crisis of 1942.
    Anatoly Kozlov put it bluntly:

The composition of our armies during the summer retreat was of great concern to us. We had a general rule of thumb – that an army needed at least two-thirds of its soldiers to be from Russia, Belorussia or the Ukraine to be militarily effective. Instead, we were finding ourselves with most of our troops from the central Asian republics – with little training or motivation, and many unable to understand even the most basic Russian words. I was given a regiment of Tartar recruits. They couldn't speak Russian, they were without weapons and equipment and had no experience of using them. I was supposed to teach them how to use a machine gun – well, that was a challenging task!

Mikhail Borisov echoed Kozlov's comments: 'On the retreat to the Don I was lumbered with a mass of Uzbeks. They were slow and apathetic – and showed no aptitude for fighting whatsoever.'

The divisions which reinforced the 62nd Army during the actual battle of Stalingrad were far better trained and equipped, but the mix of nationalities remained an ongoing problem for the defenders. Vladimir Kiselyov, a company commander in the 13th Guards Division, recalled:

There were a lot of Uzbeks amongst us – they hardly understood Russian at all. You asked a question like 'What company are you from?' and you got an entirely different answer, in virtually incoherent Russian, like 'We haven't been getting any bread for three days'.

It was a source of enormous pride that the defenders of 'Pavlov's House', one of the strongholds at Stalingrad, came from many different nationalities, but this sense of unity was forged in the most disadvantageous of circumstances.

Battle memory

German fighting always incorporated a psychological element – a wish to terrorize their opponents and paralyse their fighting will. Their encirclement tactics were designed to create fear and uncertainty, the fear felt by men when they are isolated, surrounded and facing extinction. Armies sometimes experience a kind of 'collective memory', and for the 62nd Army the terror they faced at Stalingrad echoed the earlier, traumatic defeat they had suffered on the Don – when most of the army had been encircled and annihilated. They dreaded that history would repeat itself on the banks of the Volga.

From a purely tactical point of view, these German moves became predictable and could be more easily countered at close quarters in city fighting. But in the battle of wills between the two opposing armies they retained considerable power. Mereshko related:

On the steppe they were always toying with us during our retreat. At night-time they sent out machine gunners on motorbikes, with a lot of ammunition, to create a lot of noise and make us believe we were encircled. We would call them the 'night actors'. But some of our troops were frightened when they saw flare rockets or heard the sound of firing behind them – and panicked and left their positions.

Fear persisted throughout the battle. Mereshko described the atmosphere in the army four months later, in mid-November, as its shattered remnants clung to the Volga, preparing for a last, terrible battle of encirclement within the ruined city:

Our big fear was that when the ice on the river froze the Germans would get behind our position and encircle all our troops. By this stage, we only had 7,000 soldiers left. Chuikov set up special armoured posts on the two biggest islands on the Volga, Zaitsevski and Golodny – with heavy machine guns, hand machine guns and anti-tank guns – to try and stop this threat. But our strength was so depleted. We were afraid the Germans would capture these outposts, surround us, and cart us all away.

To counter such formidable advantages, Russian soldiers longed for someone to provide leadership by example. 'We needed to become proud of our army again', said Mereshko, 'and that pride could only be inspired by the right commander.'

Ineffective Leadership – the Story of the Bear Catcher

In the terrible retreat to Stalingrad, many were struggling to keep the merest vestiges of hope alive. Men were searching for effective leadership and finding it utterly lacking.

'The majority of our commanding officers are cowards', a young soldier named Gudzovsky wrote that summer. 'Surely we do not keep having to run away – we could have stood our ground. To hell with retreating! I'm sick to death of pulling back from the places where I grew up.' When generals criticized Nekrasov's description of the retreat to the Don, and then the Volga, complaining that he portrayed 'a ragged troop of bandits rather than a heroic Soviet army', he retorted: 'You weren't around to see it – you had long since fled east with your jeeps.'

Battlefield stress was reaching alarming proportions. Alexander Fortov felt the army's ability to command and control its men dissolving around him.

We had a tractor from a nearby collective farm to help us pull our gun – but the tractor broke down and couldn't be fixed. So I walked off, found the head of our HQ, described the situation we were in, and asked for assistance. Instead of being given a decision I got a torrent of abuse. This colonel called me a liar, accused me of running away and threatened to shoot me. I went absolutely pale with shock. Finally he told me to go back and make the tractor work – which was an absolutely useless order as it needed proper repair in a workshop. I returned and told my men about this encounter. Then we heard a sound of a motor engine, and a lorry suddenly appeared. The driver got out, saluted and said 'At your disposal sir!' Apparently, the colonel had relented.

Fortov's experience was no isolated phenomenon. The Red Army was in meltdown and its commanders could no longer cope with the situation. One NKVD report observed bluntly:

There is a serious problem with the commander of the 23rd Tank Brigade, Colonel Khasin – he has completely lost authority because of extremely impolite behaviour towards his officers. He constantly threatens them with executions and demotions. His influence is very negative. He has driven the staff officer of the corps, Colonel Volkonsky, to such a condition that he is ready to shoot himself. He demotes personnel for no reason whatsoever.

Chuikov described his first impressions that summer: 'In everything I could sense a lack of firm resistance at the front – a lack of tenacity in battle. It seemed as if everyone, from the army commander downwards, was always ready to make another move backwards.' The generals he met had no idea of the situation on the ground and issued orders that were often incomprehensible. Kolpakchi, the 62nd Army's first commander, talked happily of probing the enemy's positions and making a general advance forward. Out on the steppe his soldiers wandered about aimlessly, had consumed the last of their rations, and were suffering terribly from the heat. Chuikov found divisional staffs forlornly searching for the Army HQ. 'When I asked them where the Germans were, where there own units were, and where they were going, they could not give me a sensible reply.'

Chuikov believed the Red Army's commanders had comprehensively failed to get any sort of grip on the battle. They had a limited knowledge of the enemy's movements, and were out of touch with reality, 'reckoning their obvious failures as great successes'. Kolpakchi was replaced by Lopatin. On the 28 July 1942 the new commander dispatched a resounding battle order to his troops: 'The 62nd Army is completing the encirclement of the enemy.' In fact, the initiative lay entirely with the Germans, who had already broken through the Russian lines and reached the Don. Chuikov was scathing: 'This reminds me of the anecdote about the man who caught a bear. "Bring it over here", someone said. "I can't", he replied, "it won't let me."'

In such dire circumstances, one act of selfless courage could help keep hope alive. Mikhail Borchev remembered the captain of his artillery unit taking a rocket weapon, nicknamed the 'Andryusha', across the Don on a raft.

> It was still classified as top-secret and it was vital it did not fall into enemy hands. But the captain was only a few metres from the shore when the Germans appeared with their tanks and infantry. They quickly had him within firing range and called out, ordering him back. But he blew the raft up, destroying the 'Andryusha', killing himself rather than let the weapon fall into their possession. I thought about that a lot as we fought in the ruins of Stalingrad.

Another and perhaps the most remarkable act of sacrifice was performed by cadet units. They should have been given proper leadership and training; instead, they were thrown in front of the German war machine. Mereshko commanded a company of them:

> They moved at least twenty of these regiments from various cities straight into the front line. Most of the cadets were just 18 – those boys were pushed through an accelerated, short course, and many didn't even finish it. Half our company didn't have rifles – and we only had one machine gun, instead of the normal complement of ten. They were so brave – nobody tried to run away, and no one showed any cowardice. But they deserved so much better.

'The normal strength of each cadet regiment was 2,500', Mereshko continued,

> but by the beginning of September most were reduced to barely a hundred. General Lopatin, who commanded our 62nd Army during that terrible August, said that the way these guys fought was truly heroic. But Lopatin was no longer able to lead his army effectively. Many of the soldiers and officers who had broken out of German

encirclement on the Don had completely lost hope – they didn't care anymore – and we could no longer count on them to hold back the enemy. So we took their weapons off them and armed our young cadets instead. They were left covering our retreat all the way back to the outskirts of Stalingrad.

Anatoly Kozlov remembered how 3,000 cadets were sent to Stalingrad from his college at Grozny and only twenty survived the battle:

They were too young, just 18, and without military experience. They were called to battle as ordinary soldiers, they died as ordinary soldiers; there was no time to get promoted. Their courage covering the retreat was outstanding – and while they tried to stem the German onslaught our commanders either disappeared or sat far behind the front line issuing instructions which bore no relation to reality.

The 'Not a Step Back!' Order

The powerful advantages possessed by the Germans as they advanced on Stalingrad forced their Russian opponents to draw on their deepest inner resources to sustain themselves. Every veteran of Stalingrad can identify with a journey into despair followed by the regaining of a sense of worth and value. For most of them, that journey started with a remarkable order from Stalin himself, his directive number 227, christened by the soldiers the 'Not a Step Back!' order. It marked the symbolic drawing of a line – a decision that no further retreat was possible, and that the fleeing Red Army must turn and face the enemy, and make a stand.

What exactly was Order 227? It was issued on 28 July 1942, with the Stalingrad battle only recently under way. Further south, there were rumours that Red Army units had panicked during the German attack on Rostov and had abandoned their positions – and it was now clear that much of the Caucasus would be lost. Order 227 – which was read out directly to members of the armed forces – set out clearly the danger the country was in.

Every commander, soldier and political worker must understand that our resources are not unlimited . . . To retreat further would mean the ruin of the country and ourselves. Every new scrap of territory we lose will significantly strengthen the enemy and severely weaken our defence of our Motherland.

Its rallying call was: 'Not a Step Back! This must now be our chief slogan. We must defend to the last drop of blood every position, every metre of Soviet territory, to cling on to every shred of Soviet earth and defend it to the utmost.'

To back up this order, a spirit of 'iron discipline' was brought to the army – 'panic-mongers' and cowards would no longer be tolerated. This new discipline was given teeth through forming units behind the front line – known as blocking detachments – which had power to shoot those found retreating without permission, and setting up punishment battalions – penal companies – for those guilty of cowardice or indiscipline.

These provisions were undoubtedly the reason why the order was not fully publicized at the time, and since its eventual publication – in 1988 – it has become highly controversial. This is the source of claims that the defence of Stalingrad was enforced by a gun at the soldiers' backs rather than coming about through any genuine heroism.

Some of the content of Order 227 is genuinely shocking. It was intended to shake up the Red Army and was put into effect with absolute ruthlessness As the battle of Stalingrad unfolded, on 13 September 1942, the commander and commissar of a fleeing signals regiment were shot for cowardice in front of their troops and blocking detachments prevented more than a thousand soldiers making an 'unauthorized retreat' beyond the Volga. But repression alone could not and would not have created a turnaround of fortunes at Stalingrad. Order 227 also appealed to soldiers' love of their country: 'This is an appeal of our Motherland. To fulfil it is to defend our land, save our Motherland and demolish the hateful enemy.' This evocation of deeply felt patriotism, at a time of profound crisis, began to work a transformation in the mood of the army.

Vasily Chuikov, the defender of Stalingrad, described the situation:

> At the beginning of the summer of 1942 our armies retreated to the Don and then to the Volga, and towards the Caucasus – and the country lost the Donbas, its engineering industry, the wheat of Rostov and Stavropol, and much, much more. By the middle of the summer of 1942 over 40 per cent of the population of the Soviet Union was in the occupied zone. Such a situation could hardly fail to give cause for alarm. Every new retreat by our armies had a devastating effect on the mood of our people. The army was faced with the greatest danger of all – losing the trust of the nation. In these circumstances the slogan 'Not a Step Back!' was coined.

Anatoly Kozlov remarked of the order: 'It was harsh but inevitable. The task was to stop the Germans. It was already clear that what happened at Stalingrad was critical – that everything would be decided here. There was nothing else to do.' Praskovja Graschenkova said: 'The moment we were given Order 227: we realized that we were the ultimate line of defence.' Evdokia Belitskaya, a nurse with the 64th Army, added: 'We knew that this was a time of crisis and felt the pain of our people. There were two options left to us: either to defend Stalingrad or become slaves of the Germans.'

Tamara Kalmykova recalled:

> Everybody was retreating, and that was why the 'Not a Step Back!' order was so badly needed, because lots of people, soldiers and commanders, seemed to think that as we had so much land, our country was so large, we could keep on retreating and retreating – and then, at some future date, start fighting properly again, when everyone had decent weapons and training. But that just wasn't right, because we were leaving behind so much: our harvests, our factories and our plants, our people. We couldn't keep falling back and Stalin, in his Order 227, realized this. The order was vital to restore discipline in the army and alleviate the despondency felt by the people.

In July 1942, opinions were more divergent. An NKVD report reveals some of the reactions within the army were critical: 'This order will change nothing – it has come too late. The German strength in aircraft is overwhelming. We are already defeated.' 'People put in penal units will go over to the Germans rather than face the blocking detachments. We need bread, not discipline.' 'Too many soldiers have perished – there are not enough of us left to fight now.' 'I don't believe in the force of this order. Last year we retreated. This year we will retreat again – beyond the Volga.' Yet although some soldiers voiced concern, or feared Order 227 had come too late, there was nevertheless a strong groundswell of support for it within the Red Army: 'A good order – made at the right time' was a frequent observation.

'Many of our soldiers supported the order', Anatoly Kozlov said, 'even if some feared it was too late. All of us expected a decisive response from our high command as we retreated towards the Volga.' For Mereshko it was the first crucial moment in the Russian recovery:

> The 'Not a Step Back' order has created a negative image – in the west, but also in our own press – of Russian troops being forced to

attack with machine guns at their backs. Each army had a punishment unit for officers and a penal battalion for soldiers but by 1942 we had lost 70 per cent of our economic resources. Some officers and soldiers believed that they could retreat all the way to the Ural Mountains but any further retreat would lead to the death of our Motherland. There was nowhere left to retreat.

Mereshko continued:

Order 227 played a vital part in the battle. It opened the eyes of the army and the people, and showed them the truth of the situation facing the country. It led to the famous slogan at Stalingrad: 'There is no land for us beyond the Volga.' We were no longer just fighting for a city. It inspired us to fight for very metre of ground, every bush and river, each little piece of land. Order 227 brought an incredible ferocity to our defence of Stalingrad.

Machine gunner Mikhail Kalinykov was stationed on Stalingrad's southern front. He and his fellow soldiers also felt the power of Order 227:

To be honest with you, there was considerable uncertainty about the fate of the city – whether we could hold it or not. And yet, after Order 227, we felt that we had to hold out at Stalingrad regardless of that uncertainty – somehow, we had to make our stand there. You see, the soil was now precious to us, and we had to defend every metre of it. It was our promise to the Motherland.

Veteran Vladimir Turov put it simply: 'Blocking detachments could not make Order 227 work. The motivation had to be within us.'

Chapter Two

Stalin's City

Stalin's 'Not a Step Back!' order had an immediate impact on the war effort. It stiffened the resolve of the defenders and made clear to ordinary soldiers the perilous situation facing the country. But it could not in itself transform the mood of the army. Order 227 needed a worthy objective, a place to defend of obvious importance to Red Army troops – and a commander able to reach out and lift the spirit of his men. Valentina Krutova, an inhabitant of the city, said simply: 'Stalingrad was hugely symbolic – after all, it carried Stalin's name – and there would have been an irretrievable loss of prestige had it been surrendered to the enemy.'

The city of Stalingrad was originally named Tsaritsyn. It was founded at the end of the sixteenth century as a fortress and trading outpost on Russia's southern frontier. Situated on the western bank of the Volga river, it dominated the route to Astrakhan and the southern Caspian Sea, and the arrival of the railway system at the end of the nineteenth century led to its considerable industrial expansion. During the Russian Civil War both sides realized Tsaritsyn's strategic significance and fought over it fiercely. Stalin himself played a part in organizing the Bolshevik defence and the city was renamed in his honour. It was substantially rebuilt in the 1920s and 1930s and by the beginning of the Second World War stood as a Soviet showpiece, with a population close to half a million people.

Once the war began Stalingrad's newly constructed Tractor Factory was converted to tank production. The city also boasted one of the oldest artillery-making factories in Russia, renamed the 'Barrikady' in the Soviet era, and possessed important steel production works, chemical factories and oil refineries. Stalingrad was an obvious target for Hitler – economically and strategically. Its capture would cut the transport of oil and vital resources from the south. And because it was named after the head of the Soviet Union, and strongly linked to him in the propaganda circulated by the regime, it would also be a colossal psychological blow if it fell to the enemy. Stalin would lose face utterly if he retreated from the city that bore his name.

Stephan Mikoyan, the son of the Bolshevik Trade and Supply Minister, was brought up with Stalin's children and knew the Soviet leader well. During the summer of 1942 he was an air force captain, guarding the vital Baku oilfields, and was also employed on special secret surveillance missions, reporting to the Foreign Minister, Molotov: 'We all knew what was at stake if we didn't hold out at Stalingrad', he said.

> The consequences for us were quite unthinkable. Stalingrad was a symbol of such enormous importance, both within our country and on the broader world stage. We knew that the Turkish army had mobilized in August 1942 and some their regiments had already undertaken reconnaissance missions across our border. I was responsible for tracking their movements and my reports went directly to Stalin. We had no doubt that if Stalingrad fell Turkey would enter the war as an ally of Germany. Stalin desperately wanted to hold the city.

Stalin's Railway

In their advance on Stalingrad in the summer of 1942 the Germans methodically cut its rail links. Stalin had foreseen this danger, and months earlier had ordered the construction of an emergency railroad from Saratov, further up the Volga, to Leninsk, about 20 kilometres east of Stalingrad. During the battle it carried the ammunition and heavy equipment necessary to sustain the fighting and brought in reinforcements. The secret railway was vital for the successful defence of the city.

The railway was built as fast as possible. There was a shortage of necessary materials, so sections of the Baikal-Amur railroad were taken apart and brought to the new construction sites. It was laid down just in time – there was only one track, with a few sections double-tracked, to allow trains to wait there as others passed by. Mereshko once travelled on the railway, taking 62nd Army papers and documents to Saratov, and remembered a speed restriction of 10 to 20 kilometres per hour, because there had been no time to reinforce the rails – they were just resting on the ground.

The Germans constantly bombed the railway; the Russians protected it with anti-aircraft guns and armoured trains. Repair units were sent out constantly. 'This railroad was so important to us', Mereshko said, 'for it allowed the necessary quantity of ammunition – and a huge amount was expended in street fighting – to be brought up to our frontline.' At Leninsk, lorries and horses carried the ammunition to the east bank of the Volga, where it was shipped across the river to Stalingrad. It was usual for the trains to run one after another, almost in a continuous line, bringing their vital supplies towards the city.

The construction of the secret railway undoubtedly reveals positive aspects of Stalin's leadership: his command of the economy, his foresight and his remarkable attention to detail. Veterans believe that Stalin dominated this battle from afar. Attempts to airbrush him out of the picture are therefore nonsensical. But his legacy is complicated and highly emotive, and faced with differing accounts of what happened, often driven by political ideologies, it becomes harder and harder to get a clear view.

Stalingrad was Stalin's city – he had encouraged its industrialization and rebuilding and he understood better than anybody else its economic and political significance, and the consequences if it fell into the hands of the enemy. In the summer of 1942, Germany's rapid advance into Russia and the Ukraine had left the economy struggling. Many factories had been evacuated beyond the Urals but production had only just started again. There were terrible shortages everywhere – and this disorganization hamstrung Russian resistance on the approaches to Stalingrad. But during the battle in the city the picture began to change, as the economy became fully mobilized.

Fortov said:

> Stalin ordered the secret railway to be constructed, but it represented something larger to us, the hard-won industrialization of our country. The Germans wanted to take it from us. We were all aware of what was at stake if the enemy captured Baku and our oilfields. I was a lieutenant, far away from the big political decisions. But, being a patriot, I was worried about the amount of land and resources we were losing to the Germans. We needed to make a stand and Stalingrad seemed to be the place to do that. By building the railway Stalin made that stand possible.

Anatoly Kozlov added:

> Stalin made many mistakes – but he had a real gift: he could anticipate things. He had pushed for a series of defences around Stalingrad as early as December 1941. I sometimes wonder whether, on a purely instinctive level, Stalin had this place in mind as the battleground to finally confront Fascism.

In the summer of 1942 Stalin was struggling to contain the German onslaught. He appointed a series of commanders to take charge of the Southern

Front after the military disaster at Kharkov, when nearly a quarter of a million Russian troops were encircled and destroyed by the enemy. Timoshenko was replaced by Gordov, and when the Germans reached the Don basin another commander, Yeremenko, appeared. Their military responsibilities were confusingly delineated, a sign of the crisis in the wake of the German advance. Yet Kozlov made a deeper point:

> I strongly believe the real ruler of the Stalingrad Front was Stalin himself – even though he remained in Moscow. It was his city, he had experience of fighting here and knew the region well. Stalin sent many important men to Stalingrad to report on the situation – Malenkov, Zhukov, Vasilevsky, Ustinov – because he cared so deeply about the battle's outcome.

This is all very well, but it is naive to believe that such confidence – if Stalin fully possessed it himself – could be easily transmitted to the ordinary rank and file. When the Germans unleashed their onslaught on the city many feared that Stalingrad would either surrender or perish. And there was a terrible undertow to Stalin's determination – his disregard for human life and the safety of Stalingrad's civilian population. They were thrust into the frontline of the developing battle. Nevertheless, Kozlov emphasized: 'All of us expected something decisive, a clear cut decision of some sort, as we retreated towards the Volga.'

Stalingrad had begun life as a border stronghold, and was a heroic battleground during the Russian Civil War. The city was steeped in an older, warrior mythology – its great hill, the Mamaev Kurgan, which dominated the city, was reputed to be a Tartar burial ground. Documentary footage of the battle shows an impenetrable ruined landscape, every obstacle turned into a stronghold worthy of the Tartar fighting tradition. But this was created from a starting point of great vulnerability. In the beginning the city, strung out along the western side of the Volga river for a length, including its suburbs, of about 40 kilometres, with its wide streets and avenues, lay invitingly open to German attack.

The Vulnerability of the City

General Nikolai Krylov, chief of staff of the 62nd Army, later wrote:

> The enemy broke into the city after taking control of the ridge of hills which separated Stalingrad from the steppe lands and which

overlooked the whole area. The city stretched out before them in a thin strip along the banks of the Volga. It was nowhere more than three kilometres wide, and in places was far narrower. Not only was it an easy target for artillery, it also had wide, arrow–straight streets running at right angles to the Volga bank.

'It seemed astounding to us', Krylov remarked, that 'the terrible military might of the Germans, sent to cut through this narrow strip in a hundred places, was brought to a halt here'. The creation of a redoubtable line of defence amidst the city ruins was the key factor in the ultimate success of the Red Army.

Mereshko remembered the city's vulnerability at the beginning of the battle:

> The terrain surrounding Stalingrad gave so many advantages to the Germans. The land to the west of the city was much higher than its eastern side, so the enemy could easily observe our frontline of defence, and also look deep inside our position. The river tributaries ran down to the Volga from its higher side, opening up fresh tactical opportunities for our opponents, for their infantry and tanks could easily hide in the deep gullies and dried out river beds.

When the Germans force broke through to Rynok, on 23 August 1942, they secured a dominating position to direct artillery fire into the city. Mereshko described the effect of this:

> Our soldiers' telegraph worked very precisely and we quickly learnt that the Germans had reached this high spot on the Volga – and kicked our guys off it. We counter-attacked again and again but nothing came of our efforts. The Germans held on to that advantageous piece of ground to the very end of the battle. Our emplacements were much lower than the enemy's vantage point. It allowed them to fire on us as if we were ducks on a lake.

Herbert Selle recalled:

> When our Panzers took the high suburb of Rynok, overlooking the steep western banks of the Volga, the whole army was full of hope and expectation. After the decisive victory on the Don there seemed good reason to assume that Stalingrad would fall without too much opposition and that serious Russian resistance would only begin east of the Volga.

The importance of holding the high ground at Stalingrad – both tactical and psychological – was shown in the struggle for the Mamaev Kurgan, the hill in the centre of the city. Its broad slopes were covered in parkland and on its crest were the city's water towers. Both sides fought for possession of the Kurgan with incredible ferocity. For the Russians it came to hold an almost supernatural significance – they believed that if they lost the Kurgan they would lose Stalingrad.

The battle for this hill was fought out in the open, where the Germans could deploy their air superiority to maximum advantage. The power of their bombardment was so strong, Mereshko recalled, that 'the shape of the hill would literally, minute by minute, keep changing before our eyes'. It was a contest, Chuikov acknowledged, which even by Stalingrad's terrible standards was unparalleled in its stubbornness and brutality. The commander recited what had become a sacred oath for the city's defenders: 'We decided we would hold on to the Mamaev Kurgan whatever happened.'

The Defence Lines

It was most unusual for a battle to be conducted within a major urban centre. How had this come about? Russia's major cities were normally protected by a series of semi-circular defence lines. Although Stalingrad had four of these, no satisfactory defence could be set up at any of them. Mereshko continued:

> Stalin's HQ – Stavka – had ordered the creation of four defensive lines to protect the city: an outer line, with a length of 400 kilometres; a middle line (150 km); an inner one (70km) and the city line. These were to be built with the help of field engineers and the local population. But at the time we met the enemy they were only about 30 per cent ready.

This was a race the Russians never looked like winning. 'We tried to use natural obstacles', Anatoly Kozlov recalled, 'rivers, gullies and ravines – and work around them. But we were still digging when the Germans reached us. Very little firepower – heavy guns and artillery, had been installed.' Tamara Kalmykova, a communications officer with the 64th Army, witnessed the sorry state of the defences that summer:

> They say there were strong fortifications protecting Stalingrad but many of our trenches and dug outs were not properly finished when

the Germans advanced towards the city. Old people, and even children, were working almost 18 hours a day, under constant bombing, in a last-ditch attempt to ready them.

Stalin had ordered their construction many months before, in December 1941, but as the Germans advanced towards the Don the following summer, a Red Army survey found 'defensive works on the Stalingrad perimeter have been destroyed by the spring flooding of the rivers'. Instructions were hastily issued to rebuild them, but despite the extraordinary efforts of the civilian population, this was not really possible. Krylov confessed that the ambitious system of city fortification devised in 1941 placed the perimeters too far to the west and, as a result, the belated resumption of fortification building in July 1942 was unable to stop the Germans.

Tamara Kuznetsova was one of those helping to build the trenches and bunkers.

> Many of us believed the city should not be given up. But the defence work was undertaken too late, and it put our civilians at risk. We finally finished camouflaging firing points on 25 August, two days after the Germans had begun bombing Stalingrad, and only then were we allowed to return to our homes. But no evacuation programme had been organized for us and we were left trapped inside the city.

Mereshko was critical of the whole defensive concept:

> The idea that an outer defence line to the city could be constructed as far away as the Don just wasn't feasible. The necessary field engineering work hadn't been done and there was no coherent system of defence for us to use. In addition, there had been no rain that summer, the Don had become very shallow, and its width was little more than 200 metres, so it was much less of an obstacle to the advancing enemy. And once the Germans had reached the higher western bank, they could see how incomplete our fortifications were.

While some individual strong points and sections of trenches were well-constructed, and caused the Germans considerable problems, overall they were able to make deep penetrations into the defensive echelons. Fear of enemy encirclement drove the defenders back. Suren Mirzoyan fought with the 33rd Guards Division:

From the second half of August the Germans were pushing hard towards the city. We were occupying positions on the middle defence line but we were suddenly ordered to retreat again. We heard rumours that there was already fighting in the city. We were withdrawn from our positions – which we were expecting to defend strongly – because of a fear the Germans would encircle and destroy us where we stood. So we found ourselves back in Stalingrad, with just a few paltry barricades for protection.

'Inner Defence'

Stalingrad was not prepared for defence, for a long battle or for a state of siege. No one could see how the city could be held. To make a stand against the Germans, the mentality of the defenders had to change. Chuikov said: 'We needed to believe that every house in which we had even one soldier could become a fortress against the enemy.'

Stalin's 'Not a Step Back!' order put some much-needed iron into the Russian defence, and led to some bitter rearguard actions and patches of stiff fighting. It also began to create a climate where such actions were recognized and honoured. On 23 July 1942 Petr Boloto and three other anti-tank riflemen from the 33rd Guards Division were cut off from their unit south of the town of Kletskaya. Boloto and his small group held out – despite repeated attacks by the enemy – and destroyed thirteen tanks. Then they fought their way out of encirclement and rejoined their comrades.

Later, during the fighting in Stalingrad, Boloto's feat received considerable publicity and he was made a Hero of the Soviet Union. His exploit embodied the spirit of resilience and selflessness that was spreading amongst the city's defenders. But at the time the reaction had been rather different.

Mereshko takes up the story.

After their action at Kletskaya, Boloto and his soldiers broke through German lines and reached my unit and Boloto joined my machine gun company. No one believed him when he described that fight. It was not thought possible that a small group of four men could survive encirclement: 'such things don't happen in war' was a typical reaction. But then, in August, a press article appeared describing the exploit, and things began to fall into place. The mood of cynicism within the army was changing and the valiant actions of the four no longer appeared inconceivable. Boloto proved his worth to us in the streets of Stalingrad, graduating from our 'fighting academy' with the rank of lieutenant and receiving the Order of Lenin for his courage. In November his earlier exploit was formally acknowledged and he was awarded the title of Hero of the Soviet Union.

Boloto's selfless courage came to typify Red Army heroism at Stalingrad. But the broader power of Order 227 came from its link with another directive of Stalin's, made the day after his 'Not a Step Back!' order, on 29 July 1942. He revived the military orders of Alexander Nevsky, Suvorov and Kutuzov.

Alexander Nevsky was a Russian prince who had defeated the German Teutonic knights in a famous battle in the thirteenth century. A military Order of Alexander Nevsky had been created by Catherine the First, but was abolished by the Bolsheviks in 1917, in accordance with a belief that Nevsky represented a corrupt imperial past. In 1938, as a sense of national threat increased with German military expansionism, Nevsky's exploits were celebrated in a film by Sergei Eisenstein. Now, on 29 July 1942, the order was revived to encourage army officers to perform acts of exceptional courage and leadership.

The Stalinist regime clearly recognized that a more human face of courage and national pride was needed. A medal was struck and, in a deliberate link with the film, Nevsky's likeness was based on Eisenstein's lead actor, Nikolai Cherkassov.

Cherkassov's Nevsky was an instinctive patriot. His famous words of defiance of the Germans and passionate love of his homeland spoke directly to his audience at a time of profound crisis: 'It is better to die in your native land than ever to abandon it', he said. 'He who comes to us with the sword will die by the sword.' Nevsky would become a potent symbol for Red Army troops, evoking a greater spirit of patriotism and inspiring a sacred defence of the motherland against a fearsome invader.

A sense of destiny was being evoked. Nevsky's victory against the Germans was in 1242 and the battle for Stalingrad was taking place on its 700th anniversary. Mikhail Borisov said:

Yes, of course we thought about our history that summer, for it seemed to us that without our love for our motherland there could be no victory. And the resolve to defend our motherland, and never betray it, went deeper than any political ideology. The saying of Alexander Nevsky, 'He who comes to us with the sword will die by

the sword', became a source of inspiration to us. Amidst the horror,
it expressed something real and powerful – our pride in our country.

Ivan Barykin was a marine with the 154th Brigade of Naval Infantry. In early
August 1942 one of them was the first to receive the Order of Alexander
Nevsky. 'Can you imagine what a lift that gave all of us?' Barykin said proudly.

> One of our guys was No. 1 – the first to get this prestigious award.
> We were part of the 64th Army, covering the south-western flank
> towards Stalingrad: one of our lieutenants, Ivan Ruban, with only
> forty men left in his company, boldly turned the tables on the
> enemy.

Barykin described what had happened:

> The Germans were attacking with infantry and tanks and Ruban set
> up an ambush in a gully. He hid most of his men along the top, with
> his few remaining pieces of artillery, and told the rest to withdraw
> along the gully bottom to act as decoys. Ruban's plan worked
> perfectly – the Germans were overconfident and rushed straight
> into the trap – and he destroyed their infantry with a concentrated
> machine gun barrage.

The marines were part of an army group holding positions along the Aksai
river. They stood firm against the Germans when others were falling back in
panic. Their leader – and the man who proposed Ivan Ruban for the Order of
Alexander Nevsky – was Vasily Chuikov.
Barykin continued:

> When Chuikov nominated Ruban for this new award it had a big
> effect on us. We were constantly defending, covering the troops
> retreating towards the Volga, but the mood of the soldiers began to
> change. Soon, others were trying to emulate Ruban. I remember one
> guy, Ilya Kaplanov, in the suburbs of Stalingrad. He was on fire
> from a Molotov cocktail, which had shattered over him, setting him
> alight – but he ran forward in that dreadful state and threw himself
> on a German tank.

Kaplanov's desperate courage foreshadowed one of Stalingrad's most famous
heroic deeds, when another marine – Mikhail Panikakha – destroyed a German

tank in similar, agonizing fashion in the workers' settlement of the Red October Factory.

Nevsky would become a talisman for Russian troops at Stalingrad. But at the beginning of the battle such heroism was only found in isolated incidents. Suren Mirzoyan acknowledged a sense of inferiority still existed within the army:

> Every piece of land we surrendered became a traumatic experience for us. And when the Germans reached the Volga on 23 August and bombed the city, it seemed as if Hitler would carry out his plans of conquest. I remember the confusion felt by our political commissar: he had been telling us we needed to strengthen our defence and kick the Germans out of our land, and then we were suddenly ordered to retreat again, although according to Order 227 we had no right to retreat anymore. We wondered whether our High Command felt we were weaker than the Germans and could not hold out at Stalingrad.

But Mirzoyan could feel the beginnings of a change:

> We were fighting harder than before the Don. One guy said that even if he lost all his weapons, he would hold onto our land with his teeth – he refused to yield any more of it to the enemy. Men started to talk about the importance of not giving up Stalingrad – how the whole country was depending on us.

Alexander Fortov felt the pain of withdrawing from the Volga:

> It was a heartbreaking experience for us on the retreat from the Don to Stalingrad – heartbreaking to be giving up more of our own land. All my soldiers felt like that. We were afraid, when the Germans struck towards the Volga, from the north and south, that the enemy would trap us again. They were constantly dropping leaflets on us, telling us: 'Surrender! Your days are over – you don't have a way out. Stick your bayonet in the ground.' We cursed them – used the paper to make our cigarettes – and kept retreating, with the German aircraft over our heads all the time. Then the order came through – 'Back into Stalingrad!' We moved into the city through constant bombing: everything around us was on fire. I have never felt so scared in all my life.

But Fortov also noticed something different:

> Even in those terrible conditions, people tried not to succumb to
> their fears, and pushed aside their negative thoughts. I was strug-
> gling to cope one day when a soldier came up to me and said simply
> 'Comrade Lieutenant – I still believe we can win. It will go all the
> way at Stalingrad.'

The Terror Raid

The Russians were retreating towards a living city – for tragically, it had not
been possible to evacuate most of Stalingrad's inhabitants before the fighting
began. On the afternoon of 23 August 1942 the Germans subjected downtown
Stalingrad – with its mass of residential homes – to a devastating air attack. This
was a pure terror raid – singling out the civilian population – and designed to
inflict massive casualties, to break down the city's infrastructure and create a
mood of panic and despair.

Viktor Nekrasov witnessed the terrifying moment the German planes
appeared:

> We stood out on the balcony and gazed into the sky. We couldn't
> drag ourselves away. From behind the station the planes came in a
> steady stream, just as they do in a fly-past. I had never seen so many
> of them. They flew in flocks, black, repulsive, unperturbed, at
> various levels.

Valentin Spiridinov was in charge of one of the anti-aircraft units defending
the city:

> Up to 23 August the Germans had only been doing air reconnais-
> sance – usually at night, at high altitude. But that afternoon we saw
> something terrible on the horizon – it was like dark dust clouds –
> enemy planes, masses of them. They did not bomb the factory area
> at all. They went for the living quarters. Our batteries were the only
> defence against this massive raid – and we quickly ran out of shells.
> We had made the awful mistake of concentrating all our ammunition
> in one place. The Germans had realized that from their reconnais-
> sance flights and they struck the ammunition supplies straight away.
> That was that. We worked flat out with what we had by us and then

ran out. We had over a hundred anti-aircraft units and nothing to shoot with. The nearest replacements were at Saratov, over a hundred miles away. To bring them we would need a convoy of lorries and barges and it would take days to organize. And all around us thousands of people were being killed and injured.

Andrei Yeremenko, head of the Stalingrad Front, later wrote about that terrible day:

> We'd been through a lot in the war up to that time, but what we saw in Stalingrad on 23 August was something completely different. Bombs were exploding all around us and the sky was filled with columns of fiery smoke . . . Asphalt on the street emitted choking fumes and telegraph poles flared up like matches. The earth of Stalingrad was crumpled and blackened. The city seemed to have been struck by a terrible hurricane, which whirled it in the air, showering the streets and squares with rubble.

The plight of thousands of innocent civilians struck home hardest. 'In this chaos', Yeremenko added, 'we could clearly hear the screams and curses of the dying, the cries and calls for help from women and children.' It has been estimated that more than forty bombs were dropped on the city every minute. Inhabitants of the city died in the rubble of buildings, were burnt alive in houses and in the streets, or suffocated in air-raid shelters. 'No one had any idea what was about to happen', Ludmilla Silvanova said. She was 5 years old at the time – out with her family on a picnic. 'It was the weekend, the atmosphere in the city was happy and everyone was out enjoying the sunshine. Then, suddenly, it was all gone.'

Gamlet Dallakian was on the staff of the Stalingrad Front HQ, in a bunker in the city on the banks of the Tsaritsa river.

> At least 40,000 civilians died immediately because of this raid, all of them peaceful people. War is war of course, but this was the worst act we had experienced from the Germans: they deliberately singled out civilians for mass bombing. They were not fighting soldiers but killing defenceless women and children.

For some, the bombing created a powerful hatred of the enemy. Alexander Tsygankov – a private in the 181st Infantry Division of the 62nd Army – remembered reaching Stalingrad on 24 August, with the city in flames:

We disembarked straight on the bank of the Volga, where on a patch of land several thousand civilians were gathered for evacuation across the river. There wasn't a soldier or a military objective amongst them – just old people, women and children, some wounded. The Nazi planes came right over the heads of these defenceless people, dropping bombs, and then returning to fire on them with heavy machine guns. I cannot tell you the hatred we felt for these sadists. We swore that we would be avenged for everything. For the bloodshed they had caused and the destruction they had brought, for they had almost completely destroyed the city in just a couple of days.

Over time, this wild anger became a reservoir of strength for the defenders. But in August 1942 the mood at Stalingrad Front HQ was one of grim resignation. Gamlet Dallakian remembered that everybody was just trying to hang on from day to day, but even in such appalling conditions, the humour which always forms a part of human resilience began to play its part:

We took refuge in humour, to try and deal with an utterly crushing situation. We liked our Front commander, Yeremenko, a soldier's soldier who always had time for us. He would come into the bunker on the Tsaritsa and chat with us. But the chief political officer, Khrushchev, looked right through us as if we were not there. After our meetings, we had to cross a small courtyard to get to the one decent latrine. Yeremenko would go towards it, but he had been wounded in the leg, so he was rather slow, and Khrushchev would race past and shove himself in the latrine first. We joked: 'What is worse than being caught out on the steppe with the Germans breathing down your neck? To be relieving yourself in the toilet with Nikita Khrushchev bearing down upon you!'

It was Khrushchev, of course, who was responsible, in 1963, for renaming Stalingrad as Volgograd – part of his policy of dismantling the cult of Stalin. Understandably, most veterans dislike this renaming, and resent the emphasis on Khrushchev's own role in the city's defence.

The Germans continued to bomb the city heavily over the next few days. Recently released documents show the city's administration struggling to contain the situation. They ordered the mining of key buildings, factories and installations within the city – special measures drawn up 'in case the enemy occupied Stalingrad'. On 25 August, with German air attacks showing no sign of abating, a state of siege was declared and NKVD Colonel Sarayev appointed garrison commander of the city, with powers to shoot on sight anyone found guilty of robbery of public property.

An NKVD report on the bombing showed the entire city water supply out of action, the electricity system brought down, the telephone exchange destroyed and the railway station and ferry landing stage in flames. They were fears of a drastic food shortage – many of the city's bread factories had been targeted by the Germans – and for the first time a comprehensive evacuation strategy was discussed. On 26 August, a desperate yet moving appeal was made to the inhabitants of the city, invoking the memory of the defence of Tsaritsyn in 1918: 'Comrades, Stalingraders! Frenzied bands of the enemy have reached the walls of our native city. Once again, as 24 years ago, our city is living through difficult days . . .' There was something genuinely spontaneous and powerful in the almost prophetic declaration which followed: 'We will not give up our native city, our native home, our native land. We will block every road in the city with impenetrable barricades. We will make an impregnable fortress of every home, every building and every street.'

This brave statement of defiance contained the seeds of Stalingrad's successful resistance against the Germans. But Stalingrad's defences were still utterly inadequate. Chuikov observed that the city's barricades could have been pushed over with a truck. Things were to get worse, much worse, before 'impregnable Stalingrad' became a reality. On the same day as the proclamation, a letter from Alexander Voronin, head of Stalingrad's NKVD, to Lavrenti Beria made clear that a complete breakdown in law and order was now a real possibility:

> Over the last two days of bombing all the main housing blocks in the city are destroyed or burning, most factories are unable to work properly, most workshops destroyed . . . Widespread looting is taking place within the city. Five ringleaders have been shot dead on the spot. The leadership and operative staff of the NKVD are trying to maintain order.

Mass Panic

On 28 August 1942 an event occurred which was subsequently suppressed in all post-war Soviet histories: a mass flight from the city. Sergei Zacharov had been admitted to the city's Lenin hospital that month:

Despite the bombing, enormous efforts had been made to keep the hospital functioning. Then, on 28 August, something astonishing happened. I woke up to find no one on duty: no nurses, no medical staff – no one at all. The head of the hospital came up to our ward. 'I'm sorry', he said – 'all my staff have gone, they've all run away'.

We became aware of a commotion outside and everybody who could move got over to the windows. We saw a scene of indescribable chaos – everyone out of their minds with panic – it looked as if the whole city was in the grip of some kind collective hysteria. People were looting shops and buildings. Everybody was shouting: 'What's the news?' Then there was a growing refrain: 'There's nobody in the city', 'The civil authorities have vanished!', and finally, and most ominously, 'The Germans are coming!'

We watched the unfolding drama below. People were running around, screaming and crying. Then there was a sudden surge of energy. Everyone began to flee, on whatever form of transport they could find: I remember seeing one horse-drawn cart, laden with a family and their possessions, careering down the street. Everybody was leaving Stalingrad! The commanding officer of my regiment turned up. He said 'We've got to get you out of here – the city's being abandoned.'

We gathered together everybody able to move. Just over a hundred of us left the hospital. We moved along a street, in the direction of the Volga. Then suddenly a group of German planes appeared, maybe fifteen or twenty of them. They flew straight towards the hospital and began to bomb it, continuously. All the remaining patients must have been killed there – we had only just got out in time.

Around us everything was now silent. There was this eerie sense of emptiness: everyone seemed to have gone. We knew we could only try to cross the Volga at night, so Alexei, our commander, said to us 'Guys, try to get some supplies.' It did not seem right to take food from recently abandoned civilian flats and houses. So we collected it from shops – which had just been left open, as they were, full of provisions: sweets, honey, bread, sausages. Then we reassembled by the river bank.

As we waited that afternoon, we heard remarkable news. The workers in the Tractor Factory held an emergency meeting and decided not to leave Stalingrad. They would carry on producing tanks regardless. And a determined group of citizens did not flee with the others – they refused to abandon the city and took to the cellars and shelters. The mood changed – mass panic was replaced by grim defiance. The city stayed alive.

Valentina Krutova remembered this day: 'Shops were simply left open – abandoned – as thousand of people tried to flee in any direction, to go wherever they could. But others stayed. We were still hoping against hope that Stalingrad would not be surrendered.' The mass exodus was triggered by the sudden disappearance of police and militia detachments from Stalingrad's streets. An explanation for this astonishing event is found on the Orlovka salient, north-west of Stalingrad, where Russian troops were desperately trying to break the German 'land corridor' to the Volga.

The Orlovka Salient

Vladimir Turov fought in the Orlovka salient. The rapid German thrust to the Volga on 23 August left him stunned and bewildered:

> I saw a mass of their planes in the sky, all heading towards the city. Then, quite unexpectedly, a black government car accelerated towards the head of our marching column. A man got out and I recognized him from our newsreels: it was Georgi Malenkov, secretary of the central committee and a key member of Stalin's staff. As commander of our infantry battalion I went towards him, expecting to receive a decisive command – a clear, forceful instruction to deal with the developing German threat. Instead Malenkov asked: 'Where is the enemy?' I was astonished. What hope was there for us if he, of all people, had no idea what was going on?

The conversation with Malenkov – one of Stalin's key lieutenants – became quite farcical. First, Malenkov pointed to the sky and the disappearing German planes. 'You see those enemy aircraft', he said to a bemused Turov, 'I think it means the enemy have broken through somewhere.' Turov was unsure how to respond. Malenkov then became more authoritative. Pointing dramatically at a nondescript patch of soil he announced: 'Immediately create a defence line. Your task is not to allow the enemy to reach Stalingrad – is that clear?' Malenkov drove off at speed. 'It could not have been more unclear', added Turov. 'I went back to my mates and we discussed this strange visitation. The general consensus was it was some kind of practical joke!'

That afternoon Turov and his men had no idea what to do. They did not follow Malenkov's nonsensical order – and as rumours of the German advance to the Volga reached them, they began to trudge back towards Stalingrad. Then another black car sped towards them. This time it was Colonel Sarayev, commander of the city's 10th NKVD division. 'At this moment of crisis Sarayev took control of the situation', Turov continued appreciatively. 'He was clear and decisive – he ordered us to Orlovka, first to dig in, and then to try and break the German corridor.'

There were very few Red Army soldiers in the city at this time. Most were still retreating from the Don and Stalingrad was defended by regiments of NKVD and hastily recruited workers' battalions. Sarayev was effectively commander of Stalingrad. He reinforced Turov with some of his scratch force and formed up the remainder in a defence line around the Tractor Factory.

Turov continued:

> On 24 August our group were ordered to cut off the Germans who had reached the Volga. But the enemy forestalled us, blasting our infantry with their planes. It was impossible to dislodge them. Then, on 27 August, the rest of our regiment arrived and Sarayev sent us more workers' battalions and NKVD troops. We attacked the enemy again and this time we nearly pulled it off. We captured a series of hills and were in sight of our objective. We could see the Soviet armies on the other side of the corridor, only a kilometre away. But then the German air force arrived in strength. We could not break through those last few metres.

It seemed one last push would cut the 'land corridor' and surround the German forces on the Volga. On 28 August Sarayev gambled, pulling the remaining NKVD and militia units out of Stalingrad and sending them to strengthen Turov's force at Orlovka. This was the action so badly misinterpreted by the nervous citizens of Stalingrad. They took the sudden departure of the NKVD as proof that the city was about to be surrendered to the enemy. 'Fortunately not everyone panicked,' said Dallakian, 'but the streets of Stalingrad were now virtually deserted.' The city was hanging on by its finger nails.

While the mass flight from the city was never officially acknowledged in Soviet sources, it acted as a spur to give Stalingrad proper military protection. On 29 August an army brigade – the 124th, under Sergei Gorokhov – was rapidly dispatched to Stalingrad to shore up the defence of the Tractor Factory and protect the city from the north.

Gorokhov's Northern Group

'Sergei Gorokhov was able to stabilize our defences in the northern part of Stalingrad', said Mereshko. 'He took command of the Tractor Factory and the Orlovka salient, showing the qualities necessary to rally our troops and hold off the enemy.' Gorokhov was tough but fair, with a reputation for personal bravery, and his troops were devoted to him. Evgeny Kurapatov described the profound effect of a change in leadership:

> At the beginning of September I arrived in Stalingrad. I was in charge of procuring supplies for our division and reported to our commander, Vasily Ivanov. These were the first words he said to me: 'If you spoil any operation I will shoot you dead personally'. That was my introduction to him. And where was I supposed to get ammunition from? Our army supplies had been completely destroyed by German aviation. It all seemed absolutely hopeless.

But then Kurapatov's tone of voice changed:

> When we were transferred to Gorokhov's group, everything was completely different. We were still terribly short of ammunition and supplies. But Gorokhov didn't blame or threaten us in the way Ivanov had. Instead he led by example, and through his incredible courage everybody else was uplifted. We had no strong defences to protect us – and the enemy, on the high ground at Rynok, could see the length and breadth of our position. But Gorokhov was un-moveable – he radiated a conviction that we would hold firm.

Gorokhov inspired his men to counter-attack and recapture the small, northern suburb of Spartanovka, protecting the Tractor Factory. Captain Tsibulin, commander of the 124th Brigade's 1st Battalion, led the assault. When Chuikov took command at Stalingrad he recognized Tsibulin's bravery by nominating him for the Order of Alexander Nevsky - the first of these awards to be given in the city fighting.

'A conviction that we would hold firm', Kurapatov repeated. 'This was the spirit which Chuikov later came to embody for the whole of the 62nd Army. It began with Gorokhov in the northern suburbs of Stalingrad.'

Chapter Three

Lion on the Volga

The commander of the 62nd Army at Stalingrad, Vasily Chuikov, gave a quality of leadership vital for the defence of Stalingrad. He has often been viewed critically – sometimes in Russia, more often in the West – as a brutal and ruthless figure who willingly sacrificed thousands of his soldiers' lives to wear down the Germans. If Chuikov had actually been like that, his army would not have held out at Stalingrad.

Anatoly Mereshko remembered his first impressions of Chuikov:

> I saw a fairly tall, broad-shouldered man, with bushy hair, and a very strong, decisive face. Something struck me about his face; it had a particular quality, which reminded me of a lion. The strength was certainly there. He was a man of incredibly strong will, very brave – almost desperately brave – and I think that if someone else had been in charge – someone with a different temperament – it would not have been possible for us to hold Stalingrad. Chuikov had a colossal energy, and it was very infectious – it passed on to more junior commanders.

Mereshko then repeated emphatically: 'If Chuikov's character had been different we would not have held out at Stalingrad.'

But others have used the image of a lion in a less flattering light. Here is another Russian's description of him:

> He was known to have shot down officers with his own hand. People were afraid of him, a rough, even cruel officer, the hard hero of Stalingrad, with the coarse lines of his lion's face, foul-mouthed, he walked around with a stick that he sometimes brought down on the shoulders of his subordinates. Staff personnel tried to keep out of his way.

Chuikov's leadership style has also divided Western historians. Antony Beevor, in his compelling account of the battle of Stalingrad, found him an

64

unattractive figure: 'one of the most ruthless' of the new generation of Soviet commanders, his counter-attacks against the Germans 'appallingly wasteful'. He blamed him for the draconian discipline imposed upon the army, remarking pointedly: 'General Chuikov . . . became a Marshal of the Soviet Union . . . the thousands of soldiers executed at Stalingrad on his orders never received a marked grave.' Richard Overy, in his *Russia's War*, struck a very different note. Overy called Chuikov's appointment as commander of the 62nd Army 'an inspired choice'. Chuikov was able to 'gather together scattered, leaderless soldiers and weld them into a more effective fighting force'. This 'tough, burly man . . . endured what his men endured and faced death without flinching'.

Chuikov's own soldiers are honest about his faults, but choose to place greater emphasis on his outstanding qualities, for in the burning hell of Stalingrad he reached out and inspired his men. Chuikov's remarkable rapport with the ordinary combatant, a most unusual gift for a Red Army commander, lay at the heart of his extraordinary achievement: transforming the battered divisions of the 62nd Army into a fighting force of stupendous power.

Time is Blood

Chuikov famously commented about the battle of Stalingrad, 'time is blood', and this is usually seen as a cold, calculating willingness to sacrifice the lives of his men to gain time against the Germans. Antony Beevor commented:

> Chuikov openly acknowledged that when defending Stalingrad he had followed the precept 'Time is Blood'. He had to hold Stalingrad at all costs and that meant throwing fresh regiments and divisions into the hell of the city as soon as they reached the eastern bank and were ready to be ferried across.

At first glance, this seems an understandable rendition. After all, Order 227 had just been introduced, with its blocking detachments and penal companies, and Chuikov had been instructed to hold Stalingrad or die in the attempt. In his book, Beevor revealed a shocking piece of factual evidence, that on the Stalingrad Front during the course of the battle the Soviet authorities executed no less than 13,500 Red Army soldiers on charges ranging from desertion and cowardice to incompetence, corruption and even drunkenness.

However, the Stalingrad Front consisted of a whole series of armies, only one of which, Chuikov's 62nd, was bearing the brunt of the fighting in the city. The terrible number of executions took place across the whole campaign front, initiated by the Soviet authorities and carried out by their ruthless representatives, the NKVD. It was, in other words, a product both of the system and of a time of absolute crisis.

At the end of Beevor's book Chuikov becomes both the author and the executioner of these grim statistics: 'the thousands of Soviet soldiers executed at Stalingrad on his orders'. David Barrett, the editor of an important new edition of Chuikov's *Mission to China*, an account of his time as military adviser to Chiang Kai Shek, rightly says that such censure is 'unduly harsh': the spirit of draconian discipline was exemplified by Stalin's Order 227, which decreed that 'panic-mongers and cowards must be destroyed on the spot', and this new Soviet discipline applied just as ferociously to commanders as to their men.

The insinuation that Chuikov and his 62nd Army – always outnumbered and short of men – was in a position to carry out a policy of mass executions has caused its veterans wry amusement. 'Let us be frank', said Anatoly Kozlov, '13,500 men is the equivalent of a new full-strength division and we didn't see many of those in our fighting for the city.' Recently released NKVD records show the execution rate within the 62nd Army was far lower than for the Stalingrad Front as a whole. They simply didn't have the men to spare.

At the crisis point in the fighting in mid-September an NKVD report shows that 1,218 soldiers were held for attempting to leave the city without permission – of these 21 were shot, 10 arrested and the rest redistributed to different units. The army was always desperately under-strength and the blocking detachments responsible for enforcing this policy were frequently drafted into the frontline fighting. It is true that Chuikov said: 'In the blazing city we did not suffer cowards, we had no room for them.' Men were shot for cowardice without any compunction in the 62nd Army – this was a grim reality of the terrible fighting within Stalingrad. But it was something done on the initiative of officers and ordinary soldiers as well as their commander – everybody was in this together.

Chuikov made the remark 'time is blood' after he had arrived at Stalingrad and reached his army HQ. He wanted urgently to get to work, to acquire an accurate picture what was going on in the city – this was a standard he set for himself, as a commander. In his experience on the steppe that summer he had encountered generals who made grandiose dispositions, committing masses of soldiers to battle, without taking the trouble to find out the situation on the ground. Thousands had died as a result. Chuikov did not want to risk his men's lives in such a cavalier fashion. Here is what he said:

> I listened to Krylov [the army chief of staff] and at the same time
> studied his working map, the marks and arrows on it, trying to feel

my way into the events taking place . . . The Americans have a saying 'time is money'. During those days we might well have said 'time is blood'. Time wasted [by us] had to be paid for with the blood of our men.

Leadership and the 62nd Army

Chuikov was the third commander the newly formed 62nd Army had received that summer, but the first to make a real impression on his soldiers. Vladimir Kolpakchi was dismissed during the fighting on the Don at the end of July, after being in command for just a few weeks. Evgeny Kurapatov said of him:

> Only now can I tell you who our first commander was. At the time, I wasn't even sure if we had a commander at all. We heard Kolpakchi's name mentioned – that's all: we knew nothing about him. From the ordinary soldiers' point of view, he had virtually no impact on the army he was supposed to be commanding.

Kolpakchi was replaced by Lopatin. 'Again, only a name to us', Kurapatov continued. 'He didn't seem to be directing the army in any meaningful way. We didn't feel his presence, or his actions.'

When Chuikov took command it was completely different. 'There was no official announcement, but we heard about Chuikov's appointment through the soldiers' grapevine', Kurapatov remembered. 'The news lifted our spirits. At last something was happening – we finally had someone who could actually lead us – and we started to believe that we would make a stand at Stalingrad.'

We need to understand the ghastly position Chuikov was in. He had been called to the Stalingrad Front on the morning of 12 September 1942 and offered command of the 62nd Army. Later, Chuikov recalled Khrushchev's comments:

> The Germans had decided to take the city at any cost. We should not and could not surrender it to them, we could not retreat any further, for there was nowhere to retreat to. The 62nd Army's commander, General Lopatin, did not believe his army could hold the city. Instead of fighting to the death, instead of dying in an attempt to keep the enemy from the Volga, he had been withdrawing units. He had therefore been relieved of his post.

Chuikov was asked how he understood his task, and responded:

We cannot surrender the city to the enemy, because it is extremely valuable to us, to the whole Soviet people. The loss of it would undermine the nation's morale. All possible measures will be taken to prevent the city from falling.

Chuikov concluded with the fateful words: 'I swear I shall stand firm. We will defend the city or die in the attempt.'

This conversation is recounted in Chuikov's memoirs, written in the Khrushchev era; during the battle for Stalingrad, he described it to journalist Vasily Grossman in a more matter of fact fashion:

Yeremenko and Khrushchev said to me: 'You will have to save Stalingrad. How do you feel about it?'

'Yes, sir.'

'No, it isn't enough to obey, what do you think about it?'

'It means to die. So we will die.'

Gamlet Dallakian, who was on Yeremenko and Khrushchev's staff at the time, said of Chuikov's appointment: 'In comparison to Kolpakchi and Lopatin he was a much stronger person – he had a much stronger will. We all felt Chuikov would make a stand against the Germans, even with his back pressed right up against the Volga.'

Newly available documentary evidence shows that the 'Not a Step Back!' order was invoked against Chuikov's predecessor Lopatin. On 6 September 1942 Lopatin was removed from his post 'for non-fulfilment of Order 227, for the unauthorized withdrawal of units from the 23rd Tank Brigade from the defence line', and, most ominously 'for lying to the High Command'. His case was referred to Red Army supreme command, and Lopatin was arrested and placed under the authority of a military tribunal. He was only reinstated as an army commander later in the war. Chuikov refers to a meeting with him two days after taking command (on 14 September), describing 'the hopelessness he [Lopatin] felt, his sense of the impossibility and pointlessness of fighting for the city', adding 'his feeling of depression had undoubtedly communicated itself to his subordinates'.

One wonders why this meeting took place. It may have been intended as a warning to Chuikov – that if he attempted to retreat from Stalingrad he would suffer the same fate as his predecessor. Lopatin had never got a grip on the 62nd Army. But he had also been made a scapegoat for the blunders of others and a situation that many regarded as hopeless. Shortly after taking command, at the beginning of August 1942, Lopatin had tried to prevent a military catastrophe by withdrawing his forces from the western bank of the Don, saving them from the threatened German encirclement. Mereshko described what happened:

> Our commander at that time, General Lopatin, foresaw the danger and immediately asked permission from the Front commander, Gordov, to take his troops to the eastern bank of the Don and organize his defences there. But neither the Front HQ nor Stavka gave him permission to do so. As a result, our divisions suffered heavy losses and only small groups managed to break out of the encirclement and cross the river.

Having witnessed the bloody mauling of his army it is perhaps understandable that Lopatin was in a 'pessimistic' frame of mind. Stalin characteristically blamed him for his own mistakes. When the Germans broke through Lopatin's depleted forces and reached the Volga, on 23 August, Stalin personally ordered the Stalingrad Front to establish a 'second echelon' behind the hapless army, adding: 'Lopatin, the commander of the 62nd Army, has for a second time let down the Stalingrad Front through his lack of skill and inability to organize.'

The situation at Stalingrad looked bleak. As Gamlet Dallakian admitted, most people at Front HQ thought the city could not be held: 'We had far too few regular troops at that time and mobilizing the city's population against the might of the German army was not an effective answer – in reality, we had almost nobody to defend the city with.' Valentin Spiridinov agreed with this: 'The lack of infantry in Stalingrad was a huge worry for us at that time – there were only a few units scattered over the whole city.'

A Stalingrad Front report of 8 September 1942, two days after Lopatin's arrest, recorded grim news: the entire left flank of the retreating 62nd Army had been destroyed by the Germans in violent fighting on the city's outskirts and communication with neighbouring armies was now broken. All Front HQ personnel were ordered to cross to the eastern bank of the Volga. The decision whether 'to continue the defence of the city of Stalingrad' was to be reviewed on a day-to-day basis. On 13 September, as Chuikov arrived to take up command in the city, Voronin – head of Stalingrad's NKVD – wrote to Beria's deputy, Abakumov, in Moscow: 'Having received your orders not to undertake any special measures, whatever the circumstances, I am seeking instruction as to how to act in case the city is abandoned by the Red Army.' This was the desperate situation Chuikov faced when he entered the inferno of Stalingrad.

A Crucial Confrontation

On assuming command, Chuikov was immediately confronted with a dilemma. The commander of an armoured formation in his army had crossed to the far side of the Volga without permission. How was he to respond? This was one of those challenges, thrown up in the heat of battle, which define the relationship between a commander and his men. However Chuikov dealt with the situation, he risked alienating his soldiers. It would have been tempting to take a tough stance, throwing the rule book at the errant officer and making an example of him. After all, he had withdrawn without orders at the time of 'Not a Step Back!' and Chuikov needed to quickly establish discipline in his army. A number of 62nd Army staff had found various pretexts to disappear to the other bank of the river. But this course of action carried grave risks. As Chuikov had admitted, morale in the army was low. The commander of the armoured post had genuinely been trying to re-establish communications within his unit, and his previous post had been under heavy artillery bombardment. Conditions in the city were absolutely horrifying, with many units – badly depleted in men and equipment – under constant German air attack as they pulled back into the burning ruins.

As Chuikov pondered what to do, the majority of his 62nd Army felt they had been abandoned to a ghastly fate by an unfeeling High Command. Alexander Fortov and the remnants of his 112th Division had been bombed so often that 'it felt like the Germans were laying a carpet over our heads'. On 13 September they were on the Mamaev Kurgan, in trenches only a few hundred metres from Chuikov's HQ.

> When we arrived in Stalingrad everything was on fire. We were tired and hungry – there were no field kitchens for our troops. We scavenged – took a piece of a dead horse, tried to boil it into a soup. It was clear to us that the defences within the city had not been properly organized, the barricades were laughable, there was so little protection.

The last thing Fortov and his men wanted to hear was that a new commander was imposing a regime of draconian discipline.

> We were up on the Mamaev Kurgan for over a week, feeling absolutely lost. Our spirits had plummeted to rock bottom. We never received any supplies, we were terribly short of water in the sweltering heat, no shells were brought to us and it was clear that

there were very few troops in the city. Then we heard Chuikov had arrived on the Kurgan and I sent a soldier over to his HQ. He came running back to us saying 'I saw our new general walking around outside his bunker swinging a stick [Chuikov used a walking stick after a car crash earlier that summer] – is that what they are planning to do next, to drive us into battle like pack horses?'

Given the terrible suffering of his army, and the risk of quickly alienating it, Chuikov might have chosen an alternative course, empathizing with the commander of his armoured unit and forgiving his action, acknowledging that he was doing the best he could in atrocious circumstances. By doing this, he would show himself as a sympathetic figure rather than a rigid disciplinarian. But this would create new problems, for a precedent would have been set, and as the German onslaught intensified other officers would then feel justified in leaving the burning city for the far bank of the Volga. And if their officers left, why should the ordinary soldiers feel obliged to stay in Stalingrad?

In short, Chuikov was faced with an almost impossible dilemma and one can imagine the tension in the HQ, as the army staff scrutinized their new chief's reaction. In Chuikov's memoirs he described how he invited the officer into the dug out, told everyone present to stay, and then asked him: 'What would your attitude be, as a Soviet General, in command of a military sector, if one of your subordinate commanders and headquarters left the front without your permission?' There was no answer to this question. Then Chuikov warned him that he would regard any similar act in future as desertion on the field of battle and ordered him back to his original command post. This is a blunt, matter of fact account and Soviet memoirs are often overly prosaic, omitting the vital human dynamic.

Mereshko remembered how the atmosphere in the bunker was tense and sullen: no one really knew their new commander and the officer wanted to justify himself. All around them bomb explosions were reverberating as the enemy moved ever closer. 'This was the crucial moment', Mereshko continued. 'Chuikov suddenly and dramatically pointed at the city map, speaking with real authority: "Here is my HQ – on this side of the river – 800 metres from the Germans. Here is the position you will occupy – 500 metres from the Germans."'

Suddenly everyone, including the recalcitrant officer, got the point: they were all in this mess together. The mood completely changed and a new sense of purpose and urgency arose. 'Chuikov had the necessary toughness', Mereshko added, 'but it was his leadership through example which made all the difference. The story of what happened quickly spread throughout the entire army.'

'A Son of the Century': Military Career of Vasily Chuikov

Vasily Chuikov was born on 12 February 1900 into a large peasant family in the Tula province south of Moscow. He was the eighth of twelve children and the fifth of eight sons. All the boys were to become soldiers, the oldest of them, including Vasily, fighting in the Civil War, the youngest, Feodor, serving on the 62nd Army staff at Stalingrad. Vasily's father, Ivan, was a man of considerable physical strength: a skilled wrestler and boxer, he would organize winter team competitions for the surrounding villages – man-to-man fighting, with bare fists, the two sides lined up facing each other on the banks of a frozen river. Vasily inherited his father's strength and stamina – and, with Stalingrad's savage close quarters combat in mind, with the Red Army pinned back against the frozen Volga, there is something oddly prophetic about these winter 'battles' of raw physical endurance. He also was to inherit his father's explosive temper.

His mother, Elizabeth, was another strong personality – a very spiritual person and a committed Christian. She would say firmly to her young, revolutionary son: 'I am on a different path from you, but never try and judge me for it.' She worked on the church staff in her home village of Serebryanye Prudy (Silver Ponds), and when the regime was closing down all the neighbouring churches, in 1930, family tradition has it that she walked all the way to Moscow and demanded of Stalin's minister Kalinin that it be kept open. Remarkably, she succeeded. When Chuikov's family was evacuated to Kuibyshev during the war – and her son took over command at Stalingrad – she said emphatically on receiving news of the victory, 'We all prayed for him.' She gave Vasily a talisman prayer which this tough, committed communist general carried with him throughout the battle.

It was a fusion of these qualities – extraordinary strength, resilience and remarkable faith when all around looked utterly bleak and hopeless – which proved vital at Stalingrad. As his son Alexander said

> If he had just been a tough, abrasive, ruthless leader I think the battle would have had a different outcome. But crucially he also had a most unusual quality, a kind of warmth – a special empathy for ordinary soldiers and an ability to get really close to them. I will never forget one extraordinary incident, much later. We had been travelling by military train with my father – now Marshal of the Soviet Union – and made a short, unscheduled stop. My father was walking ahead of us with his adjutant when suddenly an almighty commotion broke lose. A circle of curious onlookers quickly

gathered, with the adjutant flitting around in a state of total bewilderment.

Inside the circle I saw my father with a woman, totally overcome with emotion, her face streaming with tears, and I realized straight-away that she was a Stalingrad veteran. She kept repeating again and again 'Vasily Ivanovich, Vasily Ivanovich – God has sent you back to me!' They embraced each other – my father had also become very emotional and was crying as well. The surrounding crowd stood silent, absolutely mesmerized. Afterwards, I thought about that moment a lot, for the woman wanted nothing from my father – she was not trying to get any money or anything; she was just overjoyed to see him again. It was as if a curtain had briefly lifted, allowing me to glimpse the deep affection that had existed between the commander and his army. Later, I saw it again when veterans of Stalingrad visited my father's house. The thing that struck me most was the spontaneous warmth he evoked from ordinary people.

At the age of 12 Chuikov left school to earn his living in a factory in St Petersburg, turning out spurs for cavalry officers. In 1917 he found himself unemployed because of the turmoil of the revolution, but an older brother, serving with the marines at the naval base of Kronstadt, arranged his recruit-ment into the Red Guards. Chuikov joined the Bolsheviks because he was inspired by their vision of a new Russia, and in 1918, after attending the first Red Army training course, fought for them in the Civil War, first in the Ukraine against the Cossacks, and then in Siberia against the White Armies under Kolchak.

Chuikov remembered leaving the family home at the age of 12 as the moment when he really had to grow up, 'departure from my father's house meant for me the end of childhood'. These were uncertain times, with the outbreak of the First World War followed by revolution and turmoil, and they created in him a tough self-reliance. Alexander Chuikov spoke of this side of his father:

He was rough – and could be moody and despotic. He was incred-ibly demanding of himself – and demanding of others. This way of behaving came from his outlook on life, for he often said to me 'I want to have people around me who I can really count on'. He could 'iron people hard', and either that person showed his mettle, and could be absolutely relied upon, or they would go.

In October 1918 Chuikov saw active service when he was sent to the Southern Front to fight against the White Guards. He had been appointed deputy commander of a company and his instinctive leadership skill soon revealed itself – even at this early stage of his career –for he tried not to patronize the soldiers under him but valued their experience and always considered their opinions. Chuikov quickly developed a distinctive style of command. He tried to explain the situation with the enemy to his soldiers. He always established a clear line of defence. He trained his men in bayonet attack and became particularly skilled in night fighting. These attributes were all present during the battle of Stalingrad. As Mereshko put it: 'Chuikov was always open to new tactical ideas – but he also tried to draw upon his experience in the Civil War for the close quarters fighting at Stalingrad.'

In the spring of 1919 Chuikov became commander of the 40th Regiment – later renamed the 43rd – as part of the 5th Army under Tukachevsky facing the White Army of Kolchak in Siberia. Commanding a regiment at such a young age was a source of pride to Chuikov and he carried off his duties well. Tukachevsky reported on 19 July 1919:

> then the 43rd Regiment, the best in the division, went into the attack. The commander of the regiment, Chuikov, quickly neutralized the enemy's initiative – riding round them with his cavalry and striking them in the rear, creating panic. For this achievement the regiment was awarded the revolutionary banner.

In the fighting from 1919–20 Chuikov himself received two awards of the Red Banner – an equivalent of the Hero of the Soviet Union in the Second World War – for bravery and heroism.

When Chuikov called himself a 'son of the century' he was recalling the optimism of his generation, and their remarkable idealism, which had helped forge the Bolshevik revolution. Whatever our own reservations about the terrible and bloody course that revolution subsequently took, it is vital to remember this. As his son Alexander remarked, those who came from the ranks of the ordinary people, as he did, had a real sense of destiny: 'They created the new Russia – the USSR – with their will, talents and energy. They forged its power and made its history.' That remarkable idealism was a source of inspiration in the 1919 campaign in Siberia, and Chuikov never forgot it.

That spring, Bolshevik forces had been falling back across the entire front. But Mikhail Frunze, their commander-in-chief, then made a stirring declaration of their shared revolutionary principles. He acknowledged the need for 'colossal will' to turn the situation around, but added 'with firm faith in the rightness of our cause we can achieve miracles', ending with the rallying call: 'Soldiers of the Red Army – forward to the final, decisive battle!' The bloody fighting created a spirit of courage within the army. As historian Bruce Lincoln put it: 'The Red Army advance that summer made heroes by the dozen and earned some of the leading World War Two commanders their spurs.'

Chuikov's record of service during the Civil War was distinguished. He was wounded four times – one, in Poland in 1920, left a metal fragment in his left arm that could not be operated on. It led to partial paralysis, which in time Chuikov was able to overcome through his sheer physical strength and willpower. 'The bullet wound was in his upper arm', his son Alexander said, 'and was too close to the nerve. For a time, he lost the use of his left hand – but my father was an incredibly strong man, mentally and physically, and he regained the use of it.' But this old war wound, carried by Chuikov for the rest of his life, was eventually to lead to septicaemia, breaking open in 1981, causing a nine-month illness and finally his death. In a way, it seems fitting that, after a life defined by his consummate skill on the battlefield, Chuikov died of an injury sustained there – that in a real sense, he died as a soldier rather than succumbing to old age.

Chuikov did not rest on his laurels after the Civil War, as some Bolshevik commanders did. He left his regiment in 1921 to continue his studies at the Frunze Military Academy, graduating in 1925, and was then offered the chance to join the Chinese Department of its Far Eastern Faculty. Chuikov visited China in 1926, and again in 1927–9, and was subsequently appointed to the staff of the Far Eastern Army under Blyukher, serving on it from 1932 to 1935. After attending a further course on mechanized warfare in April 1938 he became head of the fifth infantry corps in Belorussia, and was then promoted to commander of the 4th Army. Chuikov's impressive rise up the Soviet military hierarchy combined further education and training with wide practical experience.

Colonel Weinrub served under Chuikov in Belorussia and subsequently became his tank commander at Stalingrad. He later shared his impression of him in 1938:

> Military exercises run by Chuikov were significant through their novelty: he was always seeking new approaches. Once, I participated in tactical lessons on combat shooting. Chuikov was demanding that we get really, really close to the firing line, and immediately penetrate the enemy trenches, not letting them recover from the artillery shelling. It was a novelty at the time, and not everyone approved of it. But how wonderfully it worked at Stalingrad.

In 1939–40 Chuikov was promoted to the command of the 9th Army during the war against Finland. The campaign had begun in disastrous fashion, for although the invading Russian forces were numerically superior, they were up against highly motivated defenders, making skilful use of their native terrain and exploiting the difficult weather conditions. The 9th Army was first halted and then mauled by a much smaller Finnish force. Chuikov's predecessor, Dukhanov, was to blame: he had situated his command post too far to the rear of his army, and as a result he suffered a breakdown in communications and lost control of the battle.

Chuikov, a corps commander at the beginning of the campaign, took the remarkable step of conducting his own inquiry into the debacle – independently of the NKVD – and dispatching it directly to Voroshilov, head of the entire front. His critique set out a basic principle, one which was to guide him throughout the Stalingrad battle – that an orthodox military approach would not work in an unorthodox situation. The Russians had deployed their mechanized forces in a bid to crush the enemy, but what was the point of a 'road strategy', he asked, in a region with so few roads? Instead Chuikov emphasized, again and again, that 'combat in special conditions' needed to be studied – noting bluntly that, at a time of winter warfare in the snowbound north, 'the soldiers are terrified of the forest and cannot ski'. Chuikov's forthright appraisal was rewarded with the command of the 9th Army, and Dukhanov was recalled to Leningrad, but the army's divisions were now strung out and isolated and it was difficult to do much more than stabilize the military position.

Chuikov had stepped into the breach and taken control of the situation. His son Alexander showed me a family photograph, taken of his father during the Finnish War, on 12 February 1940, proudly inscribed 'Commander of the 9th Army on his fortieth birthday'. Some historians have suggested that Chuikov's own reputation was tarnished by the overall failure in Finland – leaving a question mark over his suitability for high military command. Certainly, in December 1940 he was dispatched to China as military attaché, and despite repeated requests to return to active service, after the German invasion on 22 June 1941, he remained there until March 1942 when he was finally recalled to Moscow. But this was far from being some 'wilderness' position of exile. It was seen as a very important post, one necessary as part of a broader policy to distract Japan from attacking the Soviet Union – and Chuikov was personally briefed by Stalin before his departure to China.

After his return to Russia, in May 1942, he was appointed deputy commander of a reserve army, responsible for training. Here Chuikov suffered an awful misfortune – being seriously injured in a car accident – and it would

take him a year to fully recover. In July 1942 his force was redesignated the 64th
Army and sent to the Southern Front, throwing Chuikov, still walking with the
aid of a stick, into his first battles with the German 6th Army.

Chuikov began to draw some initial conclusions about his daunting
opponents. With the independence of spirit so typical of him, he got to know
the enemy's habits – a course of action calling for honesty and enormous
courage. As Chuikov put it: 'I felt that – inexperienced as I was – in a battle
against such a strong and experienced enemy, I would have to go through a
great deal before things got better, if I survived at all.' Yet he was prepared to
try. 'I knew I could not study the situation by sitting in the Army HQ, without
seeing the terrain of battle. I took every opportunity to be out in the field – to
learn from the experienced commanders there.' He had to unflinchingly
comprehend the menace they were all facing. 'To observe the enemy, to study
his strong and weak points, to know his habits and customs, means fighting
with our eyes open, hitting the enemy where he is weak, and not putting our
own weaknesses under his blow.'

Chuikov quickly saw one of the reasons for Germans' success was the cohesion of their infantry, artillery and tank attacks, always supported by an
incredible strength in aviation. It seemed they possessed an overwhelming
superiority. He wrote later:

> In modern warfare victory is impossible without combined
> operations by all sections of one's forces, well and efficiently organ-
> ized. The Germans had this kind of polished, co-ordinated action.
> In battle, the different arms of their forces never hurried, did not
> push ahead alone, but fought with the whole mass of men and tech-
> nical backing. A few minutes before a general attack, their aircraft
> would come in, bomb and strafe their targets, pinning the defending
> troops to the ground, and then their infantry and tanks with
> supporting artillery and mortar fire would cut into our military
> formations – almost with impunity.

Above all there was the supremacy enjoyed by German aviation. 'The enemy
had firm mastery of the air. This dispirited our troops more than anything else.'

But in the midst of such dominance Chuikov began to discern a weakness,
one born, ironically, from the enemy's over-reliance on the methods which
were working so well for him. He observed that German tanks were reluctant
to attack without infantry and air support, and German infantry would open up
on their opponents with automatic weapon fire rather than finishing them off
in close quarters fighting. He realized that the Germans had become habituated

to a particular routine. Chuikov saw that he had to get one step ahead of the enemy.

Of course, achieving this was easier said than done. Mereshko said:

> Chuikov realized how hard his task was, for pursuing such a policy was incredibly difficult in the circumstances. The Germans had two invaluable trumps: better mobility and a vastly superior system of communication – which meant they could easily anticipate our actions and neutralize them. Even if we did surprise them, the advantage we gained was usually short-lived.

Mereshko provided some statistics:

> A German division in the summer of 1942 usually had around 830 lorries, 60 towing vehicles, and 500 motor bikes. One of our divisions normally had only 150 lorries and no other form of motorized transport. The Germans provided radios for each infantry company – so that they could communicate with artillery, tank and reconnaissance detachments, and they also had radio receivers to communicate with their aviation. They could manage their advance – with all units in touch with each other – within a radius of 50–60 kilometres for their infantry and 300 kilometres for their tanks. Compared to this we still seemed to be in the Stone Age.

Chuikov was right to say 'communication was still our weak point in the second year of the war'. On 23 July 1942 he had to fly out in a U-2 reconnaissance plane to try and find the location of his troops. Chuikov's plane was attacked by German fighters, and brought to the ground, disintegrating on impact – miraculously, he and his pilot survived, suffering only minor injuries. Chuikov was then sent out to the southern flank of the 64th Army to try and stabilize its defences. He had only one radio transmitter and this was soon destroyed in a German bombing raid, leaving him with no radio communication at all. Despite this alarming handicap Chuikov kept his nerve, took all the troops in the area under his control – designated it the 'Southern Group' – and prepared to confront the enemy.

The Germans had begun to cross the Aksai river and Chuikov had to stop them consolidating their success. He decided to jolt them out of their routine and at dawn on 6 August – before the enemy's aviation had taken off, he directed an artillery barrage at the concentration of their ground forces and then immediately sent his infantry into the attack. The Germans recoiled in surprise.

Chuikov was able to push the enemy back beyond the river, frustrating their plan to build a bridge to get their tanks across. The next day he repeated the same manoeuvre, but this time at dusk, when the enemy planes were unable to retaliate. His success was a revelation to him: 'For the first time, we not only stood up to the enemy, but soundly beat him.' The bold action halted the German advance and stabilized the southern part of the front.

Chuikov's success impressed his superiors and put him in line for command of the 62nd Army. His improvised tactics contained, in their ingenious disruption of the German advance, the germ of the idea of delayed street fighting which became so effective in Stalingrad. Chuikov's personal qualities, his courage, resourcefulness and determination to hold the line, steadied his soldiers' nerves. He had demonstrated an unusual gift – a willingness to search for weak points in an apparently invincible enemy. As Mereshko emphasized: 'Chuikov would always go far deeper into events than someone of his rank was supposed to.' His ability to analyse the military situation and devise an appropriate counter was crucial at Stalingrad.

While Chuikov had gained his first success, broader events were developing ominously. After forcing the Don and breaking the resistance of the Russian troops, German forces rushed towards Stalingrad. In the north, their troops reached the Volga at Rynok; further south, at Kuporosnoye. The 62nd Army, badly battered on the Don, and retreating towards Stalingrad, was now cut off from neighbouring Russian forces and left to face the German onslaught on its own.

By 12 September 1942, the day Chuikov took command of the 62nd Army, the last city defence lines were being abandoned and his troops were falling back into Stalingrad. They were facing the constant threat of encirclement. Chuikov commented ruefully: 'Deep pincer movements – this was the basis of all tactical and operative plans of the Germans. Being more numerous in planes and tanks the enemy easily broke through our defences, making our troops retreat to avoid being surrounded by the enemy.' But space to retreat in was dwindling fast. The improvised frontline was now between 2 and 10 kilometres from Stalingrad's suburbs and the German were already poised to break into the city. The Russians could no longer manoeuvre their way out of trouble. With their backs to the Volga they faced the threat of a last, terrible battle of encirclement which would annihilate their forces.

As Chuikov travelled to Stalingrad he was desperately trying to find a way to frustrate his opponents' simple yet terrifying plan. 'It would be enough to stop one of these pincers', he thought, 'and it could be done with strong defence and counter-attack.' Remembering his experience on the Aksai river, Chuikov decided to pin his hopes on disrupting the enemy's routine. 'Their infantry would only go onto the offensive when their tanks had been committed. And the tanks would only attack when the aviation was above our troops. If we could spoil this orderly advance we might delay the German offensive and turn away his troops.' But he had so little time. His army was shattered and demoralized. Standing against him was the superb, almost instinctive co-ordination of the German 6th Army and its devastatingly powerful aviation.

Western historians are right to stress that Chuikov had to buy time for the defence of Stalingrad, and his initial efforts certainly cost many Russian lives. But as veteran Mikhail Serebryakov pointed out:

> There has been a lot of unjust criticism of Chuikov here. The policy that he formed, one of aggressive defence, was costly but absolutely necessary. The truth is that without counter-attacks the city could not be held – the Germans were simply too strong. It was vital to disrupt the order and cohesion of their offensive.

Chuikov's remarkable insight, which evolved during the fighting at Stalingrad, was that many of the advantages possessed by an apparently un-stoppable enemy might be neutralized through delayed street fighting. But, crucially, the morale and mood of the army had to change first. Such a policy would need to be enacted by a united, motivated force, displaying both tenacity and astonishing resourcefulness.

Mereshko spoke of an immediate change in atmosphere under Chuikov, which ultimately led to a unique spirit of equality and unity within the army. He gave an important practical example:

> Officers received more butter, biscuits and sugar in their rations, and also factory-made cigarettes. When Chuikov took command something astonishing happened. Commanders of units were strongly encouraged to bring their rations into the dug out and share it with their soldiers. In fact, over time, it was considered almost a criminal offence if an officer ate or smoked without sharing with his soldiers.

Mikhail Borchev, in charge of a Katyusha unit at Stalingrad, confirmed this: 'Everything changed when Chuikov took command. Our army now had a new maxim: "The regular soldier is all-important: it is he who defends the commander."' Ordinary Red Army combatants had lost their sense of self-belief. 'We had started to feel inferior to the Germans – not just as soldiers but as human beings', admitted Mereshko. 'We thought it was quite impossible to beat them.' But he, like so many others, was struck by the attention Chuikov paid to his men. 'The way he trusted us, and made use of ordinary soldier's ideas, was a revelation', Mereshko continued, 'and it began to bring back our self-esteem and pride.' He gave an example of this:

> In the early stages of the battle we dreaded German air superiority – it was without doubt the thing we feared the most. Their planes were over our heads the whole time – and we felt so desperately vulnerable. We had no anti-aircraft guns left in the city, and our own air fleet, with less than a quarter of the planes of our opponents, could not offer us real protection. Chuikov was thinking how he might reduce the deadly effectiveness of the enemy's aviation and he found inspiration in the actions of an ordinary soldier named Protodyakanov.
>
> Protodyakanov was an anti-tank gunner, who, finding himself alone with his gun in the 'neutral zone' – no-man's land – after a sudden German attack, did not fall back to the new Russian line, but stayed where he was, managing to hit a number of German tanks. When Chuikov spoke to him he was surprised that the Germans had not bombed his gun emplacement. He realized that the enemy was reluctant to send in his planes when the frontlines were really close to each other. He immediately gave the order to get nearer the German positions.

Chuikov found a practical way to achieve this.

> He ordered us to dig our communication trenches and entrances to dug outs in an elongated zigzag, with its tip much nearer the enemy line, so we could get closer to their positions, narrowing the gap between us. Our maxim became 'If the enemy is trying to create distance between our forces we don't let him do it.' This tactical device proved itself again and again.

Soldiers were struck by the new tactic's simple effectiveness – and delighted that it had originated from a fellow comrade.

> When our detachments managed to reduce the neutral zone – moving into these forward positions – we noticed that the Fascists bombed behind them, often hitting empty trenches or dug outs. Sometimes, when enemy bombers continued to try and hit our

troops, they struck German positions instead. By this simple device Chuikov reduced our losses and raised the morale of our soldiers.

Similarly, Chuikov's street-fighting tactics arose, in part, out of a genuine concern for the casualty rate suffered by his army. Mereshko emphasized:

> He and his HQ understood only too well that our troops suffered big losses during counter-attacks, seizing buildings that the Germans were using as strongholds or making attacks on house blocks that were vital for the cohesion of our line. In the course of the fighting at Stalingrad it became clear that smaller groups could fulfil these tasks much better. But these smaller groups were not able to take over and deal with all the threats on their own – that's why we created storming groups.

Chuikov realized that fighting a desperate rearguard action in the burning city of Stalingrad was a demoralizing experience – so he hit upon a psychological ploy, whereby each combatant assumed an attitude of 'permanent offensive', ready to strike back at the Germans whenever he could. 'Chuikov paid a lot of attention to developing a snipers movement in Stalingrad', Mereshko continued, 'and got his whole military council involved in promoting their achievements – so he could encourage the ordinary soldier to hit back at the Fascists.'

Chuikov had an uncanny grasp of the powerful emotions thrown up at Stalingrad. As Mereshko remembered:

> He could almost feel the mood of the battle. He always studied the state of mind of the enemy – and instinctively sensed the feelings of his own troops. He gave us reason to hope again. Our position remained incredibly difficult – but psychologically, he was able to turn the tables on the Germans.

The Achilles Heel

Every commander has a weak point – and Chuikov's was his explosive temper. 'I have his personal file as his military career developed', said his son Alexander, 'and amidst the compliments, "well-educated", "promising", "devoted to the party of Lenin and Stalin", is one warning refrain, "too explosive".' In the stress of Stalingrad Chuikov would sometimes hit officers whose reports had angered him. His soldiers expected toughness, but this kind of violence, seen as humiliating and shaming, was genuinely disliked. If Chuikov had not possessed exceptional qualities this character defect would have seriously undermined his command.

One incident quickly became notorious. When Chuikov arrived at the 62nd Army HQ on 13 September 1942 the Germans were launching an attack on the city. The new commander was desperately attempting to get through to one of his units to find out what was going on, but completely unable to make contact. The lines had gone down and in his mounting, helpless frustration he lashed out. Radio operator Maria Faustova recalled the moment: 'There was an NKVD officer, Konstantin Danilin, passing through the HQ. Chuikov mistook him for the communication officer – and whacked him with his stick!' Danilin himself confirmed the incident: 'Yes – I was hit by Chuikov. Apparently he thought I was someone else. The Germans were bombing the area around the HQ and it was chaos. I suppose you might say I was in the wrong place at the wrong time!'

So was Chuikov a bully who intimidated his men? Feodor Shatravko went with his commanding officer to see Chuikov on the Mamaev Kurgan on 13 September, and remembers talking about the incident afterwards:

> The officer was frank with me, saying it was well-known that Chuikov could sometimes be violent or abusive, but overall he was seen as fair and just. His military service in China was highly regarded, he was considered to be well-educated and very experienced and, most importantly, he was always trying to save the lives of his soldiers.

Mikhail Borchev's older brother Ivan was on Chuikov's staff and they often talked together about their commander: 'He was seen as a very talented leader – firm and courageous', Borchev remembered. 'But what struck Ivan, more than anything else, was Chuikov's concern for ordinary soldiers.'

So what were soldiers' overall impressions of Chuikov's leadership style? I have singled out four vital qualities.

Toughness in command

The commander at Stalingrad had to enforce discipline ruthlessly. Chuikov combined approachability with toughness. Sergei Zacharov, who fought with the 284th Division on the Mamaev Kurgan, came to know him well: 'Chuikov was straightforward and easy-going – it was easy for us to talk to him – and he would never be strict with you unless there was a reason, but if he gave you an order, try and disobey it!'

Mereshko elaborated on this:

> Chuikov was very tough on control. If you were on a reconnaissance mission he always expected you to reach the frontline. If someone hadn't got there but pretended that he had, he always caught them out. He would say 'Alright, you say you went into the Tractor Factory, well what shop did you go to?' And he would keep on with his questions, 'Okay, such and such a shop – well where is the place of the commander?' He would ask for minute details, down to the kind of machine tools stored, the individual soldiers that you talked to. When he got answers to all these smallest details – then he was satisfied!

This strict system of discipline was vital for the 62nd Army's survival. The HQ had to know the exact situation at the frontline, as Mereshko made clear:

> Chuikov, and his chief of staff Krylov, ordered us to report only what we saw with our own eyes, what we did ourselves. If you were ordered, say, to enter Pavlov's House – but you only saw it from a distance, and pretended that you were inside, it was considered something terrible, as a crime against the army, and those who did it were removed from the front.

'Removal from the front' was the grim euphemism for being placed before a military tribunal and shot.

Making a stand in such terrible conditions required absolute ruthlessness. Chuikov demanded the utmost of his men, insisting they hold their lines come what may. It was a pitiless edge of steel behind Stalingrad's defenders. 'At times like this he could be merciless', Anatoly Kozlov remarked, 'always pushing his men. But how else was Stalingrad to be held?' Mereshko added a chilling detail:

> Yuri Bondarev, in his film *Hot Snow*, did not hide the fact that one of his heroes, General Bessenov, was almost an exact prototype of Chuikov. The words he used when it was necessary to stop the German advance are virtually the same: 'I allow no right of withdrawal. Not a step back! The present lines must be held to the last man. For everyone, without exception, there can only be one justification for leaving their position – death.'

In tough situations, Chuikov could be abrasive and harsh. Mereshko noted:

> He could be rude to people, and this was not always justified, but in general it sprang from an unwillingness to accept cowardice, lies, or failure to take responsibility. He was rude to such people because he simply did not want them around – but if he saw that you had fulfilled your order and had genuinely done your best, it was completely different.

The fictional Bessenov embodied Chuikov's strict control, his determination to uphold the 'Not a Step Back!' order and willingness to arrest and court-martial for cowardice those who left their defences without permission. But Bessenov also led by example – personally going to the most dangerous positions and encouraging his men. He went to great pains to reward his soldiers' courage and bravery. 'The words of Bessenov are exactly those Chuikov used, when he gave me the medal "For Courage"', Mereshko recalled. 'He said "It's all I'm able to do" – it was the only medal he could present personally – "and I wish I could do so much more." But his words were more than enough, for we felt valued again – as soldiers and as human beings.' Chuikov understood strict discipline could only be effective at Stalingrad once he had lifted the morale of his army.

A distrust of blueprints

'The most important thing I learnt on the banks of the Volga', Chuikov later wrote, 'was to be impatient of blueprints. We constantly looked for new methods of organizing and conducting battle, starting from the precise conditions in which we were fighting.' This flexibility – and freshness of approach – was to become one of the 62nd Army's great strengths. From it evolved their street-fighting tactics, their use of storm groups, and systems of strongpoints, to wear down the strength of the attackers. 'Chuikov made remarkably creative use of the initiatives of soldiers or small army units', said Mereshko, 'he was always open to new tactical ideas and – if they worked – prepared to use them for the whole army.' Let us take one example – the first successful night attack conducted by a Russian storm group.

Alexander Rakitsky was head of operations for the 37th Guards Division, stationed in the workers' settlement of Stalingrad's Tractor Factory. On 8 October 1942 the order had been given to storm a group of houses, to straighten out the front, and Zholudev – the divisional commander – had decided on a night attack to achieve this. This was something of an experiment, for the only previous night attacks conducted by the 62nd Army had ended in failure. Nevertheless, Chuikov approved the plan and declared he would come and watch the attack in person. Rakitsky remembered:

> Chuikov arrived at our divisional HQ at 10.00 p.m. that night. The assault was to be launched against a residential complex known as the 'six-house block', six big houses in the shape of a hexagon, on a high piece of land, overlooking the workers' settlement, factory and Volga. Chuikov asked about the flashing red lights – our units had flashed red torches as a signal they were ready – and we explained that our storm groups were now in position. 'Fine', he said, and picked up the phone and got through to the artillery group, stationed on Zaitsevski Island, mid-way across the Volga. 'There will be a concentrated artillery barrage on the six-house block for ten minutes', he told us. 'When our artillery finishes, go straight into the attack.'
>
> We went to an observation point to try and follow the progress of the assault. Chuikov was standing next to me and he was asking about everything. During the artillery barrage our paratroopers crawled up close. When it stopped we heard a sudden, short series of explosions. 'What's happening?' Chuikov said. I told him that it was our soldiers' grenades, probably thrown at a distance of about 20–25 metres from the house, adding that when we heard the noise of intense machine gun fire our guys would already be in, jumping through the windows. There were short, sharp machine gun exchanges, isolated shots and grenade explosions, and the cries of those wounded. Tough fighting was clearly going on inside the building. Then came the flares. I explained to Chuikov that we used a system of signals – by torch or flare – to show which parts of the building had been liberated.

The crucial thing in night fighting was to have agreed passwords – something you could quickly shout out to ascertain, in the darkness, whether it was your fellow soldiers or the enemy ahead of you. 'I explained our own password system to Chuikov', Rakitsky continued.

> In night fighting, when we opened the door to a room, we immediately called out 'I am the first!'. 'What's the reply?' asked Chuikov. It would be unfortunate if there was a German inside who knew a little Russian and could improvise 'I am the second'. 'It's a little

different', I continued, 'if one of our guys hears the password he calls out "I'm the first!" as well.' Chuikov paused, and then burst out laughing. 'Clever guys', he said, 'Clever guys!'.

The Russians managed to capture one of the houses in the block. 'Chuikov was really satisfied', Rakitsky recalled. 'He called us together and said "We have successfully started night counter attacks against the enemy, using storm groups. This is really important!"' This telling vignette captures Chuikov's attention to detail, openness to new ideas and willingness to apply them to the whole army.

Chuikov's ability to 'think outside the box' – unusual within the Soviet system – was vital at Stalingrad. It provoked a confrontation at the very start of his command over the best way to use artillery against the German attackers. 'Chuikov was forced into a serious argument right at the beginning of the battle with the Stalingrad Front's artillery commander, General Matveyev', Mereshko acknowledged.

Matveyev demanded that all artillery regiments arriving with their divisions were shipped across the Volga, with the rest of their troops, to the western bank of the river, right into the city. This was the conventional approach – but Chuikov strongly opposed it. He wanted all heavy divisional artillery to remain on the eastern bank.

This calls to mind Chuikov's statement: 'We opposed the Germans with our own tactics of city fighting, not according to any blueprint, but as we worked them out in the course of the battle, perfecting them all the time.' Chuikov quickly realized that routine artillery deployment would not work in the terrible conditions of Stalingrad. Mereshko recalled:

There were no horses or tractors left in the city for us to use, you couldn't hide them from the German bombardment, and it was completely impossible to move heavy artillery through the ruined streets, with all the bomb and shell holes. Wheeled manoeuvring had become impossible within the city. And delivering shells was incredibly difficult in the second half of September 1942. During the daytime the enemy saw everything – anything approaching from the eastern bank of the Volga – and kept every boat in their sights and under fire. Night time crossings were also very risky, for the Germans lit up the river with flare rockets. They knew the locations of our ferry crossings and kept them under constant artillery barrage. It was not that difficult to deliver ammunition to the Volga – what was exceptionally hard was to transport it across the river, to the western bank.

The Stalingrad Front came to accept Chuikov's view and all heavy artillery was left on the eastern bank of the Volga. 'It was clever', said Mereshko,

> because now there was far more chance of our artillery surviving. And every commander – whether of a division or a battalion – could call up our artillery for support. Chuikov realized that on the western bank we only had room for light, portable equipment – anti-tank guns and mortars – and observation posts, to call in accurate artillery fire from the other bank. His flexibility of thinking paid off – it gave us an opportunity to manoeuvre with supporting fire power and General Pozharski – the head of 62nd Army's artillery – could concentrate this fire, in the right place, at the right time, all over the city.

The ordinary soldier is closest in my thoughts

'In the forefront of my thoughts is the individual soldier', Chuikov wrote.

> He is the main hero of war. More than anyone else, it is he who has to meet the enemy face to face. And often, he knows more about the psychology of the enemy troops than the generals who are observing them from afar. The soldier learns about the character of the enemy and, at the end, he knows his moral strength in the field of battle. In the final analysis this is the decisive factor in any combat.

Veterans of the 62nd Army like to draw to my attention to this quotation. As Mikhail Borchev emphasized, 'When Chuikov took over, the army's maxim became: "The regular soldier is all-important."' Chuikov fully understood the value of reaching out and motivating his men:

> Even in the toughest fighting, a well-prepared soldier who under-stands the morale of the enemy is not afraid of him – even if his opponent is numerically superior. There is nothing wrong in the fact that a soldier, who is fighting in a basement or under a staircase, and who knows the general task facing the army, is left on his own initia-tive, to accomplish his own task on his own. The soldier is often his

own general in street fighting. You can't be a commander if you don't trust your soldiers' skills.

Chuikov realized a fundamental truth – at a time of absolute crisis 'every man is his own commander'. Chuikov's stroke of genius was to 'hide' his army's weaknesses, the constant shortage of ammunition and vital supplies, its lack of formal training, by creating room for the life experience of the ordinary soldier. He listened to his men's ideas and tried to incorporate them. By allowing his men an unusual degree of combat initiative, the great strength of his opponents, their well-honed, methodical and disciplined approach, began to turn into a weakness, an over-regimented and inflexible way of fighting.

When Chuikov generated a spirit of inventiveness in his army – encouraging a different way of fighting – it shook the enemy. German soldiers began to complain of 'hooliganism', the 'gangster methods' employed by Red Army troops. They didn't like being jolted out of their routine and were unsettled – not knowing what to expect next.

To promote such inventiveness Chuikov decided to break up the traditional army formations – and alongside battalions, companies and platoons introduce new units: small storm groups. Chuikov was tough on discipline – but he was also prepared to trust his soldiers. And that trust arose from his remarkable empathy with the fighters in his army: 'How important it is for senior commanders to chat with the troops in the frontline', Chuikov later said.

> I know from my own experience that when you talk to soldiers in a dug out, share their grief and happiness, smoke each other's cigarettes, weigh up the situation together and ask their advice about operations – then the soldier will inevitably feel: 'If the general was here that means we need to hold firm!' The soldier will not retreat without being ordered to do so, and will throw everything in his power into the fight against the enemy.

The small groups he created allowed him to keep contact with his men in this way, and powerfully fostered this spirit of mutual trust.

Chuikov understood the importance of morale: 'If you rely on an order, without preparing the morale of the men who will carry it out, then those men will swim not towards the battle but back to the bank they have set out from. In this situation, posters and slogans won't help you.' Transformation of morale required a spirit of comradeship in the army.

Lyubov Isayevna was a volunteer nurse, who worked to organize the evacuation of the wounded from the Barrikady Factory area. Her 2-year-old daughter had been killed in the German air-raids, just as she had been starting kindergarten:

> Chuikov was always prepared to give responsibilities to us – ordinary soldiers or civilian volunteers. I remember going to see him at the Army HQ and being struck by the alertness of his face, as if he was always waiting for his soldiers' reports. I found him attentive and kind. He would chat – make some hot tea, share his advice with me. It was the same with other liaison people.

'He was extraordinarily approachable', Sergei Zacharov recalled. 'There were no affectations with him – he was down-to-earth and straightforward. Stalingrad fighters were so special to him. We could come to him as if he were our own father.'

Leadership from the front

Chuikov led from the front – and this was so important at Stalingrad. 'We all felt the force of Chuikov's will, his sheer determination', Mereshko recalled. 'With all the problems we had, and it was a desperate situation, we knew our commander would stay with us, defending and protecting Stalingrad, with all the resources available to him, and this conviction radiated out and reached all our soldiers.'

Chuikov was personally very brave. He would not ask his soldiers to undertake a task unless he was willing to face similar danger himself. But he also had a larger vision, one of a spirit of courage and comradeship within his army. As he wrote in his memoirs:

> It is important for every soldier to feel that his exploit will not pass unnoticed. One can then rest assured that the order will be carried out. Of course, there is no need for, let us say, a divisional commander to spend all his time in the forward trenches – his place is in the command post, from which he has to direct the fighting. I stress, however, that in the face of danger the commander must be near the frontline, as close to his men as possible. In that situation the soldiers will not disappoint you – they will do the job you call on them to do.

This was leadership through personal example, as Chuikov made clear: 'I learnt this at the school of the battle of Stalingrad. We called on all commanders to be in the frontline. They needed to explain to everyone that there could be no retreat.'

It was an obvious risk for a commander to go so close to the fighting. 'I remember one time I met Chuikov at our divisional HQ', recalled Alexander Rakitsky. 'He had asked me to take him to the frontline positions. It was incredibly dangerous, and I remember protesting "You are too precious to lose", but my appeal fell upon deaf ears!' Mereshko often accompanied his commander into the thick of the action:

> Against all regulations, our Army HQ was less distance from the enemy than a battalion HQ should be. And Chuikov would frequently get even closer to the frontline, suddenly turning up where things were most difficult, with a small group of staff officers. We often found ourselves drawing pistols, fanning out, and making a 'circular defence' of our commander, with the Germans right under our noses. That was very characteristic of Stalingrad.

But Chuikov's decision to personally appear where the fighting was toughest had an enormous impact on his men. Konstantin Kazarin, a company commander from the 308th Division, remembered the ferocious attacks launched by the Germans in the Barrikady Factory in the later part of October:

> Things were really hard and we were struggling to keep on going. I was called to report to our regimental commander – and at this stage the command post was on the frontline, and the commander was fighting with his men. I entered the dug out, and saw our divisional commander, Gurtiev, there, and also Chuikov himself. He was standing in a black greatcoat, with a few of his personal guards, chatting to the officers, seeing what conditions were like, asking what he could do to help. The impact on us was colossal: our own chief was there with us, in the middle of this hell. We gained fresh determination to hold onto our positions.

'We need to remember that Chuikov was almost willing people to hold their ground', Mereshko said. 'He passed this on to other commanders and to ordinary combatants. If a soldier sees a commander – a general – next to him, he gains new certainty that he can stand it, that he can maintain his defence.'

One particular moment stands out – at the beginning of October 1942, when the Germans set alight the oil tanks above the Army HQ. A sea of burning oil descended to the Volga, leaving the command post surrounded in a mass of flames. But surrounded by fire, Chuikov and his staff stayed where they were, administering the army. This was the moment, as Anatoly Mereshko recalled, where they reconvened in the surviving dug outs, covered in soot and oil, with 'an entirely Afro-Caribbean flavour'. Chuikov spoke in private about the 'absolute hell' of that time, when for four days they worked in stifling heat and fumes, unable to sleep at all: 'I don't know how we survived that – but, somehow, we knew we had to get through it.'

Stephan Guriev, commander of the Siberian 39th Division, said at the end of the battle:

> How could we, as divisional commanders, even think of retreating across the Volga when the most senior command was in as desperate a position as we were? 'It's difficult for you', we said to our soldiers. But then we pointed to the burning dug outs of our army HQ, 'It's just as difficult for our leaders – they are being attacked, bombed and burned, the same as we are, and even worse . . .' This had the strongest effect on the troops, and they all fought to the bitter end.

Chuikov and Krylov: A Vital Partnership

Chuikov and his chief of staff Krylov formed an indispensable partnership. Mereshko recalled:

> They worked together as a team at Stalingrad, and became almost indivisible, like two soldier's boots, marching to the same step. Krylov was a big, strong man – like Chuikov – and once he had worked as a porter on the Volga, which was tough, physical, strong work. That kind of physical toughness was so important at Stalingrad. He was also a very calm person and in difficult situations he always managed to retain his self-control – he could appear relaxed even in a most terrible crisis. On many occasions he calmed Chuikov down. When the oil went up in flames above our HQ, and some were panicking and running around outside, it was Krylov who kept his head. He saw the danger – the surrounding trenches were quickly flooding with burning oil – and told everyone to stay where they were: he ordered them to stay in their dug outs and continue working. A lot of lives were saved by his quick thinking.

Krylov had valuable experience in defending a city, first at Odessa, and then at Sevastopol. 'He was Chuikov's "thinking mate" – always thinking what else can we do against the Germans?' added Mereshko.

> They complemented each other: they both had the same thoroughness, the same attention to detail. Krylov's maxim was: 'The staff officer should know about everything on the frontline.' I remember once coming back from the factory district – it was in October 1942 – and Krylov started asking me about conditions on the defence lines: 'How many bullets do the soldiers have left? How much tobacco? When was the last delivery of vodka?' They were very detailed questions – and because of the danger and tension in getting to these places, I had forgotten to find out some of these things. I didn't make that mistake again – we used to say that Stalingrad was a very good school for us!

Krylov's firmness was absolutely necessary. 'He was direct and forceful in asking for what he wanted', Mereshko remembered.

> Our soldiers always came first, whether it was delivery of tobacco or evacuation of the wounded. Once, I heard him on the phone to the head of the Volga flotilla. Conditions around us were terrible – there was constant bombing and artillery shelling and the flotilla chief did not want to send in the boats – he said they would be destroyed if they tried to cross. Krylov was implacable: 'Well, we have the wounded – who will die if you don't!'

Krylov – like Chuikov – was approachable, and approachability was so important at Stalingrad. At Odessa, in 1941, where he was head of special operations, he always liked chatting to his staff – he would pop into the map room so that he could talk to everybody, discuss the situation with them. He would listen carefully to anyone who had come from a particularly difficult sector of the defence. Chuikov and Krylov had a special gift of empathy, unlike Gurov, the army's commissar – who was a tough man, brave and methodical, but also rather a loner: he didn't mix with other officers or communicate well.

The Rival Commanders: Chuikov and Paulus

Chuikov – a volatile, instinctive fighter – could not have been more different from Paulus, the commander of the German 6th Army. This contrast played an important part in the evolving battle. 'We paid a lot of attention to the personality of the man opposite us', Mereshko said.

> We studied his style, his manner, his habits and the way he devised his military operations. It was like a game of chess – we wanted to be able to anticipate his next move. We quickly realized that Paulus was professionally very competent: he was an intellectual, and his forte was in planning broad strategic deployments. But he was also pedantic and hesitant. He was directing a battle almost a hundred kilometres from the frontline, at his HQ at Golubinskaya, on a tributary of the Don. Of course, it was conventional practice to situate the army HQ well behind the fighting. But for us, with our commanders sometimes just a few hundred metres from the frontline, it came to symbolize something – that Paulus lacked an instinctive understanding of the fighting. I genuinely think that the German commander was unable to comprehend Chuikov's tactics – so he persisted with his own approach, regardless. We used to joke about it: 'Paulus is used to strategic thinking – well, you don't need any strategic thinking here, you just have to grasp the tactics of street fighting.'

Paulus held two aces at the beginning of the clash at Stalingrad: the professionalism, high morale and efficiency of his army and the brutal yet powerful simplicity of his overall objectives. His intention was to pin the 62nd Army against the Volga, isolate it, bleed it of supplies, disrupt its communications and finally smash it in a last, annihilating battle of encirclement.

As Mereshko commented:

> We quickly learnt to anticipate what Paulus would do next. But anticipation was not enough – his army carried out his orders with such devastating force. However predictable your enemy is, it doesn't help you if at the end of their assault you have no one left who can frustrate their plans.

Yet over time, as the terrible combat in the city intensified, Paulus's character began to tell against him.

The valour of the Guards: troops of the 42nd Regiment of the 13th Guards advance into Stalingrad on the early evening of 14 September. Their intervention saved the city.

'Sell your lives dearly': Chuikov, flanked by Rodimtsev and divisional commissar Vavilov, addresses the soldiers of the 39th Regiment of the 13th Guards before their attack on the Mamaev Kurgan.

Rodimtsev's staff meet in their improvised HQ – constructed inside a conduit pipe.

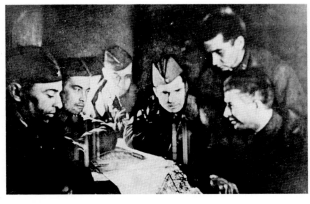

Jacob Pavlov and 'Pavlov's House' – one of Stalingrad's most famous fortresses.

A Red Army
machine gunner
in action.

Rodimtsev, Commissar
Mikhail Vavilov and Chief
of Staff Tikhon Belsky
consult a situation map.

Storm group
commander Jacob
Goldberg in the ruins of
the Red October
Factory.

Chuikov and Gurov watch the evacuation of wounded staff from the 62nd Army's HQ in mid-October 1942.

Alexei Vodnev – a 14-year-old 'son of the regiment' – who was employed on reconnaissance work in Stalingrad.

General Alexander Rodimtsev – he provided the quality of leadership vital at Stalingrad.

A Red Army soldier carries a food container to the frontline troops.

Fighting for the Red October Factory, December 1942

Rodimtsev and his staff with photographer Valentin Orlyankin (second from right, with camera). Orlyankin provided some of the best action shots of the Red Army in the 'defensive' phase of the battle.

Pavlov, Rodimtsev, Chuikov and sculptor Evgeny Vuchetich (creator of the Mamaev Kurgan memorial complex, which was opened in 1967) return to 'Pavlov's House' on the 25th anniversary of the battle.

The entrance to the conduit pipe that served as Rodimtsev's HQ.

Above and left: The 39th Regiment of the 13th Guards moves into a new defence line on the morning of 22 September 1942 – nicknamed the 'day of death'.

A storm group goes into action.

Chuikov and Gurov
admire Vasily Zaitsev's
sniper rifle.

General Stephan Guriev
(foreground) and the
staff of the 39th Guards
Division.

The 'village on the Volga'
– army dug-outs along
the river embankment.

Sokolov – the commander
of the 45th Division –
consults a map of the
city's factory district.

Mikhail Panikakha's heroic deed.

The small boats that supplied Stalingrad's defenders after Crossing 62 was lost.

Chuikov and Batyuk (far right) at an advanced observation post.

Above and right: 'The soldiers' fires are smoking': scenes from army life – preparing food, sharing cigarettes.

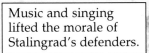

Music and singing lifted the morale of Stalingrad's defenders.

Paulus always hesitated before making big decisions, and this hesitancy began to spread within his army. 'Worthy but uninspiring', was how German air commander von Richthofen described him, adding that 'from the highest level down, attempts at motivation are only theoretical – the generals issue orders, but do not lead by example'. Richthofen was already concerned by the lack of daring apparent in the methodical German advance.

'A big victory can be won by the last battalion', Mereshko said pointedly.

> You have to take risks to finish a battle off. What we dreaded, as the fight for Stalingrad intensified, was someone like Field Marshal Rommel being sent in to take overall command. Rommel could have grasped the nature of city fighting and imposed his will on the battle. But Paulus lacked Rommel's killer instinct and this gave us hope – we could get close to the enemy, frustrate his plans with street-fighting tactics, and somehow hang on.

The German commander revelled in the planning and organization of military operations but he was not a natural leader of men. Alexander Rakitsky was struck by this:

> We knew that Paulus was originally the 6th Army's chief of staff. And to be honest, he was better suited for that position. Chuikov was careful – he was always willing to listen to different opinions, he never made hasty, thoughtless decisions, and he created a collective spirit within the army HQ – but he also had the gift of being decisive and clear. He was very decisive as a leader.

Mereshko agreed: 'Chuikov was a good communicator, who could explain why he was doing something and carry the army with him. He could make good decisions very quickly.' The key to success at Stalingrad was thus decisive leadership: Chuikov possessed that skill; Paulus didn't.

Chapter Four

The First Crisis

Chuikov's gift for summing up a situation and making tough but necessary military decisions was apparent during the first crisis at Stalingrad, on 14 September 1942. German troops broke into the city. Chuikov's courageous response undoubtedly saved Stalingrad from falling to the enemy. However, the actual course of events that day is entirely different from those given in standard histories of the battle.

On 12 September 1942, when Chuikov was appointed 62nd Army commander, two other important events were taking place. His opponent, Paulus, was visiting Hitler at his headquarters at Vinnitsa, in the Ukraine, to discuss German plans for an assault on Stalingrad; in Moscow, Soviet commanders Zhukov and Vasilevsky were meeting with Stalin, and airing the possibility of a counter-offensive on the flanks of the enemy's position, which might encircle the advancing German 6th Army.

Paulus's visit to the Fuhrer marked a shift in his leader's thinking. The campaign in the Caucasus was losing momentum and Hitler was now increasingly drawn to Stalingrad, and the political prestige to be gained by a decisive victory there. His growing obsession with the capture of the city led to a belated return of the 4th Panzer Army to assist in the offensive. The Panzers approached Stalingrad from the south, linking up with Paulus's 6th Army at the beginning of September, a success which forced the Russians to abandon the last of their defence lines and retreat into the city. Following this, the Germans quickly occupied the hills to the west of Stalingrad and prepared for a full-scale assault.

Despite the acute threat, Stalin's High Command in Moscow saw a longer term opportunity to counter-attack the Germans. They would send additional troops into the region around Stalingrad, drawn from all over the Soviet Union, and while the Germans bent all their efforts in an assault on the city, they would strike against the enemy's more vulnerable flanks, on the river Don, and the steppe lands south-west of Stalingrad. But they needed several months to enact such an ambitious plan, for sufficient reserves would not be ready before the middle of November 1942. Stalingrad had to be held first and the city's position was looking desperately precarious. When Stalin overheard

Zhukov and Vasilevsky discussing the possibility of a counter-offensive he told them to look into it further, but his immediate concern was the city which bore his name.

Stalingrad's defences were being pulverized by the Germans. It seemed impossible that it could hold out for more than a few days. To break the city's isolation from the rest of the front Stalin ordered repeated attacks on the German land corridor running through to the Volga at Rynok. Three hastily equipped Russian armies were thrown into a series of desperate offensives against the enemy – a wasteful and ultimately futile policy. But wisely the Soviet High Command also ordered an additional formation, Rodimtsev's 13th Guards Division, to be sent directly to Stalingrad to support the city's hard-pressed defenders. This reinforcement proved vital.

Chuikov's 62nd Army was by now a crumbling amalgam of battered divisions and depleted reinforcements. All his units were woefully under-strength. On 14 September he noted one of his armoured brigades had only one serviceable tank left. On paper his troop numbers looked reasonable enough but the effect was largely illusory. At full strength a Red Army division consisted of 12,000–13,000 men. Chuikov found one of his divisions numbered only 1,500 men, three others had dwindled to less than 800, and one was in reality a mere composite battalion of just a 100 soldiers. The entire left flank of the army was covered by a Guards Division reduced to 250 infantrymen.

Chuikov later explained the terrible conveyor-belt system used to keep the army fighting:

> It meant that our soldiers and small units crawled out from German tanks, more often than not wounded, to another position, where they were received, incorporated into another unit, provided with equipment and some ammunition, and then went back into the battle.

The statistics are stark. In its first assault on the city – with some of its best troops still on the Don waiting for flank cover from their Romanian allies – the German 6th Army was only employing its leading divisions. Nevertheless, it was attacking Stalingrad with double the infantry possessed by the defenders, three times their strength in artillery, five times as many tanks, and supported by overwhelming air power.

An additional concern on 14 September 1942 was the 62nd Army's desperate shortage of ammunition. An NKVD report showed it only had enough for one day's fighting in the city and the amount being ferried across the Volga was utterly inadequate. Vast quantities of ammunition were required for city fighting: in September 1942 the German 6th Army expended over 23 million rifle and machine gun rounds, around 750,000 mortar shells, 685,000 tank and infantry artillery shells and its soldiers used some 178,000 hand grenades.

Whether Stalingrad could hold out in such desperate circumstances remained unclear. The morale of many of its defenders was still poor. Chuikov's determination to make a stand had to be carried through at the divisional level of command within his battered army. The change began with the arrival of General Alexander Rodimtsev and his 13th Guards Division.

Alexander Rodimtsev: The Importance of Divisional Command

Alexander Rodimtsev was 36 years old when he led his 13th Guards into battle at Stalingrad. He had won the title of Hero of the Soviet Union fighting against the Fascists in the Spanish Civil War. His daughter Nathalia recalled:

> He got out to Spain because of his skill as a machine gunner, and at the battle of Guadalajara, where Mussolini's Blackshirts were put to flight, he manhandled a number of heavy machine guns into position, and single-handedly worked his way along the line, firing them all, as if a company were there.

His courage during the battle won him the award and Rodimtsev's bravery was never in doubt. 'On another occasion, when the enemy were attacking, he personally jumped on top of a tank to disable it', Nathalia added.

After returning from Spain Rodimtsev studied at the Frunze Military Academy, and at the start of the war gained distinction fighting his way out of German encirclement at Kiev. His 87th Rifle Division reformed as the 13th Guards in January 1942, and was subsequently reinforced and re-equipped before being sent to Stalingrad. Paratrooper Georgi Zolotovtsev came to know Rodimtsev well. They first met at Kiev in the summer of 1941, and when Rodimtsev was promoted to divisional command Zolotovtsev became his adjutant. He was on the staff of the 13th Guards throughout the battle of Stalingrad, acting as the division's cartographer and drawing up its daily situation maps. Zolotovtsev recalled:

> Rodimtsev was very direct, and if there was something he didn't like he would tell you straight away. He was tough and hardworking – and expected the same standard from those around him. He would not tolerate laziness. But he was never arrogant – and always simple

and straightforward in his dealings with his men. His two great strengths at Stalingrad were his physical bravery and extraordinary calmness in a crisis. At two moments when we were threatened with annihilation – the German attack on 22 September 1942 and their night assault on 1 October – his presence of mind was remarkable, and undoubtedly saved us from catastrophe.

Rodimtsev, like Chuikov, pushed his men hard. 'He was very demanding, both of himself and others', said Albert Burkovski, a 14-year-old who was adopted as 'son of the regiment'.

> If he gave an order, he expected it carried out, whatever the cost. I remember, at a very difficult point in the battle, one of our soldiers was sent out to capture a German. He never returned. So another was sent, and another. Five men were sent, one after another, before we got our prisoner.

Such toughness was expected at Stalingrad. Rodimtsev, like the 62nd Army's commander, was really respected by his troops. 'When a man has confidence and self-belief you can really feel it', Burkovski added. 'Some of our commanders, at company or platoon level, tried to put on an act, to appear confident – but in Stalingrad such acting didn't work and it quickly became apparent what you were really like.' Alexander Voronov, artilleryman in the 13th Guards, added: 'We all rated Rodimtsev very highly, for his personal bravery, for his heroism in Spain. We needed people like him to have any hope of winning.'

Rodimtsev and Chuikov had completely different temperaments – one was calm and unflappable, the other highly volatile. 'Rodimtsev, unlike Chuikov, could control his temper', Mereshko said simply. 'Chuikov appeared at our HQ several times', Zolotovtsev recalled, 'and he was so emotional – it was as if we had been hit by a sudden thunderstorm!' Yet the two had much in common, and both, in their different ways, struck up a remarkable rapport with their men. Rodimtsev would also turn up in the trenches to encourage his soldiers. 'He was not the kind of general who avoided the ordinary soldier's dug out', said Burkovski.

> He'd listen to our complaints – encourage us to keep going, see if he could improve things for us. He would come to us and say 'Oh guys, you have to press on. Where is the man supposed to be bringing food to you? That son of a bitch! Well, I'll have to speed him up.'

It was obviously risky to go right up to the frontline. Georgi Potanski recalled one such visit. The division had occupied a large flour mill close to the banks of the Volga and turned it in to a strongpoint. The Germans were all around, firing on them day and night.

> Rodimtsev came to visit us, accompanied by just a couple of body-guards. He was wearing an ordinary soldier's uniform – German snipers were constantly looking out for our commanders. Things were really difficult for us at that time but suddenly word passed around 'Rodimtsev's here!' The atmosphere became electric. In the midst of all the noise and shell fire there he was, chatting to his soldiers – remembering some by name – encouraging everybody. We really respected him for that!

'He had an excellent memory', his daughter Nathalia said, 'and could always recall a soldier's face and remember his name.'

Rodimtsev was the first in a series of divisional commanders who transformed the 62nd Army by leading from the front. Others, who arrived subsequently, followed suit: Gorishny, in charge of the 95th; Batyuk, leading the 284th; then Guriev, Smekhotvorov, Zholudev, Gurtiev, Lyudnikov and Sokolov. Yeremenko stressed the importance of choosing the right divisional commander for Stalingrad:

> We appointed Gorishny to follow in Rodimtsev's footsteps because he had the same leadership qualities. He was an exceptionally courageous man, who could persevere in the face of difficulty and was prepared to push his soldiers hard but remain utterly devoted to them. He had sound organizational ability, could make good decisions quickly and above all had the gift of managing his troops in almost any circumstances.

Gorishny won his reputation for bravery in the Russian Civil War. With commanders like these, Yeremenko believed the ordinary soldier would be better motivated to stand against the enemy, creating 'a stronger spirit of resistance at Stalingrad'.

Rodimtsev also had the quirky humour which came to be characteristic of Stalingrad's defenders. When Mereshko ran through Rodimtsev's leadership qualities – he was brave, democratic (he would consult with his men), his HQ was close to the frontline – he paused and smiled, 'and we all knew that he had a very good barber, Yasha, who would play on the violin before shaving the new recruits!' After a tough day's fighting Rodimtsev's hairdresser, Yasha Rubinichik, would give a soldier a shave, and play music in the men's dug outs. 'We all remembered those little impromptu concerts', Zolotovtsev added, laughing. 'Defying the horror of our situation, we would ask him to play a tune, gather round a table, find some alcohol, and sing. Suddenly, Russian fellowship reappeared in the midst of that devastated city.'

Rodimtsev had particular skills which were invaluable at Stalingrad: his previous experience of street fighting during the Spanish Civil War, at Madrid University and at Albacete, where the International Brigade was stationed. During the battle, a telegram was sent to Rodimtsev by members of the Brigade, now living in exile in London. They congratulated him on the stand at Stalingrad, and were struck by the similarities in the tactics employed in the city fighting in Madrid in 1936 and those in Stalingrad in 1942, almost as if one battle formed a continuation of the other. Rodimtsev was to be the vital partner, with Chuikov, in the development of the 62nd Army's storm groups, which were first employed in his 13th Division. 'He wasn't just a divisional commander', Mereshko stressed, 'Chuikov immediately brought him onto the military council as well. The two of them created our street-fighting tactics together.'

The 62nd Army and the NKVD

On the morning of 14 September 1942 the NKVD was still holding central or 'downtown' Stalingrad. They were performing a dual role, which came into place with the appointment of Colonel Sarayev of the NKVD's 10th Division as garrison commander, as soldiers and police. As a result, there were two over-lapping areas of military authority at Stalingrad, one held by the head of the NKVD, the other by head of the 62nd Army. Yeremenko, at Front HQ on the eastern side of the Volga, did not properly appreciate the problems this was creating in terms of cohesive command and army morale. At 4.00 a.m. on 14 September he set out his plan to defend the city, dispatching his orders to Rodimtsev, whose troops were rapidly approaching the eastern bank after a series of forced marches, and separately, to Sarayev, head of the NKVD garrison, and Chuikov. The NKVD was to take overall responsibility for defending central and southern Stalingrad. The 13th Guards were to hold the northern part of the city with other units of the 62nd Army. At nightfall on 14 September the 13th Guards would cross the river and take up position in the factory district.

These orders were a mistake. The main thrust of the German advance would be towards the centre of Stalingrad, to capture the railway station, the Mamaev Kurgan – the crucial artillery spotting point for directing fire within the city – and the main ferry embankment on the western side of the Volga, known as the central crossing. The NKVD was not strong enough to withstand them.

Ivan Schylaev, a veteran of the 13th Guards and historian of the division, summarized the problem:

> The NKVD was primarily a police force. They watched over banks, business enterprises, the local population and us. We thoroughly resented them. They might garrison a few houses, or organize some local strongpoints – but they were not up to the task of stopping the Germans. Their independent role destroyed the tactical cohesion of our command – it was as if the Red Army was not trusted to defend Stalingrad properly.

Gurov, Chuikov's commissar, was scathing about the NKVD: 'Sarayev's division was scattered all over the front, and therefore there was practically no control over it. It did not fulfil its function – it hadn't held its defensive positions, and it didn't maintain order in the city.'

On 14 September Chuikov decided to take the bull by the horns. During the night he had transferred his command post from the Mamaev Kurgan to the shelter of a large bunker on the banks of the Tsaritsa river. His previous HQ had been so heavily exposed to enemy fire that it was impossible to maintain communication with his army units. Chuikov made a laconic observation about conditions on the Kurgan:

> On 13 September all of us at the command post, from private to commander, had nothing to eat. Breakfast was prepared for us in a cottage on the Mamaev Kurgan itself, but an enemy bomb sent the cottage and the breakfast up in flames. An attempt was made to cook dinner in a field kitchen, but it was destroyed by a direct hit from a mortar bomb. After that our cook simply left us to go hungry.

Chuikov was to move to five different HQs during the course of the battle but never forgot his first command post. 'I see the Mamaev Kurgan even in my dreams', he told journalist Vasily Grossman. Years later, he would decide to be buried there.

On his arrival at the Tsaritsa bunker, Chuikov was greeted with Yeremenko's instructions for the forthcoming battle. Seeing their error, he immediately and directly challenged them, insisting that the NKVD forces be subordinated to his own authority and that he be allowed to make all decisions about troop deployment within the city. Yeremenko agreed. This action changed the way the battle was to be conducted. Sarayev was called to the Army HQ and informed of the new situation. Chuikov was ready for a confrontation but the NKVD commander backed down. 'I understand', said Sarayev diplomatically, 'I am now a soldier of the 62nd Army.'

The incorporation of the NKVD within the 62nd Army meant Stalingrad's defenders were responsible for implementing the 'Not a Step Back!' order themselves. Over time, this made a tremendous difference to morale. NKVD reports and army combat journals make clear that the blocking detachments, which were usually placed behind the army, at the ferry crossings on the Volga river bank, were now under the authority of divisional commanders. They could, in cases of military emergency, be brought into the frontline fighting. 'It felt completely different', Ivan Schylaev said forcefully, 'when the blocking detachments were no longer just sitting there, watching over us. With the Germans pushing hard towards the Volga, Chuikov made them fight with us to defend the city.'

There was an immediate shake up in the defence lines. The 62nd Army war diary recorded that by the late morning of 14 September NKVD detachments had been taken out of the frontline and replaced by regular army units, 'in order that we can make a firm stand and not allow the enemy to enter Stalingrad'. NKVD personnel were allocated a subsidiary role, to prepare strongholds and local resistance points within the city in case the Germans broke through. It was noted that Rodimtsev and his staff would report to Chuikov at 2.00 p.m., 'to obtain their combat tasks'. Chuikov was now firmly in command at Stalingrad.

The German Breakthrough

Chuikov had a clear purpose for the 13th Guards Division. 'He wanted to put Rodimtsev in the centre of Stalingrad, replacing Sarayev, and give him an independent area of command', said Schylaev.

> It was a huge compliment to our divisional commander, but events dramatically intervened. At mid-day on 14 September the Germans struck a terrible blow at the heart of Stalingrad. They broke through our defence lines, captured the Mamaev Kurgan and poured into the streets of the city.

This was the first crisis point of the battle.

That morning the Germans attacked along the entire front. For a while the Russians resisted stubbornly, even launching small counter-attacks, but the weight of the enemy offensive began to tell. The defence line was steadily pushed back and at midday two German divisions, the 71st and 295th, were ready to break into the city. Air power was employed to devastating effect. The 62nd Army war diary noted grimly that groups of fifty to sixty enemy planes would saturation bomb individual Russian units, then make way for advancing German tanks and infantry. At noon the defence line began to crack. Enemy infantry – in battalion strength – supported by tanks and groups of machine gunners, was making its way through the gullies into Stalingrad. German forces were converging on the Mamaev Kurgan, the key to the city.

Remnants of Alexander Fortov's 112th Division were dug in on the Kurgan. 'The bombing of our positions started that morning, and gathered in intensity', Fortov remembered.

> The awful cacophony of sound was swelled by enemy artillery and mortar fire. Everything around us was roaring and burning. The Germans managed to hit our transport vehicles and everything went up in flames. Our losses were mounting all the time – the conditions were absolutely horrific. And then their infantry and tanks appeared. We tried to return their fire, but more and more of them were arriving.

Fortov's last memory was of a shell exploding right next to him. He was half-buried in the earth, losing all sense of hearing. 'I was carried off the Kurgan by our retreating soldiers. It was a miracle I survived at all – so many of our guys were killed there.'

Suren Mirzoyan's 33rd Guards were also on the hill.

> From our vantage point on the slopes we could see what looked like the entire German war machine moving into the city: columns of tanks, with their soldiers riding on the top, followed by their motorized units. It looked like a terrible swarm of black insects was devouring Stalingrad. They were all so well-armed and equipped – and more and more of them kept coming: we thought they were going to roll right over us.

Mirzoyan and his unit were manning a heavy machine gun emplacement on the Kurgan.

The intensity of the German bombardment around our position was unbelievable. Their planes were flying over us the whole time. We would lie down in our trenches, with bombs exploding all around us. Then their artillery joined in. I was shell-shocked for a few minutes and lost consciousness. I came to, covered in blood, to see my mates to the left and right of me had been killed in the blast.

Red Army soldiers were no longer able to stand the strain. It looked as if the city was about to fall to the enemy. 'German Junkers were coming really close, dive bombing our trenches', Mirzoyan continued.

They switched on their sirens, making that terrible screaming sound as they swooped down on our positions. The noise was just unbearable and our soldiers' nerves started to go. One guy stood up, pulled himself out of the trench and started to walk off, ignoring all commands to stay. Another did the same, then another.

At 1 p.m. the 62nd Army war diary reported that the enemy had taken the hill.

News of the German capture of the Mamaev Kurgan had a devastating effect on the rest of Stalingrad's defenders. 'When the Germans took control of the Kurgan panic broke out amongst our soldiers', Mereshko acknowledged. 'It spread to unit after unit. We found ourselves losing control of the army.' It seemed as if the enemy had Stalingrad in their grasp. Georgi Zolotovtsev emphasized:

The Kurgan dominated the Volga, and once the Germans were on top of it, with such a commanding view of the city, they were easily able to correct their artillery fire. Their bombardment was terrible enough anyway – but now they could hit their targets with lethal accuracy. Our position looked utterly hopeless.

German machine gunners were fanning through the city towards the Volga and the central ferry crossing was now under fire. 'At that moment', Ivan Schylaev recalled 'the fate of Stalingrad – and of the whole war – was hanging in the balance. What happened in the next few hours would be crucial.'

Rodimtsev's 13th Guards – What Really Happened

At 2.00 p.m. General Alexander Rodimtsev arrived at Chuikov's HQ on the bank of the Tsaritsa. He had struggled to reach the command post amidst the terrible German bombing, crawling from shell-hole to shell-hole. One of his accompanying machine gunners had been killed in an explosion, another wounded, and his reconnaissance officer left severely shell-shocked.

Rodimtsev looked decidedly the worse for wear, dishevelled and covered in dust and patches of oil, so much so that when he gave his name at the bunker's entrance the sentry stared at him in disbelief, then called an officer over to check his papers. Chuikov's greeting to his fighting comrade – rendered prosaically in accounts of the battle as 'I see you didn't get off lightly' – is remembered differently by 62nd Army staff. It had wonderful humour in adversity. In the oppressive heat of the Tsaritsa bunker, with the sound of fighting drawing ever closer, Chuikov eyed Rodimtsev, a smile playing across his lips, then spoke with mock seriousness: 'Comrade General, do you normally present yourself for duty in such a condition?' There was a pause, followed by the robust response: 'Fuck your mother, Comrade Commander!' Everyone laughed. For a moment, the awful tension was forgotten.

There was plenty to be tense about, as Yeremenko, the Front commander, subsequently made clear:

> After the enemy captured the Mamaev Kurgan the situation in the city got harder and harder for us. There were no reserves and the central crossing of the Volga was under threat. The Germans were using the most outrageous methods of fighting to try and confuse us, changing the direction of their blows and painting their tanks with Soviet insignia. The Hitlerites were planning to break our defence in as many places as possible, isolate one resisting district from another, and then drown our defenders – separately – in the Volga.

The accepted version, while acknowledging the serious situation in Stalingrad, suggested that the defenders then courageously held on to key positions within the city – including the vital central ferry crossing – until nightfall, allowing the 13th Guards to cross over to Stalingrad and retrieve the situation. Richard Overy described the events of the latter part of 14 September as follows: 'Greatly outnumbered, Chuikov's tired troops retreated block by block. With just fifteen tanks and a handful of men he held off the furious efforts of the 6th Army to reach the central jetties.' This narrative stemmed largely from Chuikov's memoirs, written in the communist era, when it was impossible to acknowledge anything unduly 'negative' about the battle. But the Russian commander was only able to tell part of the story.

Chuikov identified the threat facing Stalingrad's defenders on that terrible afternoon: 'The situation was growing more difficult with every hour. The danger was that the enemy would cut through and reach the central landing stage before the 13th Guards arrived.' He formed two small groups from his reserves to try and stop the enemy reaching the Volga, and it is implied that they somehow hung on until dusk, when the German offensive abated and the 13th Guards were successfully ferried across. New eye-witness testimony, which fills in these vital few hours, shows the Russian position was far more desperate than Chuikov was able to admit.

It was not just German tanks painted with Soviet insignia which were causing problems for the defenders. The loss of the Mamaev Kurgan had thrown the 62nd Army into a state of despondency. In the jittery atmosphere, Chuikov's decision to transport all his heavy artillery to the eastern bank – necessary and vital in the longer term to maintain effective resistance – was seen by worried and exhausted soldiers as proof that the Red Army was about to pull out of the city. 'When our troops saw the artillery being shipped to the far bank of the Volga everyone took this as a sign that Stalingrad was about to be abandoned', said Ivan Schylaev. 'This terrible moment has been excised from our history books – no one talks about it – but removing the artillery triggered an alarming collapse in morale.'

The Army HQ was struggling to hold its scattered forces together. When Chuikov gave instructions for a counter-attack to regain the Mamaev Kurgan, his orders were not obeyed. It was feared that defenders charged with stopping the Germans reaching the Volga had simply walked off, abandoning their posts. German machine gunners were pushing towards the river embankment and had the central crossing in their sights. Chuikov was standing on the edge of the abyss.

The 62nd Army's commander had to act fast to retrieve the situation. His original intention was that Rodimtsev would take his troops across the Volga at nightfall. In fact, Mereshko admitted, it was no longer possible for the army to hold out that long: 'After we lost the Mamaev Kurgan we had to change our plans – it simply wasn't feasible to wait until dusk any more – and Chuikov and Rodimtsev decided that some of the 13th Guards would have to cross right away.' The first battalions would be shipped over immediately, in full view of the massed enemy aircraft hanging over the Volga, which were bombing and machine gunning everything that moved. With considerable courage, Rodimtsev insisted he would personally lead his men across. Their embarkation was put forward to 5.00 p.m., in broad daylight.

Anatoly Kozlov, who fought with the 13th Guards in Stalingrad, stressed the danger these men faced:

> At least 1,500 men were ordered to cross the river straight away, on the late afternoon of 14 September. We knew that night crossings were extremely difficult – but daylight ones were regarded as fatal. Most of these men would not reach the western bank of the Volga.

Mereshko also acknowledged the terrible implications of the new plan:

> It was virtually impossible to cross the Volga during daylight. There were always masses of German planes above the river. They would bomb and shoot at anything that moved – even a little boat with two or three people in it would be pursued relentlessly, and bombed until it sank. Only armoured boats could survive, and they had to manoeuvre constantly. The larger boats were bombed from the air, were shelled by artillery and mortars, and were even shot at by heavy machine guns, which the enemy had now got into position above the Volga embankment.

The weight of fire the Germans brought to bear on anything crossing the river was annihilating. And if a boat sank, it was practically impossible to swim to the bank. 'Even if you dropped all your equipment, weaponry and ammunition, then there was the weight of your coat and your boots', Mereshko commented grimly. 'Most of our soldiers who were thrown into the water drowned as a result.' It was part of the unique horror of Stalingrad that so many Russian troops died before they even reached the battle. 'Once your boat went down, you had to be an exceptionally strong swimmer to reach the bank', Burkovski added.

> Most people didn't make it. You had such a weight of stuff on you, it was virtually impossible to throw it all off and begin to swim. And even if you did, you were likely to be killed by the shelling and bombing before you reached the other side.

Everyone understood the seriousness of the situation. 'We commandeered all the boats we could for the crossing', Mereshko continued.

> And we ordered the Volga flotilla out on the river, with every boat capable of firing a gun, so that their salvoes could provide a smoke-

screen to shield our troops from German bombing. The guardsmen would cross the river under the cover of this smoke, and we would throw in all the air support we could muster.

This was a powerful example of Chuikov's bold, decisive leadership. Mereshko emphasized:

It was an awful decision to have to make, but an absolutely correct one. Chuikov was frighteningly close to the frontline, but the great advantage this gave him over Paulus was that he could react quickly to changing circumstances. Ordering in the first regiments of the 13th Guards that afternoon proved to be one of the crucial interventions of the battle.

Chuikov suggested to Rodimtsev that his troops leave unnecessary heavy equipment and supplies on the eastern bank. They would have to go straight into action as soon as they jumped off their boats. Army HQ had just heard that the Germans had reached the Volga above the crossing point. They had occupied key buildings overlooking the crossing – the State Bank, the House of Specialists – and were putting it under intensive fire and small groups of enemy infantry were approaching the landing stage. 'The situation looked really desperate', Ivan Schylaev said, 'for German machine gunners had already reached the Volga embankment. Yet somehow Rodimtsev had to get through, to lead his men into this inferno.'

The sound of fighting was drawing closer and closer to the Tsaritsa bunker. 'The Germans were now only 600 metres from our Army HQ', Schylaev continued. 'There were hardly any reserves left – just a few tanks. So Chuikov and Rodimtsev created two groups of 40 men, drawn from army staff. Their task was to break through to the crossing and hold it – at any price – until the 13th Guards arrived.'

This desperate decision left Chuikov and his HQ without protection, with the Germans just a couple of streets away. As he said farewell to Rodimtsev, it was hard to know which man's plight was worse. Chuikov's last words to his 13th Guards commander have been rendered into appropriate Soviet rhetoric: 'Will your Guards do their duty', Chuikov enjoined. 'I am communist', Rodimtsev replied, 'I have no intention of abandoning the city.'

'We recalled that conversation rather differently', Schylaev said. 'Chuikov went up to Rodimtsev, embraced him, and spoke simply and informally: "I can't see either of us surviving this. We're going to die, so let's die bravely, fighting for our country."'

The Race for the Ferry Point

Ivan Yerofeyev, an NKVD officer on 62nd Army staff, was in one of the Russian combat groups racing for the ferry point:

> We were ordered to form a group of officers and men from the HQ, armed with grenades and machine guns and accompanied by two tanks. We had to clear the houses taken by the Fascists along the Volga and reach the central crossing.

The terrible urgency of the task was felt by everyone and Yerofeyev described their advance to the Volga: 'Our tanks drove right up to German strongpoints, until they were at point-blank range, then fired through doors and windows and we jumped in after them, clearing the houses with grenades and machine gun fire.' Then the ferry crossing came into view.

> It was a scene of indescribable chaos. Through terrible smoke we saw the boats bobbing in the water, the supply vehicles parked by the jetty, the injured, laid out on the ground nearby, hoping to be evacuated. Everything was burning; everybody was shouting and screaming. German planes were attacking in relays, coming down really low, first machine gunning and then bombing.

German infantry had already reached the embankment above them. 'The chief administrator of the ferry crossing was killed by German sniper fire from the neighbouring houses, and then the commissar who took over from him was also shot', Yerofeyev continued.

> The harbour was in flames and the heat reached such intensity that the Katyusha rockets, unloaded and stacked by the quayside, suddenly ignited. They were all flying out of their boxes, exploding everywhere like ghastly fireworks. We were desperately running about, trying to separate the ammunition boxes, with German snipers picking us off all the time.

Yerofeyev and his comrades managed to put out the fire in the harbour storage area. And then, through the smoke, they saw groups of enemy infantry advancing towards them, closing in for the kill. 'We realized the Germans had completely infiltrated our position', he remarked bluntly. It seemed impossible to hold the crossing any more. Stalingrad would fall. And then something extraordinary happened: with a last, colossal surge of energy, the defenders rallied and flung themselves against the invader. 'Everybody, whatever their rank, whether they were injured or not, everybody who could move, formed into one last defence line', Yerofeyev remembered. 'We stood together, firing and firing – until our guns were almost melting from the heat.' Somehow, they hung on.

The Preparation of the Troops

On the other side of the Volga, the soldiers of the 13th Guards Division were gathering. Vasily Grossman recreated the scene:

> As the division was approaching the Volga, men saw a tall, dark cloud. One couldn't possibly mistake it for dust. It was sinister – black as death – the smoke from burning oil storage tanks rising over the northern part of the city. Big arrows nailed to the trunks of trees said 'Crossing'. They pointed towards the Volga. The division couldn't wait until night to cross the river. Men were hastily unloading crates of weapons and ammunition, and sugar and sausage.

As Grossman made clear, the assembling troops were really frightened. A daylight crossing was a death sentence: 'The enemy was everywhere, in the sky, on the opposite bank. The soldiers fell silent. Every head was turning from side to side in anxiety. Everyone was glancing at the sky.' Rodimtsev's own description to Grossman was utterly prosaic: 'We began the crossing at 1700 hours on 14 September, preparing weapons as we went along.' But it was Rodimtsev, back from the burning hell of Stalingrad, who now inspired his men.

'The saying that the soldiers were the architects of our victory was never truer than on 14 September', said Ivan Schylaev. 'But proper psychological preparation of our troops was all important.' Rodimtsev saw his men looking anxiously up at the sky, terrified of the German planes above them, and seizing upon this, turned their fear into a source of pride. Schylaev recalled:

> He stood in front of us, and pointing to the sky, asked: 'Do you know where you are now? You are in the famous Rodimtsev Division. We are paratroopers – and we fight until victory and defend to the death.' He spoke of the battles we had participated in

– and then, turning to the raw recruits, who were suffering the most, said: 'You are part of us, part of our group. You will fight as well as all the others. Combat with the enemy will initiate you.' The mood began to change.

Ahead of the soldiers was the burning city. Schylaev continued:

Rodimtsev pointed towards Stalingrad and told us: 'Fierce fighting is going on over there. The Germans have already reached the Volga. Soon they will destroy everything and Stalingrad will fall. And when Stalingrad falls, the fate of our country, our Motherland, will be different. Turkey will join the war against us; Japan too.' We didn't just hear this message – we felt it. Our terror was replaced by an incredible sense of urgency. We realized that there was not a moment to lose – if we delayed our crossing, the Germans would destroy Stalingrad. And at that moment, we were ready to sacrifice our lives for the Motherland.

Rodimtsev felt the future of his country resting on a knife edge. 'At first, he was daunted by what he had to ask of his soldiers', said his daughter Nathalia,

for it looked as if they were crossing the river and going straight to hell. He felt as if he were on the edge of a sheer precipice, and wondered whether he could muster the strength to keep on going. But then, when he looked around at the faces of his men, he suddenly understood. It was his mission to lead these people – and to turn the situation around.

The Crossing

Red Air Force Lieutenant Ivan Pstygo had just returned from another flying mission over Stalingrad. His small fleet of planes was pitifully outnumbered by the Germans. He noticed a concentration of troops near the landing strip and saw their commander arriving with a group of officers. Rodimtsev called Pstygo over to him: 'Comrade Pilot, I need to get my men across the river before evening. Provide us with as much air cover as you can muster.' Pstygo could hardly believe his ears, for German dominance of the skies was near total. He pulled himself together and replied: 'I will do my best Comrade General.' His last memory, as he got into his plane, was seeing Rodimtsev's staff car heading back towards the Volga. Pstygo held out little hope for its occupants – he thought the attempt to cross the river was suicidal.

Valentin Spiridinov witnessed Rodimtsev's men moving down to the shoreline. He and two fellow gunners had just crossed the Volga in the other direction – they were on their way to collect spare parts for their artillery.

> I saw this large body of troops heading down towards the river. They were moving incredibly quickly, and in absolute silence. I noticed that they were lightly equipped – they were only carrying grenade launchers and light infantry mortars – and I realized that they were going straight into close combat with the enemy. I carried on watching, mesmerized. There was something remarkable about them, the firmness of their step and their total concentration on the task at hand. I felt as if something extraordinary was about to happen.

In the skies above Pstygo and his fellow pilots were battling with swarms of enemy planes. For a brief moment, the smoke parted and he saw Rodimtsev's boats moving across the Volga, surrounded by the cascading water from myriad explosions. 'It was a remarkable sight – to see how they were managing to keep formation with such a terrible barrage being unleashed against them. I felt a sudden surge of admiration. I was so proud of those guys.'

But the German planes were now finding their bombing range. Vasily Grossman described the scene:

> A tall and thin bluish-white column of water sprang up about fifty metres from one of the barges. Immediately after it another column grew and collapsed even closer, and then a third one. Bombs were exploding on the surface of the water, and the Volga was covered with lacerated, foamy wounds.

Then a ferry crowded with soldiers received a direct hit. 'There was a flash of flame, dark smoke enveloped the ferry, an explosion was heard, and immediately afterwards, a drawling scream as if born from this thunder.' Ivan Schylaev has never forgotten that moment.

> The ship was manoeuvring, then a sheet of fire erupted on the upper decks: the force of the explosion shook the Volga. When it was over – and the smoke had cleared away – there was nothing, just waves where the ferry had been. The scene froze our blood.

Still the boats kept coming. The city was drawing closer – and the soldiers could hear the sounds of explosions and the rattle of heavy machine guns. The enemy increased their fire. Explosions were tearing into the water and throwing it high into the air. Albert Burkovski saw the troops approaching the embankment:

> We were lying on the ground. Everything was on fire – there was smoke everywhere. The boats were being bombed and shelled. I saw a big barge – full of soldiers, with their big coats, grenades, sapper's spades, ammunition and machine guns – go down right before my eyes. Rodimtsev's own boat was hit by a bomb and most of the people on it died, but somehow he made it to the bank. I don't know how he managed to survive, perhaps it was through sheer will power. He later told me 'I couldn't afford to get killed, I had to maintain command.' That crossing was so terrible – I think more people died than reached the other bank.

The 13th Guards had suffered terrible casualties. 'More than half those guys were drowned crossing the river', Anatoly Kozlov confirmed. 'But the rest kept coming.' The Germans held most of the embankment, and were training mortar and machine gun fire on the boats. 'There was no time to land', said Ivan Schylaev. 'The soldiers jumped down into the water and went straight into the attack.' Yet somehow, the desperate situation galvanized the men. 'The troops were so determined', Burkovski remembered. 'They gathered together, shouted a "Hurrah!", and then, with astounding force, ran forward and just kept on going. The Germans were in a dominating position, but I think they were unprepared for the sheer ferocity of that assault.'

The attacking Guardsmen were almost willing Stalingrad not to surrender. 'It is hard to find words for the fighting I saw', said Gamlet Dallakian.

> One soldier had lost all his weapons. His head was bleeding and his tunic was covered in blood. Yet he ran straight at a German and broke his neck with his bare hands. He tossed the body over his shoulder – it was as if he was drawing upon some source of incredible strength – and then, without looking back, he ran on to the next one. The Guardsmen were quite literally throwing themselves into battle – at a run – with this powerful sense of urgency, all the time saying to scattered defenders on the shoreline: 'Hold on, hold on! We are coming.'

The Germans occupied the high river embankment and brought over-whelming firepower to bear on the advancing Russians. It did not seem possible that they could succeed – and yet they did. In ferocious hand-to-hand combat Rodimtsev's soldiers recaptured a key building from the Germans – the Mill, overlooking the Volga – and secured the river crossing. That night, thousands more of the division were able to cross. As the terrible day drew to a close, Stalingrad's defenders had managed to cling on to their city.

In subsequent Soviet histories of the battle, the events of 14 September were rearranged to show that all the Guardsmen crossed the Volga at night. The mass panic – which forced Chuikov and Rodimtsev to throw their troops into battle in broad daylight – was too painful to acknowledge. The mere possibility of military failure at Stalingrad besmirched the honour of the communist state. As Gamlet Dallakian pointed out: 'We could never admit that the city might have fallen to the enemy.'

Now we can pay tribute to the leadership of Chuikov, the bravery of Rodimtsev and the heroism of his soldiers. The position of the defenders was still desperate. But looking back at the events of 14 September Ivan Yerofeyev felt a vital difference:

> General Rodimtsev had shared the same dangers as his men, and successfully organized the defence of the Volga embankment. Somehow, I felt he was organizing the defence of our Motherland itself. This was the moment when we began to stand up to the Germans and hold on to our native soil. 'Not a Step Back!' was now a reality for us at Stalingrad.

Chapter Five

Courage Born of Desperation

The September Battles

On 14 September 1942 the Red Army barely held on at Stalingrad. Chuikov and his HQ staff would later reflect on that fateful day. The central ferry crossing had been within minutes of falling to the enemy. Their Army HQ lay unprotected, only 600 metres from the advancing Germans. They had no reserves left (an NKVD report stated that on 14 September even the blocking units were fighting on the frontline). Somehow, they had survived. Decisive leadership and raw courage had played its part.

An interesting weakness in the opposing commander, Paulus, was also becoming apparent – his reliance on 'method fighting' and inability to take risks and finish things off. Chuikov had the events of 14 September in mind when he said:

> Historians maintain that in great battles outstanding generals would often have won a decisive victory if they had only had another battalion. During these days of fighting, it seems to me, Paulus had more than enough battalions with which to split the 62nd Army and reach the Volga.

The Russians now had a chance to cling on. But it was a desperate chance – and the fighting in Stalingrad in September 1942 was truly horrific. Some of the famous descriptions of combat at this time create an impression of a city already transformed into a series of formidable strongholds, and German strength and morale worn away through costly efforts to capture these urban fortresses. The reality was rather different. The Russians were struggling to form a coherent defence line and trying to disrupt the cohesion of the German advance. The enemy were prepared to sustain casualties to achieve their overall objectives. The position of the defenders remained exceptionally difficult. Yet amidst these difficulties, a desperate courage was born. It was becoming clear there would be no easy German victory at Stalingrad.

The Grain Elevator

As the Germans advanced towards the Volga, southern Stalingrad offered them a tempting target. It was without doubt the most vulnerable part of the city. The enemy had already reached the river at Kuporosnoye, splitting the 62nd Army from its neighbour, the 64th, and could use this breakthrough as a lever, driving the defenders up against the Tsaritsa gully and destroying them there. Mikhail Serebryakov emphasized that the river gullies – which ran into the Volga from the western steppe – allowed the enemy to penetrate their positions: 'The gullies were incredibly convenient for the Germans; they were like a series of roads leading to the Volga. They could rake the tops with aircraft fire, or infiltrate them with men and tanks.'

The grain elevator dominated the skyline of the southern Stalingrad. It was an easily recognizable landmark, and when Paulus planned a victory badge for his troops, to celebrate the intended capture of the city, he used the grain elevator as his background motif. But it was to become the focal point for a heroic stand against the Germans.

On the evening of 17 September a picked force of about fifty guardsmen and marines assembled in the building to confront the enemy. Lieutenant Andrei Khozyaynov, commander of a platoon of marines, described the ghastly struggle which followed:

> In the elevator, the grain was on fire, the water in the machine guns evaporated, the wounded were thirsty, but there was no water nearby. During the day many of us climbed up to the highest points in the elevator and from there fired upon the Germans; at night we came down and made a defensive ring round the building. Our radio equipment had been put out of action on the first day. We had no contact with our units.

Mereshko stressed that it was vital to hold off the attackers here.

> The Germans were searching for high points from which to control the river crossing routes. From the roof of the grain elevator you could watch over the Volga and the main ferry crossing. The enemy wanted to put heavy machine guns and light artillery on top of it. And there was another reason why this building was so important. It lay in the middle of the land corridor the Germans were widening between the 62nd and 64th Armies. They wanted to create a dead

zone, pushing the 64th Army further south, and increasing the isolation of our defenders.

Importantly, the Germans wanted to capture the grain elevator intact – so that they could use it as a stronghold and enjoy its grain supplies. They sent in some tanks and infantry, in battalion strength. On 15 September it appeared that the Russians had been caught off guard, for the Panzers pushed through to the elevator before it had been properly garrisoned. But their infantry did not immediately secure the building and it gave Chuikov a chance. Mereshko described his determined response.

> The speed of the German advance in this sector shocked us. We could see what they were trying to do – isolate us from the rest of the front and disrupt the supplies being sent to our army across the river. Their Panzers had broken through so fast that we almost lost the grain elevator straight away. Fortunately, there was a series of tunnels running from the Volga to the elevator, and Chuikov now made use of them, getting our soldiers through – behind the German lines – to garrison the building. It was a suicide mission. We knew ammunition and water would quickly run short, so we sent in a group of specially picked troops – some of our best guardsmen and marines – whom we could rely upon to make a stand.

For two days the small garrison resisted heroically, in awful conditions, until finally the Germans broke into the building on 20 September. The defenders remained defiant to the very end. 'At noon twelve enemy tanks came up', Khozyaynov continued. 'We had already run out of ammunition for our anti-tank rifles and we had no grenades left. The tanks approached the elevator and began to fire at our garrison from point blank range. But no one flinched.' One Russian machine gun was blown up by a German shell, another bent out of shape by a piece of shrapnel. 'Explosions were shattering the concrete; the grain was in flames. We could not see each other for dust and smoke, but we cheered each other with shouts.' German tanks and infantry appeared. 'Fighting flared up inside the building. We sensed and heard the enemy soldiers' breath and footsteps, but we could not see them in the smoke. We fired at sounds.'

The German troops were deeply disconcerted by such fierce resistance. 'Fighting is going on inside the elevator', one of their soldiers wrote. 'It is occupied not by men but by devils, whom no flames or bullets can destroy. If all the buildings of Stalingrad are defended like this, then none of our soldiers will get back to Germany.' Later, Chuikov spoke proudly of the tenacity shown by its defenders, but as Mereshko pointed out:

> We only found out what had happened in the grain elevator after the battle for Stalingrad had ended. At the time we heard the sound of fighting but had little idea of what was going on. The defending force had become completely cut off, and was making its own provision for water and ammunition. We heard rumours that our soldiers were suffering terribly, and that a few survivors managed to retreat to Golodny Island, on the Volga.

Mikhail Serebryakov, one of the Russians who recaptured the grain elevator from the Germans at the end of the battle, recognized its strengths as an improvised fortress and spoke revealingly about how the story of its defence was used to represent only a very partial truth about the battle.

> It was an obvious place to make a stand. It was a superb stronghold and was always going to be difficult to take. In mid-September our men fought bravely for a number of days, but their desperate resistance then became part of our propaganda myth – that from the very beginning we were superior to the enemy in fighting spirit. This was not so – we gathered ourselves, and resisted powerfully, but in the early days things were very bad for us. It is never mentioned how hard it was for us to recapture the building in January 1943 – the Germans defended it ferociously, even bringing up an armoured train and incorporating it into their position.

Serebryakov was right to stress that the defence of the grain elevator became part of a Soviet propaganda myth. Russian troops did not always resist heroically, particularly in the early stages of the fighting. As Antony Beevor said: 'It is not an insult to their courage – if anything, it confirms it – to remember the minority who would not, or could not, stand the appalling strain of the battle.' Some were guilty of cowardice; others found the city combat simply unendurable. Chuikov decided to garrison the grain elevator because Russian resistance south of the Tsaritsa was disintegrating. The 42nd Brigade's combat journal recorded the deteriorating situation in the vicinity of the elevator between 15 and 18 September. Neighbouring Red Army detachments were retreating without permission, opening the Brigade's flanks to the enemy. It was in danger of being encircled by the Germans and some of its units were already surrounded. All communication with 62nd Army HQ had been lost.

The overriding problem in this sector of the battlefield was poor morale and lack of effective leadership. Some of the 42nd Brigade fought their way out of encirclement on the night of 17 September, but lost many men doing so. The Brigade Commissar, Schapin, died of his wounds on the banks of the Volga – and panic set in. A rumour started up that other troops in the sector were fleeing the city, 'allowing a threatening situation to develop', as the combat journal laconically put it. The collapse started at the top. The commander of 42nd Brigade left the defence line, pretending that he was off to consult with the staff of the army. He never returned. Shortly afterwards, the commander of the neighbouring 92nd Brigade followed suit. Anxious soldiers, deserted by their leaders, fled to the banks of the Volga and started preparing rafts to escape the city.

Chuikov had not been able to stamp his authority here – and he acknowledged his failure: 'Two infantry brigades, cut off from the army, were fighting south of the river Tsaritsa. Officers of Army HQ sent to these brigades did not return and were presumed killed.' Chuikov subsequently found out that 'the commander and HQ of the combined brigades, abandoning their units, had left the city, been ferried across to Golodny Island, and from there were sending false reports about the progress of the fighting'.

Meanwhile Chuikov had been forced to move his own HQ again. The bunker on the Tsaritsa was simply too dangerous and on the night of 16 September the 62nd Army commander and his staff walked down to the Volga, crossed the river, and returned to Stalingrad further north, setting up their new HQ behind the Red October Factory, close to some oil storage tanks. These were believed to be empty – which turned out to be a grave error. The tanks were still half full – and at the beginning of October the Germans bombed them, setting them alight and nearly drowning Chuikov and his staff in burning oil.

The grain elevator had been defended with valour but the Red Army's hold on the city remained precarious. Chuikov was really worried about the state the army was in, and on the night of 16 September he was afraid to spend more than a few hours on the opposite bank, in case his disappearance led to a panic amongst his troops. 'What might happen to the army, to the city, if we had to spend the following day on the left bank of the river? My hair stood on end.' Racing back towards the Volga, as dawn broke, he jumped onto the landing stage followed by his staff, commandeering a last, departing ferry boat. Some of his deputies – including the heads of artillery and anti-tank units – slipped away in the confusion. Chuikov's response to this desertion was the remark: 'The air will be purer without them.' His determination to remain positive was vindicated by their replacements, Major-General Pozharski for artillery and

Lieutenant-Colonel Weinrub for the armoured units, who proved both highly competent and extremely courageous.

The Central Railway Station

On the night of 14 September thousands more of the 13th Guards were able to land in Stalingrad. Chuikov and Rodimtsev now conceived an audacious plan. They would send a force through the city that night in a bid to recapture the central railway station from the enemy. It was a desperado's throw of the dice. The troops would be cut off from their fellows, with limited food and ammunition, and if they succeeded in taking the station would have to bear the full weight of German counter-attacks. 'When these soldiers went off into the city we were moved by their courage', remarked Schylaev. 'It was an act of self-sacrifice which would buy us a little time. They were brave men and they were willing to die.' Rodimtsev later said: 'We knew what the effect of taking the station back from the Germans would be. It would provoke them – and they would throw all their manpower at its defenders.'

Chuikov and Rodimtsev resolved to send in several hundred men under the cover of darkness, hoping the enemy's guard would be down. Ivan Schylaev said:

> This was a surprise attack, and remarkably, it succeeded. We dispatched a reconnaissance battalion – and the Germans evidently didn't believe we could get through to the railway station. We were able to capture it early in the morning of 15 September.

The fierce fighting for the station, and the Russian defenders' subsequent brave retreat through central Stalingrad, became a famous episode in the battle. But it has not been easy to establish how long the Russians held the railway station for. 'We were unsure what was happening once the men were surrounded', said Mereshko. After the war, Chuikov met with one of the battalion's officers, Lieutenant Anton Dragan, and their conversation forms one of the most moving sections of his book. Dragan's powerful description of the fighting is well-known. His men moved through the city towards their objective:

> By now it was night, and the sounds of battle rolled around us. We massed near the station and moved in ready for hand-to-hand fighting. We made a sudden attack, threw our grenades, and went in

after them. The Germans ran away, firing chaotically in the dark. By the time the enemy recovered, and realized there was only one company of us, we had already established strong defence positions, and although they came back to attack us several times before dawn, they could not regain the station.

Dragan described the heroic defence which followed: 'The station buildings were on fire, the walls burst apart, the iron buckled, but the men went on fighting.'

Chuikov reckoned the railway station held out for five days before the brave force finally retreated, early on the morning of 21 September. 'But we need to remember this period of the battle is notoriously difficult to reconstruct', Mereshko warned. Nevertheless, a determined stand in one of Stalingrad's most famous landmarks had obvious propaganda value. Dragan's conversation was woven into the official Soviet history of the division, by 13th Guards veteran I A Samchuk. Russian resistance was now prolonged: wave after wave of Germans were beaten back. After several days ferocious fighting 'the Guardsmen peered out from the ruins and counted twelve burning tanks; enemy corpses lay in heaps at every approach to the building'. Samchuk made the resounding declaration:

> For ten days and nights, the encircled battalion fought off fierce enemy attacks from within the train station. For ten days and nights, a handful of resolute Guardsmen with almost no ammunition and food, under constant artillery barrage and aerial bombing, managed to hold a tactically important piece of land. This action assisted nearby units greatly.

Samchuk cited the situation report of one of the defenders, Koleganov, on 20 September. Koleganov was wounded but he and his men were continuing to hold out in atrocious conditions. The enemy was trying to encircle them. Koleganov exclaimed: 'Our Guardsmen do not retreat. Let us die the death of the brave – the enemy will not penetrate our defences. Let the entire country know of the 13th Rifle Division!'

Western historians of the battle have normally settled on a five-day period of resistance. John Erickson, in his *The Road to Stalingrad*, wrote:

> On 20 September German bombers concentrated at first light to blow what was left of the railway station to pieces. The survivors

moved out to the square facing the station and occupied part of a building – christened the 'nail factory' because of the stores of nails found there – on the corner.

Regaining Stalingrad's main station was a daring coup; to hold it for five days against the might of the German 6th Army would have been a stunning achievement. Alan Clark, in *Barbarossa*, drew upon the accounts of Khozyaynov and Dragan to demonstrate that the German offensive 'was now, undeniably, stuck fast'. Stalingrad, in his eyes, had become 'a battle of attrition' and 'it was the Germans, not the Red Army, who were being forced repeatedly to raise the ante'.

Antony Beevor agreed: 'The main station, having changed hands fifteen times in five days, ended with the Germans as occupants of the ruins.' But it had clearly been a time-consuming exercise for the Wehrmacht. Beevor linked it to other 'similarly stubborn defences of semi-fortified buildings in the centre of the town', the Univermag department store, the 'nail factory' and a 'three-storey building not far away', before concluding 'German soldiers, red-eyed with exhaustion from the hard-fighting, and mourning more comrades than they had ever imagined, had lost the triumphalist mood of a week before. Everything seemed disturbingly different.'

The impact of the furious struggle for the railway station is not in doubt. But could its defenders really have held out for so long? Mereshko emphasized:

Only certain places could be effectively garrisoned against the enemy. Most buildings in Stalingrad were easily destroyed by German bombardment. To hold out you needed a really strong construction, a mixture of brick and concrete, allowing the spine of the building to stay intact. There had to be substantial cellars too – these features were vital.

Yet the railway station had no cellars for the defenders to shelter in and was largely made of concrete and wood. It would be unable to withstand a substantial German air attack.

Ivan Schylaev spoke frankly.

I do not wish to belittle the courage of the defenders, but the accepted version of events is false. We held the railway station for less than twenty-four hours. On 15 September a number of German attacks were beaten off. But in the evening they brought in their bombers and dropped incendiaries on the station. Our men suffered terribly – many of them were burnt alive. The shattered remnants abandoned the building and fell back towards the Univermag department store.

Schylaev contacted Anton Dragan, who gave him an account of what really happened. This can now be revealed for the first time:

> During the night of 14 September our first battalion received an order to penetrate the enemy's position and take over the railway station. We fulfilled that order. But on 15 September the fighting around the station was incredibly severe and we suffered terrible losses. We were reinforced by a regimental machine gun company. It helped. Then the third company of Koleganov reached us. The station passed from Russians to Germans and back again. In the evening the building burst into flames and fighting continued on the platforms and track. But the Germans brought up a reserve unit and we were forced to abandon the railway station.

The remnants of the battalion were now stranded behind German lines without shelter. Dragan continued:

> We rushed into the 'nail factory', but were only able to take over one workshop. Fighting carried on inside the building. Our battalion commander, Chervyakov, was shell-shocked there on 17 September and command was taken over by his deputy, Fedoseyev. Koleganov was wounded on 18 September. On 22 September the remnants of the battalion split into two parts.

Dragan's chronology of events shows that Koleganov's situation report of 20 September, cited by Samchuk as proof of continued resistance in the railway station, was actually dispatched from the 'nail factory'. In his conversation with Chuikov, Dragan spoke of the desperate fighting in its workshops:

> The Germans were pressing the battalion back on three sides. The position with ammunition was serious, and there was no question of food or sleep. The worst part was the thirst. In our search for water we fired at drain pipes to see if any dripped out. The fighting would die down and flare up anew. In short skirmishes we used knives, spades and the butts of our rifles.

Dragan explained to Chuikov the mood of angry defiance which lay behind Koleganov's report. The lieutenant was wounded and concussed, but determined not to surrender:

> He said to battalion HQ that the position was difficult, but that as long as he lived the scum would not get through. Fierce fighting went on into the night. Small groups of German snipers and machine gunners began to penetrate our rear. They hid in garrets, ruins and sewer pipes and proceeded to fire at us.

The raw courage of these men is undeniable.

Dragan's new account has a more matter of fact tone. As what remained of the battalion dropped back, Fedoseyev, the acting battalion commander, attempted to establish an HQ in the cellars of the Univermag department store; however, his position was quickly overrun:

> The Hitlerites surrounded the Univermag and took over the HQ of the first battalion. Fedoseyev was killed. From this moment I took over as commander. We now consisted of roughly a hundred people: a mortar company, led by Bodunov, a machine gun company under Dilenko, a political officer, Sterlev, and myself, as commander. The Fascists had us surrounded in the 'nail factory' and were squeezing us back towards the Volga.

This was an astonishing rearguard action, but one quickly isolated by the enemy, and only covering a small area of the city centre. The men broke out, and made a last, desperate stand in a ruined house on the Volga embankment. The Germans had reached the river in this sector, so they remained isolated from the rest of the army:

> Only about forty people reached the Volga bank. Bodunov was killed. We took over a house that became our last strongpoint. We defended that house for five days and nights on Krasnopiterskaya Street – just twelve of us remained, and the Germans were constantly attacking us.

In his conversation with Chuikov, Dragan described their last acts of resistance, and these have become justly famous:

> We decided to raise a red flag over the building, but we had no red material. Understanding what we wanted to do, one of the men, who

was severely wounded, took off his bloody vest, and after wiping the
blood from his wound with it, handed it to me.

The defenders were desperately short of ammunition. Dragan told Chuikov:
'We beat off the next attack with stones, firing occasionally and throwing our
last grenades.' The Germans reckoned they had run out of bullets, and came
out into the open, moving down the street.

I put the last belt in the heavy machine gun at the semi-basement
window and sent the whole of the 250 bullets into the yelling, dirty-
grey Nazi mob. I was wounded in the hand but did not leave go of
the machine gun. Heaps of bodies littered the ground. The Germans
still alive ran for cover in panic.

But the enemy's armour returned.

Again we heard the ominous sounds of tanks. From behind a
neighbouring block, stocky German vehicles began to crawl out.
This, clearly, was the end. The guardsmen said goodbye to one
another. With a dagger my orderly scratched on a brick wall:
'Rodimtsev's guardsmen fought and died for their country here.'

In the aftermath of victory, Dragan's testimony had enormous symbolic
power. The Germans eventually destroyed his shelter with concentrated tank
fire. Remarkably, six of the defenders, buried alive in the rubble, later managed
to escape the building. Chuikov used the story to pay tribute to his troops:
'Alone, isolated, in small groups, they fought for every building, fought to the
last round of ammunition, inflicting enormous losses on the enemy.' But at
the time, this story of heroic resistance against the odds was not known to other
fighters, who could have drawn inspiration from it. As Dragan confided to
Schylaev: 'Only six of us – all wounded – survived from a large, reinforced
battalion. And during our desperate resistance we remained so utterly alone.'

Just one fragment of information got through to the rest of the army:
Koleganov's situation report. Although the full text was set out in the combat
journal of the 13th Division the communist state heavily edited it. All swear-
words - such as 'Fucking Fritz' – were removed by its political censors. The
exhortation 'Our soldiers are making a final stand for the victory of our people'
became 'The Guardsmen will give everything for the complete victory of the
Soviet system'. As veteran Anatoly Kozlov wryly remarked, 'To recapture the
raw, authentic language of Stalingrad we have to take out the communist rhet-

oric and put in plenty of swearing.' Worst of all, Samchuk, or his editors, deleted Koleganov's final, proud declaration to the rest of the army – the last message this desperately brave soldier wished to convey to his comrades. Perhaps his powerful human spontaneity unsettled a regime founded on Marxist dogma. His words – typed in the journal in block capitals – were simply: 'LET US BE HEROES WHILE DEFENDING STALINGRAD.'

Storming the Mamaev Kurgan

The most powerful act performed by the Red Army in mid-September was to launch an aggressive counter-attack to recapture the Mamaev Kurgan. The clash was fought out in the open, with all the advantages held by the Germans. The Russians made their assault in daylight, attacking up the slopes of the hill towards a well-defended enemy position, in the teeth of a devastating air and artillery bombardment. The attack could not possibly succeed.

And yet somehow, it did. Incredibly, the red flag was hoisted above the water towers on the Kurgan's summit. The message to doubters in the army was unmistakable: we are here to stay. As Chuikov said: 'We decided that we would hold on to the Mamaev Kurgan, whatever happened.'

Ivan Schylaev was artillery co-ordinator for the attack and watched the whole assault through his binoculars: 'The story of how we recaptured the Kurgan is usually told incorrectly', he said. Unfortunately, Chuikov made a slip in his memoirs, muddling up different regiments of the 13th Guards, and this mistake has been repeated in subsequent histories of the battle. Speaking of the night of 15 September, the 62nd Army's commander recollected: 'We were all concerned about the fate of Mamaev Kurgan. I ordered Yelin's 42nd Regiment, which was still on the other side of the Volga, to be ferried across that night and to be sent to the Kurgan.' He then added: 'On the morning of September 16 Yelin's 42nd Regiment took the Mamaev Kurgan. Close engagements, or rather skirmishes to the death, began and continued on the Kurgan until the end of January 1943.'

Schylaev clarified the situation:

> The leading battalions of the 42nd Regiment crossed the river on the afternoon of 14 September, and the remainder that same night, along with the 34th Regiment. Their task was to erect a defence line in the central part of the town and stop the Germans reaching the Volga, and it was a reconnaissance battalion from the 42nd Regiment which briefly recaptured the railway station during the night of 14 September. But it was my own regiment, the 39th, which crossed

the Volga twenty-four hours later, during the night of 15 September, and took up positions close to the Mamaev Kurgan, ready for an attack the following morning.

In the early hours of the morning Chuikov met with the regiment and explained the importance of his daunting order. Schylaev recalled:

> He talked informally with our regimental commander and was frank with him – Chuikov was under no illusions how difficult this was going to be – promising him all the support he could muster. We would be reinforced by a tank brigade and an infantry regiment from the 112th Division. Then he walked round, speaking simply but forcefully to clusters of our soldiers. I heard snippets of his conversation: 'We have to retake the Mamaev Kurgan – everything depends on it', 'If you are going to sell your lives, sell them dearly.'

Over the passage of time Chuikov became unsure of the regiment's number, but he never forgot the experience of meeting with its soldiers. In private, his son Alexander related, he spoke about the heavy weight of responsibility he bore:

> I saw those troops arrive in Stalingrad. I saw their faces and I looked into their eyes. They were strong guys, tough and handsome. They were all readying themselves for the attack. And as I talked to them, I knew I was sending most of them to their death. Can you imagine what that felt like? And yet, there was no other way. We had to get the Kurgan back.

The attack was scheduled to start at 9.00 a.m. The Germans clearly had no idea of what was coming. 'They didn't expect us to go over to the offensive in that sector', said Schylaev. 'I remember they were heavily bombing the Red October Factory that morning. Our troops approached the slopes of the Kurgan through a gully and were not spotted by the Germans. Then the enemy suddenly saw them and all hell broke loose.'

Everything seemed to go wrong at once. 'To have a chance of taking the hill our attacking infantry needed to be supported by a concentrated artillery barrage', Schylaev continued.

> We only had a few pieces of light artillery on the western bank: some anti-tank guns and 120mm mortars. Most of our heavy guns were on

the other side of the Volga but their supporting fire just wasn't accurate enough. Then the so-called tank brigade arrived. Our men were expecting about fifty tanks to appear – that's the normal strength of a brigade – but only four showed up, and they were in a terrible condition. Within minutes all of them had broken down on the slopes of the Kurgan. They could still shoot but they couldn't move. Our tank force was supposed to support a massed infantry assault but it was now completely immobilized.

German planes began to appear above the slopes of the Kurgan, bombing the assembled soldiers. The Russians needed to attack in strength but some of their infantry still hadn't arrived. Eventually the reinforcements from the 112th Division turned up. 'It would have been nice to have been joined by a full strength regiment of several thousand men', continued Schylaev. 'Those men were late – which delayed our attack – and when they finally appeared there were only 120 of them.'

The guardsmen prepared to move up the hill. But the Germans were now aware of their opponent's intentions and brought the full force of their air power to bear. Heavy artillery and mortars joined in. Vladimir Kiselyov was a company commander in one of the advancing battalions. 'It was as if we had been hit by a tidal wave', he recalled. 'There was a sudden deafening roar. Shells and bombs started exploding all around us. Many of our guys were killed or injured in that terrible bombardment – our casualties were horrific.' The attack was on the verge of disintegration.

Rodimtsev now arrived on the Kurgan. He had been watching the preparations for the assault and saw his soldiers faltering under withering German fire. He realized he needed to step in and somehow rally his men. It was near-suicidal for a divisional commander to appear at the frontline in such conditions but Rodimtsev disregarded the danger. He recalled an encounter which followed:

> I saw a young lieutenant who had frozen in terror. His troops were standing behind him, hesitant and uncertain. I told him to move forward but he seemed oblivious to my command. He began to fumble for something, dropped his water flask, and then started to shake uncontrollably. I had never hit a soldier under my command and I never wanted to again. But I grabbed hold of that lieutenant, shook him hard, slapped him twice across the face, and yelled 'Get going!' Suddenly, he woke up, pulled himself together and sprinted forward, followed by his men. He won a medal for courage that day.

Rodimtsev's frank account was shared in conversation with veterans he liked and trusted. There seems no reason to doubt its authenticity. It is understandable that the young lieutenant had succumbed to shock in such terrible conditions – so much was being asked of these men. Yet in battle psychology, combat can sometimes hinge on moments like this. A different commander could have provoked a mutiny by publicly striking one of his officers. Chuikov's worst character trait was hitting his subordinates. But the desperate urgency of Rodimtsev's slap galvanized his troops and the whole attacking force surged forward and charged towards the enemy.

The Germans had dug a system of defences on the summit of the Mamaev Kurgan and set up machine gun emplacements there. They raked the attackers with a hail of bullets. As Kiselyov neared the enemy he counted only a dozen survivors from his 120-strong company. His remaining men grouped together, flung their grenades and jumped into the trenches. Chuikov was watching the assault through his binoculars. Later, he told his son Alexander:

> I will never forget their heroism. The enemy was pulverizing the hillside around them, yet they kept going, fixing bayonets and closing in for hand-to-hand fighting. I saw one of our soldiers bayonet a German and toss him up in the air. They all kept moving forward with such incredible determination. For an instant, I imagined I was watching a line of *Bogatyr* [legendary Russian warriors of old] destroying their foes.

The vicious struggle for the top of the hill swung backwards and forwards. 'I saw the most savage fighting', Schylaev remembered. Kiselyov was caught in the middle of it. 'A group of us jumped into a trench. There was a German soldier about to fire a machine gun. I punched him and knocked him backwards. Men were clubbing each other with rifle butts and frantically stabbing with their bayonets.' The Russians seized the trenches but the enemy immediately struck back. 'A whole mass of them came running towards us', Kiselyov remembered, 'it was really terrifying'. Some of his comrades were unable to withstand the strain, and ran off in panic. But a young lieutenant, Timofeev, manhandled a captured German machine gun into position and turned it on the enemy, mowing them down. The men's spirits suddenly lifted. A guardsman hauled down the German flag and trampled on it. 'Just after 11.00 a.m. we saw the red flag raised above the summit of the Kurgan', Schylaev recalled, 'and word of this quickly spread throughout the army.'

The hoisting of the red flag was a gesture of heroic defiance. Stalingrad's defenders were determined to hold on to that hill. Later in the battle they would be pushed off the summit again, but they remained entrenched on the slopes. Rodmitsev's guardsmen would be replaced by the men of Gorishny's 95th Division, and then Batyuk's 284th – but the Kurgan was never again surrendered to the enemy. Once, Gorishny reported to Chuikov a fluctuation in his frontline of about a hundred metres. Chuikov warned him to be careful – the loss of a few hundred metres could lead to the loss of the Kurgan. 'I shall die rather than abandon the hill!' Gorishny replied emphatically. That was how important it was to the Red Army.

September Snapshots

Regaining the Mamaev Kurgan was a vital morale booster, for conditions in the city were atrocious. The smell of burning and stench of death were everywhere. Leonid Gurevitz recalled:

> It was an utterly disorientating landscape, with endless ruined houses, broken windows and rotting piles of rubbish that no one took away. Once we came back from an operation and could not find our shelter. We wandered around for a while, feeling quite lost, before realizing that it had been destroyed by an enemy bomb. We were always short of food and water and there is one scene I will always remember. There were two soldiers sitting in a courtyard. They had made a bonfire, managed to get hold of a frying pan, and some flour and oil, and they were making pancakes. All around them were heaps of dead bodies, just lying there: no one bothered to take them away. And in the middle of this pile of corpses these guys were shouting at us, 'Hey, comrades – come and have some pancakes!'

On the Mamaev Kurgan the dead were everywhere. The intensity of fighting was unbelievable. 'I remember walking on the dead, decomposing bodies on the Kurgan', Burkovski said. 'Imagine it – I put my foot on the ground and when I lifted it was filthy with somebody's intestines. It will never be erased from my memory.' By the time the 95th Division took over from the 13th on the hill, Nikolai Maznitsa recalled the slopes of the Kurgan were completely covered in corpses. 'In some places you had to move two or three bodies aside even to lie down. They quickly began to decompose and the stench was appalling.' At the end of September, Batyuk's 284th had arrived on the Mamaev Kurgan. 'The hill was wreathed in smoke', said Vasily Gorokhov.

The Germans were bombing and shelling us all the time. We felt as if we were on a volcano. There was a constant, terrible noise, and the acrid stench of burning – which made it so hard to breathe. And every time a shell landed, fountains of earth, mixed with fragments of people's bodies, would fly up in the air in front of us. We prayed that this situation was only temporary, that reinforcements would arrive and somebody would get us out of this hell.

'I felt an overwhelming sense of despair', said Gurevitz, 'a sense that we were finished with, that our fate was decided, and we would never see our families again. To keep going I focused on simply trying to survive, one day at a time.' The vodka ration of 100 grams a day was vital. Gurevitz added:

It took the edge of our tension, otherwise you would go mad. It was just the right amount. Because of the high daily losses there was a discrepancy between the amount of vodka issued and the number of men able to receive it – and it was always possible to get more. There were some guys downing half a litre a day. They just wanted all the stress to go away. But drinking that amount was always fatal – you lost your sense of danger and the ability to fight properly.

In such conditions, the 62nd Army practised a ruthless discipline to survive. At times, this was brutal and pitiless. Gurevitz continued:

Of course, there was Order 227, and I saw myself how people were shot dead for disobeying orders. I was supposed to carry a heavy coil of communication cable. There was a kid with me, helping, from central Asia. He was just eighteen and had never seen any shooting before – and had no military training to speak of. He had been partially deafened by the constant explosions and couldn't take any more. There was a period of intense fighting and our cable got cut, and the battalion commander ordered me to restore it. We had to run the cable line through intense enemy fire. But the boy just sat huddled up in the trench, shaking, like a frightened animal. The commander gave the order 'Go!' and just he didn't react – so he pulled out his pistol and shot him.

Some of these memories are particularly painful. Georgi Potanski said:

We would let ordinary citizens go down to the river to get water, mostly women – they would come from the part of the city occupied by the Germans, cross our lines, and go down to the Volga. This little ritual took place every morning. Then something terrible happened. Our troop concentration points and supply depots were concealed under the steep river embankment. They were well hidden, but when the women reached the water's edge they could see where they were. And after they returned to the city the Germans opened up an artillery bombardment at precisely the places where our soldiers were concealed. We realized the Germans had planted a spy amongst these women. The next morning, when they came down to the river as usual, we received an order to detain them and then take them across the Volga. Can you imagine what it was like to carry that out? The women were shouting and screaming at us – saying they had left their children behind, that their kids were thirsty – and many became absolutely hysterical. They were put under military escort and taken away by force.

Potanksi struggled to continue. 'We forced them to abandon their children – I still have nightmares about it.'

Amidst this horror, Russian soldiers began to gain a grim sense of solidarity: they were all in this hell together. Chuikov said to Vasily Grossman.

Once you are here, there is no way out. Either you will lose your head or your legs. Everyone knows that those who turn and run will be shot on the spot. Retreat means ruin – if you retreated you would be shot; and if I did, I would be shot as well.

Order 227 imposed draconian discipline on Red Army soldiers, but Chuikov's flexible interpretation of it was all important. Previously, blocking detachments had existed solely to stop people running away. Chuikov put the detachments under the authority of divisional commanders, and brought them into the fighting at moments of crisis. It created a different atmosphere in the army. 'When we fought for the Mamaev Kurgan in the middle of September we all knew that there were no blocking detachments behind us – and everyone capable of carrying weapons was in the frontline', said Kiselyov. 'It made an enormous difference to morale.'

There were also the penal companies. After Stalin issued Order 227 those guilty of criminal or political charges could be placed in a penal battalion and sent to the front, as an alternative to serving a prison sentence in the camps. The death rate in these units was virtually 100 per cent, for their missions were suicidal and there was no training or proper weaponry. The only realistic chance of survival was to be seriously wounded in combat, and, to use the awful phrase current at the time, expiate one's sins through blood. But at Stalingrad Chuikov ensured they operated differently.

'The penal companies did not form a regular part of our army', Mereshko said. 'Instead, they were kept under Chuikov's personal authority.' Georgi Zolotovtsev described how they were used.

> There was one company – the 110th – under Chuikov's direct command. It fought on the Mamaev Kurgan. There are rumours that it took part in the storming of the hill on 16 September but that is not true. It was brought in later in September and moved into the line alongside Batyuk's 284th Division.

Zolotovtsev told a remarkable story about a soldier who briefly fought in it.

> There was a private in our division of whom we were very fond – his name was Vasily Prognimak. He was bit of a rogue, but a lovable rogue nonetheless. Once Prognimak was sent to the far bank of the Volga to get some supplies. Normally we were stuck with this sort of millet 'soup' for breakfast, lunch and dinner. But suddenly we had this wonderful lamb stew – it created a sensation! We found out that Prognimak had commandeered a car, driven off to a collective farm and grabbed a few sheep. But stealing was a serious offence and somebody reported him, so he had to be sent to the penal unit. We thought that was that – no one came out of those alive – but within a week he had rejoined us. He had fought bravely in an attack and Chuikov had him released. Chuikov's intervention had an enormous impact – we felt that acts of courage were seen and really valued by our commander.

Chuikov enforced iron discipline and those who deserted their positions would be shot. But he also created a spirit of unity in his army by praise. He instinctively understood a timeless military truth, put well by the Roman writer Vegetius: 'soldiers are corrected by fear and punishment in the camp; on campaign, hope and rewards make them feel better'. The 'Not a Step Back!' order was the bedrock of the Russian position at Stalingrad, but it could not create a fighting spirit in the army. Coercion was not enough.

'We were not forced to perform heroic deeds at Stalingrad', Mereshko emphasized, 'or pushed into them by commissars or political officers. Over time, our men felt proud to be part of this army – and courage became our watchword.' Chuikov said with real satisfaction to Vasily Grossman: 'On other parts of the front they are worried that cowardice will spread amongst the men; here at Stalingrad it is courage which is infectious.'

The Day of Death

On 22 September 1942 the 13th Division faced a battle for its very survival. The Germans planned a major breakthrough to the Volga – encircling the defenders of central Stalingrad and destroying them on the banks of the river. This was an all-out offensive on the 62nd Army – and it came very close to success. Yet the courageous defiance of the 13th Guards – pushed back to within 200 metres of the river, prevented catastrophe. Their heroic stand planted a powerful idea amongst the entire army: it was still possible to resist the enemy, even if thrown back to the very edge of the Volga.

The Germans had been advancing steadily through the centre of the town. 'On 16 September I was asked to draw up situation maps every two days', said the 13th Division's cartographer Georgi Zolotovtsev, 'but the enemy's progress was so remorseless that my instructions were changed to providing one every day, and finally, on 20 September, one every six hours.' Herbert Selle recalled that the 6th Army was poised for a major breakthrough:

> On 14 September two of our divisions, on about a one-mile front, had forced their way into the city and through to the Volga. For the continuation of the attack on Stalingrad, additional forces were prepared, including three divisions of the 4th Panzer Army – which were now placed under Paulus's command.

The general position in Stalingrad at this time was bleak. An offensive launched by the Russian armies north of the city, on 19 September, had failed to relieve the defenders, or stop the enemy bringing in more of its troops to crush the 62nd Army. Chuikov saw the danger clearly. On 14 September the Germans had deployed only a small proportion of their troops: 'Paulus needed a pause in order to rebuild his battle formations and deploy his main forces. To bring up his reinforcements, and to organize combined operations of infantry, tanks, artillery and aircraft, the enemy required about five to seven days.' Chuikov predicted that the Germans would be ready to launch a major offensive against him on 22 September.

Stalingrad's defenders were now utterly reliant on a counter-attack by other Russian armies on the front to head off this offensive. 'It could have changed the situation in our favour', said Chuikov, 'But this did not happen.' His criticisms are trenchant:

> Our counter-attack was made along a broad front – a fifteen-mile frontal attack – and not at the enemy's weak point. Instead of taking on the flank and rear, the assault was made against the head of a powerful battering ram, consisting of four army corps. It is also impossible to understand why this and subsequent counter-attacks were launched in the daytime – when we had no way of neutralizing or compensating for the enemy's superiority in the air – and not at night, when the Luftwaffe did not operate with any strength.

Herbert Selle, of the 6th Army, provided the German view:

> The Russians launched numerous attacks on our 'land bridge' because it was clear that a breakthrough or even a deep penetration at this point would force our troops to yield ground further south – a transfer of forces which would seriously, if not decisively affect the fate of Stalingrad. However all attacks against the 'land bridge' failed. The Russians employed masses of infantry and hundreds of tanks – but they were no match for our professionalism. The combined operation of our ground forces and aviation was the vital factor.

To no one's surprise, the Russian attack was blasted to smithereens by German air power. This soon became apparent to the beleaguered 62nd Army. Chuikov said:

> We could tell what was happening by the behaviour of the enemy's air force: from noon [on 19 September] there were only a few dozen planes in the sky above the city, but by 5 p.m. there were already as many as three hundred. The returning planes had accomplished their mission – the Russian assault had ground to a halt.

It is unusual for a Soviet general, writing in the communist era, to be so forthright about his own side's military failings. But Chuikov's anger is only too apparent. The 62nd Army had been hoping against hope for support from its fellows – now it was facing a ghastly alternative: it would have to take on the assembled might of the Germans on its own.

Its sense of isolation worsened as the enemy intensified his bombardment of the Volga. German artillery commenced night time firing on the main ferry crossing. Chuikov continued:

> The Germans did everything they could to prevent fresh Soviet forces being ferried into the city. From dawn to dusk enemy dive bombers circled over the Volga, and artillery opened up at night. The ferry moorings and approaches to them came under fire day and night from enemy guns and six barrelled mortars. The job of ferrying men and goods across the river for the 62nd Army became as difficult as it could possibly be.

Chuikov was honest about the cumulative strain his men were under. They had neither horses or trucks – there was nowhere to hide them from German bombing – so all the supplies that reached them had to be distributed – at night – on the backs of his soldiers: 'During the day they fought off fierce enemy assaults, and at night, without sleep and rest, they had to carry ammunition, provisions and engineering equipment. The result was exhaustion.'

German fire on the ferry crossing was devastating. A fresh division – Batyuk's 284th – had reached the eastern bank of the Volga. The 62nd Army was desperate for reinforcements but could not get these men across. 'We had awaited their arrival impatiently', said Chuikov, 'but the central crossing was now completely paralysed and not a single group of soldiers was able to use it.'

The force of the Germans' scientific method of fighting rested on their remorseless application of a simple plan: to isolate the 62nd Army from its fellows, deprive it of supplies and reinforcements, and then, bringing up their main strength, smash it against the banks of the Volga. They had not won Stalingrad quickly on 14 September: now they would deploy the full might of their army to finish the job.

We have been overly influenced by dramatic descriptions of the Russian defence of the grain elevator and the 'nail factory'. Alan Clark and subsequent historians have declared that on 22 September 1942, when resistance in these redoubts finally ended, the Germans were bogged down in city fighting, and their offensive 'undeniably stuck fast'. Chuikov saw it rather differently. The Germans 'no longer particularly feared an attack from the Soviet armies north of the city' and as a result, did not have to withdraw their units northwards to meet this threat. Events were developing a terrible momentum. 'The enemy was trying harder and harder to untie his hands on the Volga, in order to destroy the 62nd Army. For the first time the Germans threatened to break our forces in two.' Chuikov added: '22 September would be the critical day for the

62nd Army.' Ivan Schylaev put it more bluntly: 'Our soldiers called it "the day of death" – we were all expecting to be drowned in the Volga.'

Chuikov anticipated where the main German thrust would be. He had rein-forced the Mamaev Kurgan with Gorishny's 95th Division. Further south, things were also looking serious. The best Red Army division south of the Tsaritsa was Dubyanski's 35th Guards. A group of these fighters, together with a handpicked force of marines, had held the grain elevator with such desperate courage. But now the elevator had fallen – and the division was so weakened that its HQ and staff had to be sent across the Volga to be regrouped. Its remaining men amalgamated with the 92nd Marine Infantry Brigade but it was doubtful whether this composite force could withstand a major German attack. If the enemy broke through, he could push along the Volga, rolling up the flank of Rodimtsev's 13th Guards as they clung to a diminishing strip of land in central Stalingrad.

'We knew how difficult the position of Rodimtsev's division was', said Chuikov in helpless frustration, 'but we did not have a single battalion we could send to his aid.' On this sector of the front things were deteriorating rapidly. On 20 September a group of German machine gunners broke through close to the central ferry and the division's command post came under direct fire. Communications with the rest of the army were continually breaking down. Chuikov knew where the enemy would launch his attack but was powerless to prevent it. 'The only help we could give the division was artillery backing from the left bank', the army's commander commented grimly, 'but this was obvi-ously not enough.'

At first light on 22 September wave after wave of German bombers began to pound the 13th Division's positions. Groups of twenty planes gathered over their targets, unleashing a hailstorm of incendiary, fragmentation and high explosive devices on the Russian troops below. It seemed everything that could burn – wooden shacks, even the soldiers' ammunition cases – was going up in flames. Units of Schylaev's 39th Regiment were ordered to race through the midst of this inferno. 'We heard that the left flank of the army had completely collapsed', he recalled. 'The 92nd Brigade had abandoned its positions, fleeing from Stalingrad on a flotilla of boats and barges and leaving the Germans as our new neighbours on the Volga!' Men stationed on the Mamaev Kurgan were desperately shuffled into a makeshift defence line along the Volga embankment. 'We had to stop the Germans advancing further', Schylaev continued. 'Our division was holding a very narrow defence line, about 5 kilometres long and around 400 metres wide. There was no margin of error at all – we were right up against the river.'

Chuikov gave Rodimtsev what little help he could. Schylaev explained:

Our soldiers on the Mamaev Kurgan were under his direct command. But because of the scale of the threat he immediately transferred them back to Rodimtsev. We heard that the enemy were already moving along the Volga. It was chaos down there. We left the hill at a run, with the enemy's aviation already overhead.

Schylaev's unit reached its designated position, in a ruined building, and was assembling on the second floor when a German shell exploded.

> Several of our guys were killed. Our radio operator was bleeding heavily but we had no bandages: there had been no time to gather medical supplies. We had to pull him down the stairs and out of the house, screaming in agony. And then the Germans attacked. Through the smoke, we saw their infantry advancing along the street. They were closing in on us and, for the first time in the battle, I saw the faces of the enemy.

Savage street fighting began. Schylaev continued:

> We fixed bayonets and turned to face the Germans. The road was pockmarked with shell-holes – and we joked that we were looking into our own freshly dug graves, but all of us had one thought – that somehow, we had to hold our ground.

Along the defence line the enemy was attacking with tanks and infantry, but they aimed a particularly hard blow at Rodimtsev's HQ. They wanted to kill the 13th Division's commander. 'All our determination flowed from Rodimtsev', his soldiers would say – the Germans knew how important he was to his men.

Rodimtsev's HQ was justly famous – it was situated inside the entrance to a large conduit pipe, running under the railway embankment which crossed the Banny Gully and then down to the Volga. Albert Burkovski described its appearance:

> Engineers built a wooden structure over the running water to act as a floor. It was very humid there and very damp – and the smell was unpleasant. There was a lack of oxygen – and although the conduit was twenty metres deep, you couldn't breathe easily inside it, so the HQ was situated close to the opening. They thought they were safe there. The walls were very thick and no bombs or shells could penetrate them. It was fitted with desks and bunk beds – everything

was made of wood. You could squeeze between six and eight people in it: Rodimtsev, his head of staff, a few communication and liaison officers: the staff would change over and work in shifts.

On the morning of the 22 September the HQ was busy. 'I remember the scene', said Georgi Zolotovtsev,

I was working on one of the desks, mapping German positions. Someone was typing next to me. And Rodimtsev was on the phone – the 34th Regiment had just come under strong German attack. Over the last few days something strange was happening, but we hadn't the time to give it much thought. Normally there was a steady flow of running water under the slatted floorboards. Then the amount diminished, and finally stopped running altogether.

The explanation soon became apparent. The Germans had discovered the location of Rodimtsev's HQ and had built a dam further up the gully. They were gathering a huge mass of water behind it.

The enemy plan was brutally simple. They would launch a powerful infantry attack on both sides of the conduit pipe, pushing past the 34th Regiment stationed there. Once behind Russian lines, with their machine gunners overlooking the entrance to the gully, they would blow up the dam and flush out Rodimtsev and his staff.

Zolotovtsev continued:

It was just before 9.00 a.m. when suddenly there was a huge explosion. It was as if the ground beneath us had suddenly erupted. A huge torrent crashed through our HQ and we were immediately waist deep in surging water. I grabbed my maps, the guy in front of me lifted his typewriter, and we all waded towards the entrance. Rodimtsev led the way, holding his machine gun aloft.

Fortunately, some of the 34th Regiment had managed to hold back the Germans. Outside the gully people were running about in bewilderment. Zolotovtsev said:

Rodimtsev remained incredibly calm and quickly restored order. He gathered together what forces he had – there was a cadet battalion, kept as a reserve, and a group of field engineers nearby. He took command and led them to the assistance of the 34th Regiment.

Remarkably, Rodimtsev managed to beat back the Germans. The turnaround of fortunes left a deep impression on his men. 'He demonstrated the most incredible calmness under pressure', Burkovski remembered. 'One moment I saw our general, soaking wet, evacuating his staff: a few seconds later he was leading a successful counter-attack. The Germans wanted to do away with him – well, they utterly failed.'

Russian field engineers subsequently explored the ruined pipe. When the Germans exploded the dam, the construction had collapsed inwards, its shattered bricks partially blocking the conduit. 'If not for that stroke of fortune the flood of water would have been even stronger', Zolotovtsev remarked, 'and German infantry could have pushed through after it.' Their commander's steadiness delighted his soldiers and was celebrated with wonderful humour. On the division's situation maps, the point where the explosion of water occurred was marked in blue as a river tributary. The new waterway was christened the 'Rodimtsev'.

'On 22 September, when the enemy broke through the defences of the 13th Guards, the personal bravery of its commanders prevented a rout', added Mereshko. 'We were all aware of the danger Rodimtsev's HQ was in – it was less than 300 metres from the German front line. And for the first time we were struck by how far Paulus was from the scene of the fighting.'

Over the next few hours savage combat continued. In one sector, the Germans broke through to the last residential streets and squares before the Volga. The 34th Regiment's HQ was completely cut off. Leonid Gurevitz recalled:

> Our regimental commander got a final message out to Rodimtsev. It simply said 'Our situation is critical'. It was – the Germans were right outside! We all took up defence positions – and everyone who could shoot began firing at the enemy. We were desperately outnumbered and I thought we would all end up in the Volga!

Groups of Russians were falling back to trenches and dug outs right on the edge of the river embankment. But there was no longer the strength to resist effectively, and the Germans, sensing this, brought up their armour to finish the defenders off. One private – Viktor Malko – ran forward in a crazy act of defiance, got an anti-tank rifle into position and destroyed several advancing tanks. German machine gunners quickly surrounded him. Malko ran out of ammunition, hurled a few grenades, then was overwhelmed by sheer weight of numbers. It looked as if nothing could stop the Germans reaching the Volga. But Malko's lone stand had been witnessed by others – and the mood of the defenders suddenly changed. Machine gunner Alexander Orlenok ran forward, recaptured Malko's trench and sprayed a mass of German infantry with machine gun fire. Three enemy tanks rumbled towards him – the first only 30 metres away. But other defenders – disregarding all danger – were now pitching in to help. Two anti-tank riflemen ran through a hail of fire, jumped into Orlenok's trench, then opened fire at point-blank range. The German vehicles burst into flames. More Russians appeared, opening up on the enemy with machine guns and rifles.

Rodimtsev sensed the critical moment had arrived. He sent his entire reserve to the aid of the beleaguered 34th Regiment, leaving himself with just a couple of machine gunners. His men counter-attacked ferociously, launching a mortar barrage then rushing into hand to hand combat with the surprised German infantrymen. The enemy were pushed back into the gully and finished off with hand grenades, and the breach in the defence line was repaired.

'We suffered terrible losses that day', Ivan Schylaev recalled. 'Everyone was fighting, including all of our wounded who could still move or shoot.' Accurate casualty figures are hard to come by. Schylaev reckoned that after the storming of the Mamaev Kurgan on 16 September the division's overall strength had already dropped from 10,000 to under 3,000. But after 22 September it was reduced to just a few hundred men. 'At the end of that terrible day, we returned to the house we had reached at the start of the German onslaught to retrieve the bodies of our comrades. We crawled up the stairs on our knees because of the danger of German sniper fire. Blood was everywhere.'

The 13th Guards had survived everything the enemy could throw at them. Schylaev felt something remarkable had happened.

Before I went off to fight my mother gave me a written prayer, to act as a talisman. I put it in my breast pocket but never looked at it – I was, after all, a communist. But something was going on at Stalingrad which I couldn't explain. I felt it when we took the Mamaev Kurgan, and more strongly when we held out on 22 September. All our soldiers were talking about it – that something bigger was happening, something we could not fully comprehend. We knew that churches were being reopened and the ancestral heroes of our country were being invoked. I was an atheist. But being an atheist at Stalingrad was no longer enough. I could not explain how I was still alive or how our army was continuing to fight. The Germans should have destroyed us all that day. Reluctantly, I took out the prayer, opened it and gave thanks to God.

The German Night Attack

The Germans never undertook another attack against the 13th Division on that scale. Instead, they reinforced their strongholds along the river embankment and maintained their fire on the central crossing. The weight of their assault would now be directed further north, towards Stalingrad's factory district. Rodimtsev had won a hard-earned reprieve.

Over the next few days, frantic work by the army's engineers brought an alternative ferry crossing – the 62nd – into use further north. Batyuk's 284th Division was at last brought into Stalingrad and stationed on the right flank of the 13th Guards.

On 1 October the Germans made a last effort to push Rodimtsev's men into the Volga. They attempted a night attack. This was a Russian speciality – the Germans disliked night-time combat and preferred to fight in daylight, with full air support. Wanting to take their opponents by surprise, they now committed two specialist engineering battalions to the assault, and one of their best infantry regiments. They were methodical – attacking where the defenders were most vulnerable, at the junction point of the 34th Regiment and Batyuk's newly arrived 284th Divison, and distracting them with a diversionary attack further south, on the 39th Regiment. The Russians were taken by surprise. The Germans got through the Krutoy gully and reached the Volga.

Once again, a threatening situation had arisen but the defenders did not panic. Instead, they fought back with incredible force. Rodimtsev personally organized the counter-attack, sending two combat groups to stop the incursion. With Germans bearing down on him, a regimental communications officer, Nikolaev, called in an artillery strike on his own position. This inflicted terrible casualties on the advancing enemy. A rain of mortar shells descended on the surprised Germans, then the combat groups plunged in, putting their opponents to flight after fierce hand-to-hand fighting.

Russian resistance in this part of the city had gained an iron backbone. The 13th Guards Division's combat journal proudly noted that their actions were now being covered by a newspaper correspondent from the *Red Star*. The Soviet press had realized that something exceptional was taking place. The next day the paper gave an overview of the September fighting. Underneath the rhetoric, it caught an emerging truth about the battle:

> Every day these Guardsmen are repulsing countless attacks by German infantry and tanks, supported by artillery and planes. They defend their positions to the last man. They realize in their hearts and minds that there is nowhere left to go. They will not yield their

ground to the enemy and they stand like an impassable wall. Steely determination and the ability to counter-attack in the face of heavy enemy pressure has become the trademark of the soldiers of General Rodimtsev's division.

Mereshko agreed:

Rodimtsev's 13th Guards played a crucial part in our defence in September 1942. They are usually remembered for the fight for the railway station and other buildings in central Stalingrad. Yet their storming of the Mamaev Kurgan was far more important. And their greatest success was on 22 September – when they were pushed back to within 200 metres of the Volga, and all seemed lost, they stood their ground against the enemy. Their achievement had a huge impact on the rest of the army.

The German war machine ground relentlessly on. But 22 September – 'the day of death' – represented a missed opportunity for them. The central river ferry had been put out of action, with no alternative yet in place. The Russians had been at their most vulnerable. A different commander than Paulus would have thrown in everything to finish them off – but this had not happened.

The Red Army's position remained so precarious that the Germans may still have believed the fall of the city was inevitable. But the psychological balance had begun to shift. On the steppe that summer, Russian soldiers feared their heroism would not be enough to stop such a formidable enemy. But in September 1942, Chuikov and Rodimtsev had fashioned that heroism into a formidable will to resist. Superior organization and masses of tanks had not pushed the Red Army into the Volga. Its soldiers had made a stand and defied the enemy. A new spirit of indomitable defiance had taken root.

Later, when Chuikov wrote about the battle, he sent a copy of his book to Rodimtsev, enclosing a warm note of appreciation. 'If not for you and your 13th Guards Division I dread to think what would have happened to us in September 1942.' Together, the two men had provided the inspirational leadership necessary to hold off such a powerful enemy. At Rodimtsev's funeral, in 1977, Chuikov paid a personal tribute: 'His bravery was extraordinary and it had an incredible effect on his soldiers. He powerfully motivated his men – and this was the vital factor for us at Stalingrad.' Rodimtsev was a genuinely heroic leader – and now other divisional commanders, moved by his example, sought to emulate him.

Chapter Six

Pavlov's House

After the dramatic day of fighting on 22 September 1942, the men of the 13th Guards Division acquired a ferocious will to resist. Determination on the battlefield can sometimes exist in elite units yet fail to spread to the mass of ordinary soldiers. But over the next few weeks the whole Russian army at Stalingrad began to discover similar power. Chuikov and Rodimtsev provided the leadership necessary to forge this new spirit; their troops found inspiration in the heroism of their comrades. One example of this heroism – which made a deep impression on the whole 62nd Army – was the plucky defence of a stronghold known as 'Pavlov's House'.

The army's chief of staff, Krylov, put it like this:

> As the house continued to hold out it became a symbol of the city's determination not to give in, a sort of Stalingrad within Stalingrad. It was a part of our defence which most clearly displayed the main features of the whole. And the importance of this strategic point was not confined to the territorial and tactical advantages of having held it. Just think how much inspiration we received from the fact that an ordinary dwelling house had been turned into a bastion on the front lines and that the Germans were unable to take it!

Mereshko described the effect on morale: 'The house was well-known within our army and its defenders knew that everyone honoured them for holding out so long.' Although the house was sometimes cut off from the rest of the army, and encircled by the Germans, it was part of an integrated defence line and could easily be seen from other Russian strongholds. Its visibility was crucial, for unlike the defence of the grain elevator, or the railway station, onlookers could see what was happening and spread the word to their fellows.

'I remember one example', Mereshko continued.

> The enemy was attacking Pavlov's House, and I was in a nearby building at the time. Some of the garrison were shooting at the Germans and throwing grenades, others – short of ammunition –

had climbed onto the upper floors of the damaged building, and were hurling stones and pieces of masonry. I was particularly struck by that – as if, quite literally, they were fighting for every stone.

The defence became a legend: 'For more than fifty days, with little opportunity to sleep or rest, a handful of men held out', Chuikov wrote proudly. 'The Germans could not break the stubborn defence of its heroic garrison. Pavlov's House remained impregnable.' But its story has become distorted by propaganda, and many of the ingredients presented to us are misleading or wrong. Telling of the events as they actually happened, far from lessening their impact, as the Soviet authorities feared, deepens our understanding and sense of their significance.

The Emergence of Storm Groups

Pavlov's House was seized on the night of 27 September 1942 by a reconnaissance unit led by Sergeant Jacob Pavlov. The capture of the house took place against the backdrop of an experimental use of storm groups by the 62nd Army.

The first storm group was used in Stalingrad on 18 September, in a night-time attack on the State Bank. After a short but concentrated artillery barrage, which forced the German garrison into the cellar, explosives were used to breach the wall and the group burst in, clearing the building of the enemy after a three-hour fight.

Suren Mirzoyan, who had joined the 13th Guards in mid-September, took part in the assault.

> The attack was organized by a battalion commander, Borisov, and the group was just a couple of dozen strong. The idea of a storm group was a novelty – but it was immediately popular with our soldiers. We could pick the people we wanted to be with, and choose a fighting buddy – the idea was to look out for each other, and watch each other's back. It was not done by rank, which was another thing we really liked – I was a private, but the guy I was with, Afanasiev, who later fought in 'Pavlov's House', was a lieutenant. Best of all, it was aggressive, using night-time fighting, which we knew the Germans disliked. Our storm group was based on one, simple idea: to give the enemy a shock, to jolt him out of his comfortable routine. We had noticed that if we struck hard at the Germans, and took them by surprise, they tended to pull back, almost as a reflex

reaction. Well, there was no shortage of volunteers to give Fritz a taste of this medicine!

Russian reconnaissance found out that about thirty Germans were holding the State Bank, so the attack relied on speed and surprise. 'We hid in a nearby gully while our sappers laid down explosives', Mirzoyan continued.

The blast tore a hole in the wall, and we followed up fast. We raced across the square, tossed grenades through the windows, let off bursts of machine gun fire and then all charged into the building. Inside, rubble was everywhere. There was a sudden collision of bodies – our people and the enemy, re-emerging from the cellar where they had taken shelter. Fist fighting started immediately. To the left of me, Afanasiev knocked out a guy, then another German jumped on him. I turned to help, but one of the enemy threw himself on me first. It was a chaotic swirl of bodies and shouting. I felt hands on my wind-pipe and struggled to breathe, but my instinct for self-preservation took over: I found the strength to draw my knife and bring it down hard on my attacker's back. Afanasiev was still in trouble, so I slashed at his opponent with my knife, hacking his legs and bringing him down.

The fighting was savage. Mirzoyan emphasized:

This kind of close combat is unlike anything else. Once you are inside a building a machine gun is no longer any use, there is no time to load it, and no room to use it effectively. Knives and small, sharp spades are the best weapons for storm group fighting – it is all about physical toughness and quick reflexes.

The house was fought for floor by floor. 'The Germans made a last stand at the top of the building', said Mirzoyan, 'and we finished off about thirteen of them there. We were in a frenzy – it was kill or be killed.' The State Bank was now in Russian hands, but it was a fleeting success. Within hours, the enemy counter-attacked in force and regained the building. Mirzoyan said:

There were masses of them.We were overpowered by sheer weight of numbers. We had a saying: 'Death lurks behind every corner at Stalingrad.' It was certainly true that night. Most of my group were killed – I was wounded, but managed to get out of the building.

The attack of 18 September was at best a limited success. Chuikov and Rodimtsev were unsure whether to pursue the idea of storm groups: they feared the unit was too small to be successful. Later, it was realized that such groups needed several detachments to be fully effective, with further troops following up behind the initial assault party. But these vital refinements were not made until December 1942. In the early stages of the battle it was a radical – and risky – decision to suddenly break up regular army formations. However, the events of 22 September – the day of death – encouraged Chuikov to persist with the experiment.

Mereshko said:

> On this day, a German weakness became really clear to us – their dislike of hand-to-hand fighting. We had noticed this before, on the steppe, and in Stalingrad itself, but wondered whether these were isolated examples. But the attack on 22 September made a strong impression. At close quarters, the Germans' strengths in aviation and artillery were useless, but they still should have finished our guys off. To our amazement, they didn't. A grenade, a bayonet, a knife, a shovel – and Russian bravery won this battle. After fierce hand-to-hand combat the German infantry pulled back. Our men began to feel a new strength in this kind of city fighting. Chuikov was encouraged, and decided to use small attacking groups more often.

On 26 September Chuikov sent out an order recommending that commanders should not just rely on regular army formations – battalions and companies – but also consider attacking operations 'on the basis of small groups, armed with machine guns, hand grenades, Molotov cocktails and anti-tank rifles'. Chuikov had the storming of the State Bank in mind when he added the brutal piece of advice: 'light artillery should be used to support the attacking groups by firing point-blank into windows'.

Over the next few days Chuikov and Rodimtsev developed storm groups further. The 13th Division was badly depleted by German attacks, and using small groups seemed a sensible way of reducing casualties. But these early efforts were largely unsuccessful. The Germans held a number of buildings along the Volga embankment which they had turned into strongholds, surrounded by barbed wire and minefields. These strong, well-built houses overlooked the main ferry route – the central crossing – and from them, the enemy's artillery kept the crossing under constant fire. To the south of the 13th Guards the enemy held the House of Specialists and the recaptured State Bank, to the north the House of Railway Workers and the L-Shaped House.

On the night of 27 September, the main Russian effort was directed against the House of Railway Workers. Several storm groups were deployed against this formidable fortress but all attempts to seize it failed. Three separate assaults were beaten off. German resistance was simply too strong. The following night, attempts to recapture the State Bank and the House of Specialists were also beaten back. The enemy was now prepared for storm group tactics and brought devastating fire power to bear on the assailants. And at the House of Specialists the storm group got a particularly unpleasant surprise.

Suren Mirzoyan was in this assault group:

> The Germans pulled back inside the house – so we rushed forward, into large ground floor room. It was a trap. The enemy had a couple of our captured tanks inside, hulled-down, in the far-corner, and these raked us with fire at close range. We fled the building in disarray. They used our own weaponry against us.

Mereshko added:

> Our plan was to take the House of Specialists with a fifty-strong storm group, but the attack failed. Chuikov was in a nearby observation point. He talked to members of the group afterwards, asking what had gone wrong. Their answer shocked us. They said they couldn't take the house because the Germans had installed several tanks inside – well-hidden – and these had suddenly opened fire. To destroy these tanks, artillery pieces would have to be added to our assault groups. But that option was simply not feasible, for the whole point of the storm groups was to keep their equipment light: they had to be fast moving. The Germans had got one step ahead of us – we were amazed by their resourcefulness.

These reverses were depressing, but the capture of 'Pavlov's House' provided a much-needed morale booster. Here everything went right. Georgi Potanski, one of only two surviving members of its garrison, took up the story:

> Chuikov ordered us to seize that house because it was a superb vantage point: you could keep the whole surrounding area under observation, and fire from all sides of the building. Rodimtsev decided to try and capture it by stealth – the enemy garrison there

was relatively small – and the Germans were distracted by the attacks on the House of Railway Workers. A small group of six soldiers, led by Sergeant Pavlov, crawled towards the house. They were lucky – astonishingly, no one was on guard at the entrance. Pavlov left two soldiers there, and moved quickly down into the cellar. He found a number of Russian civilians sheltering there. Pavlov saw a chance. He chatted with them, found out which room the Germans were in, and kicked the door open. There they all were, drinking and playing cards. He finished them off with grenades.

Pavlov's quick thinking won the house and within hours the Russians got reinforcements in. The Germans tried to recapture it, but were beaten off. The defence of Pavlov's House had begun.

In purely military terms, this was a small-scale action. Pavlov and his men had overcome a surprised house garrison of at most a dozen or so German soldiers. Just over a hundred metres away, well over a hundred Russians lay dead, and many more wounded, in the unsuccessful attack on the House of Railway Workers. But its psychological effect was enormous. 'The storming of "Pavlov's House" depended on surprise', said Mereshko. 'We loved Pavlov's ingenuity in getting hold of the place. It was something our soldiers could identify with.' Potanski fought next to Pavlov: 'He was tough, straightforward and brave – but also a bit of a character, with his faded tunic, covered in dust, dandyish fur cap and quirky sense of humour.' When Pavlov and his men set up their machine guns, and readied themselves for the inevitable German attack, a handful of reinforcements managed to get through and join them. The odds against them were still great, but Pavlov's cheery rejoinder became famous: 'Excellent – this is a big old house and we could use a little help. The more, the merrier.'

On 30 September a further attack by a storm group, on the L-shaped House, was rebuffed by the Germans. But the decision to entrust combat initiative to junior officers and ordinary soldiers remained a popular one. As Chuikov related: 'The soldier in a storm group must have initiative and boldness, must rely on himself alone and believe in his own powers . . . In an assault, he is very often left to his own devices, acts alone, on his own responsibilities.' The men appreciated this, feeling that their commanders really trusted them.

Pavlov and his men used grenades to finish the enemy off, and Chuikov remembered this for future operations: 'When our troops stormed "Pavlov's House", their experience taught us: two of you get into the house together, you and a grenade; both be lightly dressed – you without a knapsack, and the grenade bare.' A grenade became the storm group soldier's constant companion. 'No one carried packs', added Mereshko, 'it was grenades and knives. And Chuikov taught us a simple trick: release the pin, wait a moment and throw your grenade about four seconds before it is due to go off, so the enemy can't throw it back at you.'

Storm groups characterized Chuikov's principle of aggressive defence – and Red Army soldiers relished the chance of striking back at the Germans. Pavlov had interrupted the enemy's card party with an impromptu demonstration of grenade throwing – and his example quickly inspired others to leave their visiting cards. In early October 1942, Lieutenant Miroshnichenko decided to organize a night-time reception of his own, in the workers' settlement in front of Stalingrad's Red October Factory. His 'guests' were some recent German arrivals – reinforcements sent to the 6th Army from France. Fellow fighter Dmitry Lutsenko took up the story:

> Lieutenant Miroshnichenko had been studying to be a teacher before the war. He turned to me and said jokingly 'Now these Fritzes are all lovely and fresh from their time in Paris, so I think I'll give them a little lecture in grenade studies.' The lecture took place at night. Comrade Miroshnichenko, with the help of his assistants, personally conducted the demonstration of grenade throwing, as a result of which fifty-three Fritzes received an education. By the time dawn came around, Miroshnichenko and I were sitting having a quiet smoke and discussing what an impact our lecture had made on the new students.

Jacob Pavlov's bold capture of the house caught the imagination of Russian soldiers, and its defence became renowned within the 62nd Army; it was also extensively reported within the Soviet press. A journalistic desire to simplify the facts, along with the workings of communist propaganda, created the version of the story always repeated in the West.

John Erickson, in *The Road to Stalingrad* described how: 'Pavlov's House covered the approaches to the whole square . . . for fifty-eight days Pavlov beat off every assault.' William Craig, in *Enemy at the Gates*, gave the total strength of its garrison as twenty-four men, 'drawn by chance from all regions of the Soviet Union, Georgia, Kazakhstan, Uzbekistan, and the Ukraine'. As 'Pavlov's House' continued to hold out, Craig added: 'On all battle maps at the 62nd Army's HQ the house in no-man's land was now referred to as "Dom Pavlov" ("Pavlov's House"). Pavlov revelled in his new-found importance.'

Antony Beevor summarized it all as follows:

One of the most famous episodes of the Stalingrad battle was the defence of 'Pavlov's House', which lasted for fifty-eight days. They seized a four story building overlooking a square, some 300 yards in from the top of the river bank. Their commander, Lieutenant Afanasiev, was blinded early in the fighting, so Sergeant Jacob Pavlov took over command.

'Yet many veterans want the house renamed', said Anatoly Kozlov, 'because what is endlessly said about it by so many sources is wrong.' What really happened?

The Commander

Jacob Pavlov was made a Hero of the Soviet Union after the battle, and the story of the defence of 'Pavlov's House' built up around him. Soviet accounts always referred to him as leader of the small garrison. But Pavlov was never the commander of the house. Mereshko said:

> He held it for just a couple of days until more senior officers took over. Because the stronghold was so important to us, we wanted someone with more military experience in overall charge – someone who had already commanded at company or battalion level.

Georgi Potanski, one of the survivors of 'Pavlov's House', added: 'Pavlov was the most junior officer in our house garrison. We were commanded by Captain Naumov – he was the real hero of our defence.'

The Fifty-Eight Days

Once the story was constructed around Pavlov, it followed that the house had to hold out for fifty-eight days – for on the night of 24 November Pavlov was wounded in an attack on a neighbouring German stronghold (the 'Milk House', across 9 January Square) and evacuated from Stalingrad. 'I was right next to him when it happened', said Potanski, 'and saw him carried off – he took no further part in the battle. But the defence of the house continued.'

'Everyone keeps saying fifty-eight days, fifty-eight days', said Ivan Schylaev. 'What was supposed to happen then? – the battle for Stalingrad was still going on. Nobody mentions the other life of Pavlov's House after those fifty-eight days were over.' The house's real commander, Naumov, was killed in the attack of 24 November, and the house was then taken over by Anton Dragan, who had earlier fought for the railway station and 'nail factory'. Dragan commanded the house until 10 January 1943. On that date, his force of seventy men was transferred, with other 13th Guards Units, to the Red October Factory. Only a couple of soldiers were left in 'Pavlov's House'. When Dragan returned on 30 January he found that the Germans had reoccupied it: 'They were in the house and basement. We had to cleanse it of Fascists all over again.'

The Garrison

The garrison of the house is usually given as twenty-four men, drawn from all the republics of the Soviet Union. This is wildly inaccurate. 'We never had fewer than seventy defenders, and sometimes over a hundred', said Potanski emphatically, 'and the garrison was mostly Russian.'

The House's Name

The stronghold was never officially called 'Pavlov's House' during the battle, much less marked up as such on all 62nd Army maps. It was usually referred to as 'The house on Penzenskaya Street'.

'I was in the Mill when we heard 'Pavlov's House' had been taken', Potanski continued.

> We got another seven men in within a few hours, and the next day sent another thirty. A further force of fifty, and then another seventy, followed shortly. Our field engineering unit had constructed a 100 metre trench from the cellar of the Mill to 'Pavlov's House', and we moved in reinforcements: machine gunners, anti-tank gunners, infantrymen and artillery spotters. I was one of the artillery spotters for the house. On the night of 28 September I went with a communication officer to the far end of 'Pavlov's House', got up to the top of it, and cut a hole through to the roof, and set up our spotting position. We had to work really quietly – there were Germans in the square down below us.

Potanski spoke about the valiant twenty-four defenders celebrated in Soviet accounts:

Those propagandists were always shooting themselves in the foot. Our defence of the house was heroic – but not in the way they described it. They wanted to create an impression of a tiny band of soldiers holding out against the enemy, and decided it would look better if the garrison consisted only of infantrymen. But that meant our group of spotters, who fought alongside everyone else, and called down artillery fire on German attacks, was airbrushed out of the picture. Yet our role was vital – I personally received an award from Chuikov for my part in the defence.

Potanski believed that twenty-four names were deliberately selected from the larger garrison to make a propaganda point – showing the defenders of the house were a small band, recruited from all the Soviet republics, fighting harmoniously, side by side. Whatever was intended this image of unity of purpose was somewhat unrealistic:

In reality, most of our garrison was Russian and relations with those from the other republics far from easy. The commander of our artillery unit was an Armenian, Nikolai Sarkisan. The square in front of the house was covered in bodies and one night Sarkisan ordered me to go out and clear some of the corpses away. This was a typically stupid assignment – the Germans sent flares up all the time, and I was quickly seen. A volley of machine gun fire burst out, and I took shelter behind a pile of dead bodies. I could hear the sound of bullets ripping into my protective wall – but then it stopped: the enemy clearly thought I was dead. I crawled round to our defensive trenches on the outside of the house. I was challenged, but Sarkisan had neglected to provide me with a password.

'I was lucky', Potanski continued.

If the sentry had been an Uzbek or a Tartar I would have been shot – they understood so little Russian, it would have been impossible to communicate with them. Fortunately, the guy was a Russian. I was escorted to Naumov. 'Potanski', he said, 'looking up in surprise. What on earth are you doing here?' When he heard about the Armenian's instructions he picked up the phone straightaway: 'Sarkisan – you absent-minded Fuckwit! Why did you send this guy on a mission without a password – he was nearly killed.'

Red Army soldiers loved the way Pavlov had seized the house, but they also admired Naumov's skill in holding it. The propagandist decision to emphasize Pavlov's role in its subsequent defence and to completely ignore Naumov perpetrated a considerable historical injustice.

'Naumov fought side by side with the rest of us soldiers, repelling German attacks', said Potanski. 'He was an incredible hero.' Ivan Schylaev agreed: 'Naumov would not just say the words "For the Motherland!"', he recalled, 'he embodied them. He was always in the forefront of the action – his courage was inspirational.' The writer Konstantin Simonov spent a lot of time with the 13th Guards during the battle, and his novel about house-fighting at Stalingrad, *Days and Nights*, caught this quality of leadership:

> To say that during these hours he commanded his troops wouldn't be entirely accurate. He was alongside them, and they – without needing orders – did everything that was necessary. And what was necessary was to hold one's ground, fire, and keep firing at the Germans.

Naumov fought bravely, and the way he died strongly affected everybody. On 24 November the garrison of 'Pavlov's House' was ordered to attack across the square and seize a neighbouring stronghold, the 'Milk House', from the Germans. 'It was a very difficult assignment', said Schylaev.

> They managed to take it, but there was not enough support, and the Germans counter-attacked in force. Most of the garrison of 'Pavlov's House' were overwhelmed there, either killed or wounded – in a completely different house! In this terrible fight, Pavlov was carried off on a stretcher; Ilya Voronov, another famous defender of 'Pavlov's House', was caught by an explosion – they found twenty-one shell fragments in his body, but somehow, miraculously, he survived! Naumov tried to rally his men, but then he was killed, in front of everyone.

The shattered remnants of the garrison regrouped back in 'Pavlov's House'. Naumov had died on the far side of the square, and the Germans were now there in force, but his men could not stomach leaving their fallen commander behind. 'We swore we would not abandon his body', Potanski remembered, 'even if it meant that we would all perish trying to recover it.' Everyone fanned out, slowly crawling across the square. When the Germans opened fire, they hid under the bodies of the dead. Finally, they discovered Naumov. Potanski continued:

> Then our elation turned to despair. There was no way we could lift his body up and carry him back without making ourselves an easy target for the enemy. We were right under their noses. Then someone had a brilliant idea – let's use rope! So we tethered Naumov to several long pieces of rope, and slowly, painstakingly, began to haul him back to our side of the square. Eventually, we got him inside 'Pavlov's House'. We put his body on a greatcoat, carried him down to the cellar, hacked out a grave for him and gave him a proper burial. Our soldiers just stood there and cried.

Schylaev said:

> The burial of Naumov was an exceptionally powerful moment, although it never appeared in histories of the battle. More than anything else, it symbolized the determination not to surrender 'Pavlov's House'. Shortly afterwards, Captain Dragan brought in reinforcements, and took over the command.

Strongpoints

'Pavlov's House' was a strongpoint within a larger, integrated defence system. Chuikov explained how the system worked: 'The army's basic defence position was the centre of resistance, comprising a number of strongpoints. Buildings, especially good stone and brick buildings, were used as strongpoints – and linked up by means of trenches.'

'Pavlov's House' was fortified at the time when centres of resistance were being created. 'In the past our commanders have relied on blood to stop the Germans; here, we prefer to use barbed wire', Chuikov told Grossman bluntly. Army Order 179 was dispatched on 1 October 1942:

> Every trench and every dug out should be reinforced and each building shall become a towering fortress. To fulfil this task, new engineering works and obstacles must be built, buildings and houses turned into firing points for heavy machine guns, communication trenches dug, and minefields and barbed wire emplacements set out. Our strongpoints must also be equipped with anti-tank guns and mortars.

Then Chuikov used a powerful metaphor, which was to catch the imagination of his soldiers: 'All these measures are aimed at making our defence unbreakable – for all the furious attacks of the Fascist troops will shatter upon these obstacles as sea waves are broken by granite rock.'

'Pavlov's House' was linked by trenches to another ruined redoubt, Zabolotny's House, and to the Mill, behind it. One could easily imagine the house as a rocky promontory, jutting out from the main Russian defence position, and appropriately – in view of the stark imagery of Order 179 – it was given the code name 'lighthouse'. '"Lighthouse" was absolutely correct' said Mereshko. 'It was a superb vantage point, offering us a shooting range of up to 1 kilometre.'

Chuikov had made a good choice: 'I could see why our commanders felt this building was so significant', said one of the defenders.

> From the fourth floor you could observe not only the whole of Ninth of January Square, but also all the ruins beyond. It stuck out into the German defences. To the left and right of us were Germans. To the rear of us, towards the Mill, was the area occupied by our own men.

The Mill was the large brick grain store first captured by Rodimtsev's men on 14 September. It was about 100 metres from the house, and the same distance from the Volga, and acted as an important supply and staging post. 'The whole area was like a fortress complex', said Potanski proudly.

Anton Dragan, who took over the defence, described how the system worked:

> We put up barbed wire around the house, and laid out minefields. At night we lit up the area with flare rockets. We placed our machine guns and anti-tank rifles at openings on the upper floors. And when the Germans attacked, we called in an artillery barrage.

The key to the defence of 'Pavlov's House' lay in these co-ordinated, highly accurate artillery strikes.

'The enemy was reluctant to use heavy bombing', stressed Potanski,

> because of the risk of hitting his own forces at the nearby House of Railway Workers. But as soon as the Germans started an infantry attack – coming out of their cellars, running and shouting – we called in our artillery units on the far bank, and brought an immediate bombardment down upon our assailants. I was perched up

on the roof of the house, to see where our shells were exploding and correct our fire. I was even able to judge by the sound the shell made when it screamed through the air. Our minefields and accurate artillery shelling prevented the Germans from using their tanks *en masse* and we were able to inflict heavy casualties on their infantry.

The Soviet authorities chose to omit the artillery spotters from the official list of defenders. Yet without them the successful defence of 'Pavlov's House' becomes difficult to understand.

In one skirmish, four tanks came into the square, but the defenders moved up to the fourth floor, above the angle of elevation of their guns. A single shot from an anti-tank gun put one Panzer out of action; machine gun fire scattered the infantry, and the rest of the attackers retreated. It is an appealing vignette, showing the heroic defiance of the defenders, yet it could never have taken place without artillery support. The defenders were so short of ammunition that without this vital protection a massed attack would have finished them off. 'I heard this story from Pavlov himself', said Anatoly Kozlov, 'and it seemed well-rehearsed. I don't doubt something like that happened, but unless you tell the whole story, it makes little sense from a military point of view.'

Supporting artillery fire was the vital factor. During the battle, Chuikov awarded Potanski a medal in recognition of his services:

> I was summoned to the Army HQ, at night, with my fellow artillery spotter from 'Pavlov's House'. Chuikov wanted to thank us both personally. But it was a dangerous journey to undertake. We went back to the Mill, and then began moving along the river embankment, when suddenly a flare rocket lit everything up – and the Germans opened fire with mortars. We both fell to the ground. A shell exploded to the left of me, showering dirt everywhere. I picked myself up and called out to my mate 'Stand up – let's go!' but he didn't move. His whole left side had been blown away.
>
> Finally, I reached the HQ and reported to the guards on duty. I was led in to Chuikov. He looked up at me: 'Where's the other guy?' I told him he had been killed. For a moment, Chuikov struggled to speak. 'What a pity, what a pity!' he repeated, his voice choking with emotion. Then he gathered himself, and looked me straight in the eye. I felt this incredible fighting spirit – it was almost tangible, as if

I could touch it. 'Thank you', he said simply, presenting me with my medal, 'Thank you for your courage.'

'Pavlov's House' was not an isolated redoubt held by a tiny, defiant garrison. It was a strongpoint – part of an integrated defence system. The garrison acted as a storm group centre – defending the house, but also attacking nearby German strongholds, the tactics envisioned in Order 179. And the defence line was protected by a system of minefields, barbed wire and rapid artillery strikes.

Chuikov's decision to leave his heavy artillery on the far bank of the Volga had paid off. 'Machine guns and anti-tank guns would not have been enough', Potanski emphasized. 'Some days we faced ten or a dozen German attacks. Without the artillery strikes we would have lost the house.'

Everyday Life

Potanski recalled:

> We ran the house on a shift system, while one group of between thirty to forty men would be on duty, watching for a German attack, the other would be busy gathering wood or preparing food. When I was not artillery spotting, I kept watch with the rest of the soldiers. I occupied the same vantage point as Pavlov – we threw grenades together and ate from the same ration tin. The tension was constant. The sound of gunfire was always around us – there was rarely any silence. We would joke that if we sat down, shared a cigarette, or some tea, the enemy would be bound to attack.

'The staircase was still intact', Potanski continued,

> although it was only safe to use it at night – then we would forage through the rest of the house. In the cellar we had an iron stove and some mattresses put out. We did everything here: washed, boiled water in a big metal pot, heated up our food – usually condensed soups. We had to be constantly vigilant – if we slept, we always had our boots on. We hardly had time to speak and yet it felt like we knew each other well. A principle of equality operated in the house. Everyone shared the same tasks – and no one pulled rank. There was an incredible sense of comradeship.

'In the rare moments of calm', Ilya Voronov recalled, 'we would sit together, and say, almost praying: "We won't let them through."'

Communal Singing

On a foraging trip within the house a gramophone was recovered. Only one record was with it, and in the midst of battle it seemed a most incongruous companion – a Neapolitan aria about love. Potanski said:

> One of our guys translated snatches of it, 'Girls, tell your friend I am not sleeping at night, I am thinking of her.' At first, we looked at each other in disbelief. And then it occurred to us this would be a great song to play to the Germans! We were having a few 'sleepless moments' of our own at night – so after a tough enemy attack we would always put it on at full volume. It became our ritual.

Potanski continued:

> But when we started playing that record something changed. In the brief intervals between the fighting, we gathered together and sang – old Russian songs, romances, and of course 'Katyusha'. It helped so much. We forgot that death was stalking us and cheered up. It was our way of regrouping!

Singing in 'Pavlov's House' delighted Stalingrad's defenders. 'All our troops began asking for singing competitions during breaks in the fighting', said Rodimtsev's daughter Natalia. 'They would take popular melodies and put in their own words about fighting the Fascists.' Here is one such version – its rough-hewn lyrics carry genuine conviction:

> Every day, every hour, bravery grows stronger in us
> Our young soldiers are going fighting
> The bastards in the black swastikas
> Will receive fresh gifts from our rifles.
>
> Comrade, fight the enemy without mercy
> Become a hero in this hard struggle
> In the turmoil of Stalingrad
> We will beat the hated Fascists.

If the order comes, we are ready
We will triumph over death
We are united in courage – that's why we are strong
We are proud of our iron glory.

A Tale of Two Pavlovs

One of the strangest stories told about Sergeant Pavlov was that he later converted to Christianity and became a monk:

> Jacob Pavlov, made a hero of the Soviet Union, became the Archimandrite Kyrill in the monastery at Sergievo – formerly Zagorsk – where he attracted a huge following of the faithful that had nothing to do with his fame at Stalingrad. He is now very frail.

So wrote Antony Beevor in 1998 (a 'fact' invariably recycled in subsequent histories of the battle). 'All very interesting', retorted Pavlov's widow, 'but to the best of my knowledge he was still a communist when I buried him – in 1981.'

Beevor confused Sergeant Jacob Pavlov with another Stalingrad veteran, Private Ivan Pavlov. This Pavlov found torn pages from the Gospel amongst the debris lying in the streets of the devastated city, picked them up and began reading: 'It became a consolation to me at that terrible time – I started seeing things differently.' He kept them with him for the rest of the war and subsequently took his vows, and the church name of Kyrill, becoming confessor at the monastery of Holy Trinity Saint-Sergius.

In the basement of the house, a number of families were sheltering, trapped by the fighting, including a mother and her two-month-old baby girl. The little girl – Xenia Seleznyova – was very sick, but there was no medicine to give her. 'It seemed hopeless, but we were willing her to hang on', said Potanski. 'When we demolished a small section of the house, to make a firing position, Ilya Voronov found a wooden casket, with a small icon inside. We hung it round her neck. Incredibly, the baby stayed alive.'

Stalingrad's streets were littered with bodies of civilians and soldiers and the city's defenders had become inured to them. But the tiny infant's struggle for life amidst this horror moved even the most hardened soldier. Schylaev said:

> We all got to hear about that little girl and the icon, and it had a profound effect on us. She came to symbolize something – that

perhaps there was hope after all. She was a fighter, fighting for life, and we resolved to fight with her. Our soldiers worked flat out – ignoring the danger of enemy fire – and dug a special, deep communication trench to 'Pavlov's House'. Then, we managed to get her to safety.

Krylov was right to say that 'Pavlov's House' became a symbol of the city's determination not to give in. The slogan cleverly coined by Chuikov – 'Every man a fortress!' – had become reality.

Chapter Seven

Mikhail Panikakha

Anatomy of a Heroic Deed

On 1 October 1942, in the workers' settlement of the Red October Factory, a young soldier named Mikhail Panikakha died with extraordinary valour. Burning in agony from a shattered Molotov cocktail, he seized another incendiary and flung himself onto a German tank, destroying it and killing himself in the blast. His selfless act of courage became Stalingrad's most famous heroic deed.

Soldiers learnt about Panikakha through leaflets entitled 'Read this and pass it to a friend' that were soon circulating throughout the army. They bore the caption 'Immortal heroic deed of a Red Fleet Sailor', and displayed a dramatic picture of a man engulfed by a sheet of flame running towards a German tank. Underneath was a description of Panikakha's fate, set out in blunt, staccato sentences:

> His position was attacked by tanks. The marines met the enemy with fierce fire from anti-tank rifles and grenades. The Germans had the advantage of numbers and rushed forward. Their tanks 'ironed' the trench Panikakha was in. In the fight, he ran out of grenades. Looking around, he saw two Molotov cocktails. He got out of the trench and tried to light one of them – but the bottle smashed open. The liquid set him alight. He was like a liquid torch when he rushed at the tank. He realized that he would not survive. One last thought moved him – to destroy a German tank. When the vehicle was close enough Panikakha rushed forward – paying no attention to the hellish pain – and hit the second bottle over the engine.

The leaflet concluded with the exhortation: 'Comrades – Annihilate the enemy! Draw inspiration from this soldier's honour, courage and discipline in your fight against the Fascist bastards.'

Panikakha had shown desperate courage. His story profoundly affected the army, and inspired other soldiers to sacrifice their lives in order to bring down as many of the enemy as possible. 'There were many Panikakhas at Stalingrad', Mereshko said simply. The proliferation of such actions became a remarkable feature of the battle.

Each heroic deed tells a tale of exceptional bravery. Yet the official record does not truly honour those who fell – instead their exploits are often recited in a tone that is both jarring and strangely impersonal. To understand how the Red Army found its courage at Stalingrad we have to get beneath the surface of these stories, and connect with the power they had to transform the mood of the defenders.

The Battle Situation

Timing is the key to understanding a heroic deed. These stories of courage were circulated at critical moments of the battle, when the morale was faltering. Earlier in September, in the outskirts of Stalingrad, a soldier from the 154th Brigade – Ilya Kaplanov – had also destroyed an enemy tank by throwing himself at it when on fire from a Molotov cocktail. But it was Panikakha's deed, not Kaplanov's, which caught the imagination of the defenders.

Mikhail Panikakha's 193rd Division had been flung in to stop a ferocious German offensive on Stalingrad's northern factory district, on 28 September 1942. The day before, the enemy had launched a fresh assault on the 62nd Army, swinging to the north of the city, away from Rodimtsev's division entrenched in central Stalingrad. A withering bombardment had pushed Gorishny's forces off the summit of the Mamaev Kurgan and left them clinging to its north-eastern slope, then a massed German assault broke through the 62nd Army's northern defence line, pushing back the Russians up to a mile. Stalingrad's defenders were running out of space.

Surveying the events of 27 September Chuikov commented ruefully: 'One more battle like that and we'll be in the Volga.' At this moment of crisis, with his own HQ under attack, and communication with other units breaking down, he had taken a brave and entirely characteristic action – deciding that the leaders of the 62nd Army would now move forward, closer to the enemy, and reassure their soldiers. Gurov, his commissar, went to the HQ of the hard-pressed armoured brigade; Krylov, his chief of staff, to the HQ of Gorishny's 95th and Chuikov himself to Batyuk's 284th.

Chuikov was taking a considerable risk, for the army's HQ could not function in his absence. But he felt that leadership through example was more important. Mereshko emphasized: 'This decision demonstrated our commander's determination to keep fighting for Stalingrad. At particularly difficult moments Chuikov, Krylov and Gurov would leave our HQ and go to the sectors most threatened by the enemy. It was an instinctive reaction.'

The Russians were holding on – but only just. Chuikov was seriously concerned that the Germans would break through and capture the Red October Factory, splitting the 62nd Army in two. Fortunately, fresh reinforcements were now available. On the night of 27 September General Feodor Smekhotvorov's 193rd Division reached the river, ready to take up positions in the Red October workers' settlement.

Viktor Katashev recalled the troops assembling at the Volga crossing point:

> The city was burning – lit by an enormous glow. Neither the moon nor the stars could be seen, only the bright lines of the tracer bullets rising up in the sky, looking like some sort of strange fan made by multi-coloured fireflies. Searchlights swept the sky, looking for their victims.

Then the Germans spotted them. 'All of a sudden, it became as bright as day. Dozens of parachute flares were hanging in the night sky, illuminating the whole of Stalingrad and the crossing.'

The 193rd Division was heavily shelled and bombed as it made it way over the Volga (the Germans were now bombing the river at night) and lost men, officers and vital equipment, with some of its units landing in the wrong place. It now had to find it defence lines in the darkness. Smekhotvorov put it bluntly: 'Taking up positions in an unknown city – at night – without preliminary reconnaissance is a matter of immense difficulty.'

Smekhotvorov set up his HQ in the boiler room of an engineer's house near the Volga embankment. He used tracing paper to sketch out a battle plan over copies of a city map, and handed them to his regimental commanders. He was most worried about Captain Maxim Nasteko's 883rd Regiment, which had to hold the left flank of the defence line, from Zuyevskaya Street, in the workers' settlement, to the Banny Gully. On the other side of the gully were the troops of Batyuk's 284th Division. But the Germans would almost certainly try to disrupt their link-up, and strike hard at the junction point of the two divisions. The signals battalion, with all its radio equipment, had been sunk by enemy bombers, leaving Smekhotvorov unable to make contact with his neighbours.

Interrogation of some captured prisoners revealed a worrying development: three German infantry divisions and one Panzer division were converging on the Red October Factory. A colossal attack was planned for the following morning. 'Their intention was clear enough', Smekhotvorov commented grimly, 'to throw us all into the Volga river. The Nazis had failed to do this in downtown Stalingrad – now they were doubly determined to succeed.'

The men of the 193rd Division began fanning out amidst Stalingrad's ruins. Their commander watched their progress from the upper floor of the engineer's house. 'After a while my eyes became more accustomed to the darkness', Smekhotvorov continued. 'I began to distinguish some of the nearby buildings. I could tell where my men were moving from the sudden fire fights which would flare up and then die down again.'

For a few moments, in the first light of morning, the mist from the Volga lifted, and Smekhotvorov glimpsed a scene of eerie beauty. He saw the ruins of the factory district, and on its outskirts, vegetable gardens, fields and woods. And then he heard the slow rumble of the enemy's artillery barrage. He glanced at his watch – it was 8.00 a.m. sharp. 'All of a sudden, masses of German Junkers were hovering over us, the black dots of their bombs streaming down from their underbellies. A huge cloud of smoke, soot and brick dust covered the factory blocks. Explosions sent up pillars of sparks and blazing splinters.' And then a runner from Nasteko's regiment got through: 'Enemy tanks and infantry are assembling in a grove opposite us – request supporting artillery fire.'

This was the 193rd Division's introduction to Stalingrad. Smekhotvorov was struggling to hold back the Germans:

> The enemy flung everything against us – they were determined to capture the workers' settlement and Red October factory and reach the Volga. They threw in masses of infantry and tanks, while their aviation, in groups of twenty to thirty planes, continually bombed our frontline and supply areas. The non-stop explosions of bombs and shells caused everything to shudder and collapse. The settlement was in flames – and it seemed as if the earth itself shook and burned.

Chuikov paid tribute to the commander of the 193rd Division:

> In the bitterest fighting Smekhotvorov never showed any sign of faint-heartedness or confusion. I can still recall his measured voice, while hundreds of German planes were over his division and enemy shells were bursting around his men. In a telephone conversation with him you could hear, in the background, the wail of the enemy's dive bomber sirens. Yet he remained completely calm.

Such calmness was vital, for the position on this sector of the front was desperate. It truly was touch and go whether the German assault could be contained. Smekhotvorov acknowledged that on 28 September alone losses were so high that 'our rifle and tank units were no longer able to maintain a coherent defence line'. Within a further twenty-four hours all three regimental commanders of the 193rd Division and a further three battalion commanders had been killed in the fighting. Yet somehow, in the midst of this carnage, a stand had to be made. At 7.30 p.m. on 28 September Chuikov issued a desperate command:

> It must be explained to every soldier that the Army is fighting on its last line of defence – there can be no further retreat. It is the duty of every soldier and commander to defend his trench and hold his position – not a step back!

The onslaught continued. Smekhotvorov's division had arrived in Stalingrad with 5,000 troops but by 1 October it had been reduced to 600 men. Battered Red Army soldiers had somehow to summon the will to fling back the enemy. In this desperate situation, details of Mikhail Panikakha's furious stand began to spread amongst Stalingrad's defenders. Mereshko recalled:

> The story first circulated by word of mouth, then I remember reading about it in our army newspaper. Leaflets were brought out soon afterwards. It was felt that Panikakha's desperate heroism embodied the spirit of Chuikov's order: to hold firm against the might of the German offensive, whatever the cost – and stand until death.

Tank Fright

A heroic deed needs to strike a chord with the ordinary soldier. Panikakha's story was so powerful because Stalingrad's fighters could identify with his last terrible moments, with enemy tanks right on top of him, 'ironing' his trench – rolling over it, and then reversing, to bury the defenders alive. By now, everyone in the army knew the meaning of tank fright.

'I have to admit that at this stage of the battle our soldiers were really afraid of German tanks', confessed Mereshko:

> We didn't think we had a good way of fighting them. Our heavy artillery was on the other bank of the river. We had anti-tank guns, supplemented by special rifles, fitted with 2–3 metre long tubes [the

PTRF 14.5mm anti-tank rifle] and these were effective against light tanks. But our anti-tank grenades were heavy and difficult to throw out of the trench, and their range was only about 15–20 metres. Molotov cocktails were hard to use properly. They were effective up to a range of 20–25 metres, but it was very difficult to throw them that far. When we gained more experience in fighting tanks at close quarters we held our fire until they came closer – but imagine just waiting there while a huge tank is rumbling towards you . . .

Alexei Voloshin of the 10th NKVD Division said simply:

My heart sank when tanks were advancing on us and I had to hold my fire, waiting until they got closer. I couldn't show my men that I was frightened. But it was only when the tank was knocked out and on fire that I could recover any sort of equilibrium.

Viktor Katashev of the 193rd Division remembered a German tank attack on the Red October factory canteen:

A cloud of dust soon appeared from the west. Fascist tanks were coming, and behind the tanks, infantry. Several of the tanks turned and started heading straight towards us. It's difficult to describe a man's feelings at moments like this. There's a continuous rumble in the air, the ground seems to be alive and groaning. The tanks were firing as they went, from every gun they had. Shells and mines were exploding close to us, throwing up huge quantities of earth. All around there was hissing, roaring and wailing. Thousands of splinters and bullets were flying through the air.

Katashev recalled isolated moments of combat with terrible intensity: the belt in the machine gun running out, the stench from exploding shells, tanks firing on their trenches, hurling the last of the anti-tank grenades. They were desperately short of ammunition, but a group of anti-tank men from a nearby battalion came to their rescue and the attack was beaten off, leaving piles of dead and wounded.

But no help had been at hand for Mikhail Panikakha and his comrades. Mereshko continued:

We could all identify with Panikakha, out of ammunition and clutching his two Molotov cocktails. He had clambered out of his trench and it is said that a German bullet shattered one of the incendiary devices, spilling liquid all over him. To be honest, it was just as likely to have leaked when tilted – many of our Molotov cocktails were poorly made and accidents were frequent. On the steppe we lost two of our cadets who burnt when the liquid leaked – it was impossible to put out the flames.

This was a ghastly way to die. But the image of Panikakha, on fire, still advancing towards the enemy, caught the imagination of the army. 'Those nearby saw a man in flames leap out of the trench, run right up to the German tank, and smash the remaining bottle against the grille of the engine hatch', recalled Chuikov. 'A second later an enormous sheet of flame and smoke engulfed both the tank and the hero who had destroyed it.'

It seemed quite unbelievable. 'We thought about the sheer willpower necessary to perform such an act of heroism', said Mereshko. 'It was hard to imagine – yet, somehow, Panikakha did this. His courage became a source of inspiration to our soldiers.'

A Broken Chain of Command

Panikakha's desperate heroism was made all the more poignant by the startling fact that his regiment – the 883rd – was no longer receiving any effective leadership. Panikakha's first battalion had been left to face the advancing Germans without orders or instructions – its soldiers were simply flung back on their own resources. What had gone wrong?

Leadership from the front – the Russian creed at Stalingrad – carried enormous risks. At times of intense fighting the regimental commander – in close proximity to the enemy, and often fighting on the frontline – became terribly vulnerable. Within a day, Panikakha's regiment had lost three command posts. They were set up, one after another, in different locations, and just as quickly destroyed by the Germans.

The 883rd Regiment had rushed into Stalingrad so fast that some key units – including its reconnaissance and field engineering detachments – were left behind on the far bank of the Volga. Its command post was set up hastily, without proper preparation. The German response was unerring. On 28 September the regimental HQ came under heavy fire. The following day it was moved – only to be immediately struck by an enemy mortar bombardment. Eight regimental staff were killed, including the commander, Captain Nasteko. The commissar took over – the HQ moved again – and straightaway a German artillery bombardment killed the commissar and destroyed the new HQ. All communication with the regiment's battalions was lost. On the morning of 30 September a replacement arrived – Captain Martinov – and an attempt was made to re-establish the command post at another location. It was immediately flattened by the enemy and Martinov died of his wounds.

'After the third destruction of our command post', the regimental journal noted grimly, 'it was moved to the basement of a workers' club.' But effective control of the regiment was not re-established – its new commander, Lieutenant-Colonel Panschin, gave up and hit the bottle instead. He was found in the basement on 2 October in a state of abject paralysis. 'Panschin failed to show any leadership', the journal related laconically, 'and lost control of the regiment through his irresponsibility and drunkenness.'

An explanation for this terrible sequence of events began to emerge. The Germans had been able to recruit a number of agents from the civilian population still living in the workers' settlement. The regimental journal recorded:

> In many cases, our civilians are helping the enemy and actually informing them of the location of our troops. In the evenings, 'civilian shooters' mark our positions with tracer bullets. Other bastards are firing flare rockets to signal where our regimental command post is located. This enables the Germans to keep bombing and shelling it so effectively.

The presence of these collaborators was deeply disturbing. And then, while Panikakha and his fellow fighters were facing a German tank attack, their new acting commander was drinking himself senseless in the basement of a workers' club.

Although shocking, it is perhaps not so very surprising that some civilians, overwhelmed by the seeming hopelessness of their situation, sought to bring the appalling fighting to an end as soon as possible. German victory still looked inevitable.

Order was restored on 2 October by General Smekhotvorov – who turned up at the impromptu command post with an escort of machine gunners to find out what was going on. Panschin was immediately dismissed and replaced by the commander of the division's training battalion, Lieutenant Osyko. It was during this visit to the 883rd Regiment's positions that Smekhotvorov first heard about Panikakha's heroism. Smekhotvorov told Mereshko:

> At first it was even difficult to find out his name, for those guys in the frontline were dying so fast – the life expectancy of our soldiers

at that time was just one day. But I spoke to people who remembered him. He was a marine from the Pacific fleet, based in Siberia. He had a 'relaxed' way of talking, with a quirky mannerism of breaking up his words, saying something like: 'I am ly-ing down, I am ly-ing down, I kill a German, I am ly-ing down.' This amused his fellow fighters. From such little fragments he started to become a real person to us.

The awful fact that Panikakha and his comrades had been left to fight alone stayed with Smekhotvorov. He realized that the effectiveness of personal leadership at Stalingrad depended on the decisions of army and divisional commanders being carried through at regimental level. He now took action. Mereshko said:

Smekhotvorov changed the system we used, recognizing that the demands of city fighting placed too great a burden on regimental staff. The cumulative strain of their responsibilities – carried out in atrocious conditions – alongside repeated clashes with the enemy on the frontline, was simply too great. Men were burning out with fatigue. Seeing this, Smekhotvorov made a crucial refinement.

In the heat of battle, the 193rd Division's commander introduced a striking innovation. 'He decided to employ a system of rotation', Mereshko continued. 'When he saw a regiment losing its energy and strength, he sent its HQ staff to the far bank of the Volga for a few days and brought in different people. He rotated his regimental commanders all the time.' The risk of this approach was that the troops would resent people taking a break while they had to carry on fighting, but Smekhotvorov dealt with this head on, discussing the situation with his men. Mereshko added:

He made it a democratic process and listened to the views of his soldiers. He canvassed their opinions, asking them who might make a suitable replacement, and sometimes acted on their recommend- ations. The troops felt part of what was going on.

The benefits of the new regime were soon felt. Mereshko continued:

Chuikov was initially taken aback, but to his credit, he chose to trust Smekhotvorov, and allowed him to continue with this new approach. When it became clear it was militarily effective other divisional commanders began to do the same thing. Panikakha's ghastly fate had taught us an important lesson. Regimental command now became a strength rather than a weakness.

The Impact of Smekhotvorov's Leadership

Feodor Smekhotvorov is one of the unsung heroes of Stalingrad. Mereshko said:

> Very little has been written about him, in contrast to other, more well-known divisional commanders, but he had an enormous impact on the battle. He was a modest, unassuming man, yet incredibly brave. After his division moved into the factory district he found communication with nearby troops disrupted because of the intensity of the fighting. That night he walked along the line, accompanied by a just few machine gunners, and personally visited neighbouring divisional command posts to discuss fighting methods with them and properly co-ordinate the defence.

Chuikov praised Smekhotvorov's intelligence, quick thinking and his knowledge of modern warfare. These qualities were resoundingly displayed in the first week of October 1942, when, despite the terrible German onslaught, he managed to hold back the enemy, introducing for the first time the system against massed tank attack which became standard at Stalingrad.

Smekhotvorov created a system of defence in depth. His plan was that, if German tanks broke through a first echelon, they would then face a second, and a third. He deployed small groups of defenders in a checkerboard formation. Tank fighters, armed with grenades and Molotov cocktails, hid in small crevices in walls and foxholes. About 50 metres behind them Smekhotvorov put a line of soldiers armed with anti-tank rifles. Another 50 metres behind these men, he positioned the anti-tank guns. Heavy machine guns and groups of riflemen were on the flanks, to stop the enemy's infantry infiltrating the position. In between the defence lines lay a succession of obstacles: minefields, barbed wire – and nets.

This was a new invention, introduced by Smekhotvorov's engineers – heavy, netted cable, attached to an electricity source, that could suddenly be pulled up in front of German tanks, letting a very high current pass through it to short-circuit the engines. The overall effect was formidable. The 883rd Regiment's journal proudly stated that for the first time a system of defence had been organized that could stop the enemy's armoured formations attacking *en masse*.

To reinforce his new system, Smekhotvorov used a series of artillery spotters, watching from factory chimney stacks and other vantage points and also getting as close to German lines as possible. Once the enemy was entrapped by this series of obstacles, massive artillery strikes were called in. Mikhail Rabinovich was one of the spotters:

> Smekhotvorov put us in 'advanced observation posts', right along the defence line – mine was in a school building in the Red October workers' settlement. Our task was to correct our artillery strikes and make them as accurate as possible. I was armed with a machine gun, grenades and Molotov cocktails, so I could support our infantry whenever the Germans attacked.

Smekhotvorov realized that the kind of heroism shown by Panikakha could only flourish with Red Army soldiers properly protected. Without such protection, individual examples of bravery, however stirring, would ultimately be futile against the might of the enemy.

The Last Hours of Mikhail Panikakha

On 1 October 1942 Panikakha's 2nd Company – reduced to a few soldiers, armed with anti-tank rifles – was a beleaguered outpost in a creaking defence position. The entire first battalion had been reduced to a mere 45 men and there was no communication of any sort from the regimental HQ. Left to its own devices, the battalion attempted a reconnaissance of the enemy position. On 30 September it sent out a small group but it was quickly captured by the Germans. One of the reconnaissance team – a private named Shastakov – made a remarkable return. The men were left dumbfounded by what he told them.

Shastakov had been kept in a dug out very close to the frontline. His conditions of captivity were relaxed – the Germans seemed confident of success – and once disarmed he was able to move around with little supervision. Shastakov's curiosity was aroused by the sound of Russian voices at a nearby gun emplacement. Wandering over, he spoke to the three men loading and firing shells at the 193rd Division's positions. They were Red Army soldiers, captured only a few days earlier, on 27 September, when the Germans first attacked the Red October Factory. Now they were bombarding their compatriots. A sudden distraction along the line, caused by a small Russian counter-attack, prompted Shastakov to try and make a run for it. 'Come, join me', he said to the other Red Army soldiers, not quite believing what he had just witnessed. They laughed at him, and chose to stay where they were.

On the train from Saratov to Leninsk the soldiers of Panikakha's company had busily cleaned their equipment and checked their ammunition, carefully counting the number of grenades, bullets and Molotov cocktails. They had swapped exhortations. 'The sooner we get into combat the better', 'Why are they bombing Stalingrad – the barbarians!', 'Let's crush the Fascist ogre!' Now these certainties had vanished. To their horror, they had found that civilians in the workers' settlement, far from welcoming them as rescuers, were helping the enemy. Some, armed by the Germans with machine guns, even emerged from cellars and took pot shots at their unit. These 'shooters', lurking in the ruins, had already killed or injured several Red Army soldiers. It was no longer safe to cross streets during daytime – even behind the Russian lines. This problem was only solved when the entire civilian population of the workers' settlement was forcibly evacuated later in October.

At 8.00 a.m. on 1 October the enemy began shelling 2nd Company's position. The bombardment went on for one and half hours. Then the Germans attacked. Their tanks and infantry were beaten off, but ammunition was now running low and a platoon of enemy machine gunners severed communications with the rest of the battalion. The Germans attacked again from a ruined school building ahead of 2nd Company and the gullies to its left and right. Panikakha's anti-tank rifle crew managed to hit two advancing tanks before running out of ammunition. A third now approached and began 'ironing' the trench. Panikakha grabbed Molotov cocktails in both hands and faced his assailant . . .

The regimental combat journal noted simply yet powerfully: 'This is how the valiant defender of Stalingrad – tank destroyer Comrade Panikakha – died the death of a hero.'

The Inspiration

Panikakha died in agony – but not in vain. His divisional commander was profoundly moved by his act of courage and decided to publicize it. Smekhotvorov was a brave man and he wanted to motivate his battered force to stand and fight. He did not tolerate cowardice, in any form, because of its corrosive effect on Stalingrad's defenders. When a company commander in Panikakha's 883rd Regiment, Junior Lieutenant Solodilov, 'lost control' in the heat of battle and ran away, his soldiers immediately began to retreat. Solodilov was arrested, brought back and shot in front of his men. Further retreat was no longer an option.

Smekhotvorov well understood Chuikov's guiding principle, that the only effective way to negate cowardice was to counter to it through honouring acts of courage. Here lay the force of Panikakha's heroic deed, and soon others were following suit. Smekhotvorov recalled its effect:

> A similar exploit was made shortly afterwards by a soldier from a mortar company in Panikakha's regiment – Konstantin Kazakov. His fellow soldiers were out of ammunition. With a stack of grenades in his hands, Kazakov moved towards a German tank which had broken through his company's position. He was spotted and hit by a burst of machine gun fire. Overcoming the pain, and gathering his last remaining strength, the heavily bleeding Kazakov detonated the grenades and threw himself under the tank – destroying it in a huge explosion.

Panikakha was in a hopeless situation – but he was determined not to let the Germans pass. Soldiers would say of such an act: 'He refused to bow his head to the enemy.' Chuikov popularized the expression, and the defiant bravery which underlay it, remarking to Vasily Grossman during a bombardment: 'A commander must feel it is better for him to lose his head than to bow it to a German shell. Soldiers notice these things.'

In October 1942 a saying of Dolores Ibarruri, leader of the Spanish communist party during the Civil War, began to spread amongst the troops. Her resolve to fight Fascism was well-known amongst the defenders, for Ibarruri's son, Ruben, had joined the Red Army as a volunteer in the summer of 1942 – pledging to continue the fight against 'Nazi barbarism and enslavement'. He had died on the outskirts of Stalingrad. Now soldiers recalled the powerful words of his mother: 'Better to die on your feet than live on your knees.'

Smekhotvorov said simply: 'This is how the widely known sacrifice of a soldier in the 2nd Company of the 883rd Rifle Regiment, Mikhail Panikakha, became the inspiration for heroism.'

Chapter Eight

The Birth of 'Sniperism'

One of Stalingrad's most famous episodes is a duel between two opposing snipers, recently portrayed in the film *Enemy at the Gates.* The film's Russian ace is based on the sniper Vasily Zaitsev, from Batyuk's 284th Division. The German is an expert from the Berlin sniper school, named Major Koenig. A sniper duel definitely took place during the battle. It was on the Mamaev Kurgan – although it lasted hours rather than days – and it was well-publicized within the army. Vasily Gorokhov, a fighter in Batyuk's Division, remembered hearing about it:

> A German sniper was shooting at us from the Mamaev Kurgan and causing a lot of problems. He had made a 'good lair' and was really difficult to track down. But Zaitsev stalked him, finally found him and finished him off. He did a good job.

At the time, there was no comment about the identity of the opponent. 'Our political staff spread the word about it', Gorokhov continued. 'Nobody mentioned an expert from Berlin. Zaitsev was praised for his persistence – he didn't give up when his task was hard to achieve.'

'Perseverance was one of Chuikov's strongest qualities', Mereshko said simply, 'and one he sought to inculcate in his army.' Many of the new Soviet recruits to the fighting were Siberians – tough, self-reliant hunters. The 27-year-old Zaitsev was a payroll clerk in the Pacific fleet, but he had trained as a hunter since boyhood in the forests beyond the Ural Mountains – and the contest pitted his patient, home-spun skill against the polished professionalism of a Wehrmacht expert. The duel on the Mamaev Kurgan – and Zaitsev's eventual victory – became an affirmation of the defenders' native resilience.

Vasily Zaitsev became one of Stalingrad's best known defenders. His contribution was real – he was an excellent sniper, who dispatched over 200 German victims, and he taught many others to shoot. He was subsequently made a Hero of the Soviet Union, and rather like Jacob Pavlov, a story was built up around him by the Soviet propaganda machine, in which Zaitsev became the creator of a sniping movement within the defending army.

Antony Beevor is rightly sceptical of the story that the Germans brought the head of their sniper school to Stalingrad. He nevertheless credits Zaitsev with beginning 'sniperism':

> The most famous sniper of them all was Zaitsev in Batyuk's Division . . . News of further additions to his score passed from mouth to mouth along the front. Zaitsev, whose name means hare in Russian, was put in charge of training young snipers, and his pupils became known as *zaichata*, or 'leverets'. This was the start of the 'sniper movement' in the 62nd Army.

This is a wonderful myth – but nevertheless propaganda rather than truth. Zaitsev was a skilful teacher, but he did not initiate the sniper movement. 'Sniperism' – a mass movement of ordinary Red Army soldiers, who volunteered in their hundreds to go out and hunt down the enemy – was spreading like wildfire when Zaitsev joined its ranks. The real originator is as little-known as Zaitsev is famous. He began this popular movement, which gave Red Army soldiers a sense of purpose and self-belief, and taught Zaitsev the skills of his trade.

'My First Ten'

Vasily Zaitsev was a soldier in the 1047th Regiment of Batyuk's Division. Recently, one of the regimental staff, Nikolai Aksyonov, discussed 'sniperism' in his book, *On the Mamaev Kurgan*. He claims it did not originate with Zaitsev, but from another, little-known soldier in the same regiment, Alexander Kalentiev. Kalentiev fought in Stalingrad for less than two months – he was killed on 17 November 1942 – but in that time he inspired Zaitsev and countless others.

An account of how Kalentiev started sniping was reported in the 284th Division's newspaper in early October 1942. It was entitled 'My First Ten'. Kalentiev's actions were attracting considerable interest:

> My comrades were killing Germans but I was a communications officer – so I hadn't killed any Fascists myself. I really wanted to be on the frontline – I didn't want to be stuck behind my friends. Before the war, I had attended shooting courses and now I wanted to do something. My commander supported me and let me go to the frontline with my rifle and hunt for Fritzes. I searched for a place

which would make a good observation post, where I could see the enemy and they couldn't see me. I climbed up to the first floor of a partially ruined house, lay down and began my watch. After fifteen minutes three Germans appeared – about a hundred metres from me, close enough to see the details of their uniform. I had a telescopic lens, and I chose the middle German of the three and got him in my sights. For a moment I wondered whether I would miss him or get him – then I pulled the trigger. The German fell and my heart surged with joy – it was my first kill. The two others ran away. Soon a second group arrived. I was already calmer. I got one more in my sights – another kill.

The next day our unit was supposed to launch an attack. My commander gave me a special assignment, to try and get some of the German machine gunners – they were creating big problems for us. I got inside a house and looked around to see where they were shooting from. They were firing from railway carriages on a siding. I waited for one to climb out and dispatched my bullet. The German fell out onto the rails. I wanted to run over and take his machine gun, but the political officer, who was accompanying me, didn't let me, saying: 'I don't think he was on his own.' He was right. Another German opened fire from another carriage. I finished him off as well. In a few minutes I got rid of the third machine gunner. The political officer approved my sniping. He said 'Continue doing the same thing.'

In two days I encountered nine Fritzes. The tenth was an officer. I had got inside a nearby train. I thought it would make a good shelter for me – it was like being inside a tank. When it started to get lighter some Germans appeared, just 25 metres away – too close! You can't open fire at that distance – your position will be revealed and you will be caught. I waited for them to get further away. And then I saw this big officer – a huge man – shouting commands to his men. I took aim and shot him. He fell. The Germans opened fire on our soldiers and our machine gunners retaliated. Under the cover of this noise I left my train and rejoined my guys.

This is how I killed ten Fritzes. This is my first ten. And I hope to increase my fighting account many times before the anniversary of the October Revolution.

Kalentiev's account shows how 'sniperism' emerged from an ordinary soldier's desire to do something, to hit back at the enemy. Kalentiev's commander allowed him to go 'hunting for Fritzes' as an experiment. When he was successful he was given a specific military assignment – and a political officer was sent with him. When Kalentiev killed the German machine gunners he was given formal approval to continue with his sniping. The anniversary of the October Revolution (which fell on 7 November) was a marker for him to raise a substantial tally.

Letters Home

On 11 October Kalentiev, excited by his success as a sniper, sent a letter to his parents. Kalentiev came from a small Siberian village near Maryensk. He could not write – so he dictated what he wanted to say to a friend, who was barely literate himself (the letter lacks punctuation and is full of spelling mistakes). Some of Stalingrad's famous snipers were well-educated. Anatoly Chekhov, the 13th Division's famous marksman, had been a top pupil at school and Vasily Zaitsev had trained as an accountant. But Kalentiev's simple, almost child-like efforts were far more typical of the majority of Red Army soldiers:

> Hello my dear parents – mum and dad, and sister-in-law Zoya, and my brothers. I bow before you and send you my regards. Now I am going to tell you about my life, my dear parents. I want to tell you about my life. At this particular moment I live well. But I don't know, my dear parents, how you carry on, because I haven't received any letters from you. I don't understand why, mum and dad.
>
> I want to tell you I am fighting the Fritz without mercy. I finish with them – and return victorious.
>
> Also I inform you, mum and dad, that there are only three of us left: myself, Maltsev and Shuvalov – we often meet, and Petra Shuvalov is injured. So my dear parents, don't forget about me, write to me more often. Don't forget.
>
> (Written by my friend Trushin)

On 4 November Kalentiev dispatched another, very short letter home. He was now wounded, and although still on the frontline, unable to continue with his sniping: 'At this particular moment I am alive and healthy. Maltsev is also alive and healthy. I am slightly injured in both feet – but I am being treated on the frontline.'

Alexander Kalentiev died in Stalingrad on 17 November. His sniping had already made him famous – and his regimental commander wrote a letter of condolence to his father:

> I am passing on to you the very sad news that your son Sasha was killed by those damned bandits while defending _____ [censored]. But Sasha did not lose his life for nothing – he destroyed 24 Fascists with his sniper rifle. For heroism – for courage – our commander nominated your son for the award of the Red Banner. Those awful bandits did not escape punishment – and our regiment took good revenge for our fallen comrade, who died defending his motherland. We took revenge for Sasha Kalentiev. Father, we will carry on taking revenge for all our fallen comrades.

Opening an Account 'of Revenge'

Kalentiev's sniping exploits had a huge impact on his fellow fighters. By the second half of October many ordinary soldiers were following his example. It was a completely spontaneous movement – seen as a way to strike back at an arrogant, all-powerful enemy. Sergei Kozyakin described a meeting with two volunteer snipers:

> They are two ordinary Red Army soldiers – but now they have a sense of pride and purpose. When asked what they do, they say: 'We are hunters – come and see how we work.' They took me to a small tongue of sand on the Volga river and then pointed at some shattered grey buildings nearby. I could see smoke from a number of small fires. 'The Germans are there', the snipers told me, 'they have reached our Volga river. They behave as if they have already won the battle: we saw them washing themselves, drying their clothes by the fire. So we went to our commander and asked permission to hunt for Fritzes. He agreed to our request. On our first outing we killed two Fritzes. We were really excited and told all our mates.'

A simple idea was circulating amongst Red Army fighters – to open up an account. It was like a bank account – but the deposits, made on pieces of paper, would be sniping kills. Soldiers called it the account 'of revenge'. Here is a 'deposit' from one of the snipers Kozyakin met – a small, torn scrap of paper, handed to a political officer: 'My account of revenge – 25 October. Today I killed a fucking Fascist using a sniper's rifle. The Fascist came to the shore to get water. Next instalment tomorrow – Viktor Tetnyuk.'

Very soon dozens of soldiers in Tetnyuk's regiment were doing the same thing: 'The excitement was incredible', he remembered.

> Our guys would come up to each other and say 'Have you opened your account yet?' Our tallies were normally handed in to the representative of our divisional newspaper. We nicknamed our collection of German kills the 'Bank of Revenge'. We saw it as revenge on the Fascists for all the terrible things they'd done to our land – for the blood of our relatives, for the sorrow they'd caused. We were avenging the wronged dignity of our people.

This was the essence of 'sniperism' – a remarkable popular movement which sprang up amongst Stalingrad's fighters, fuelled by deep anger and a desire to hit back at the Germans. Feelings of despondency changed to rage as men took a sniping gun in their hands and went to hunt for Fritzes. 'A wild hatred of the enemy had spread amongst our soldiers', said Mereshko bluntly. It now had an outlet.

Chuikov's Decision

No one in the 62nd Army had expected sniping to catch on so fast – and many were unsure what to do with this burgeoning phenomenon. Some of the army hierarchy felt the situation was getting out of hand – for as soldiers wandered off, unsupervised, it was hard to keep control over what was going on. There were complaints that some over-enthusiastic amateurs were a downright hindrance – they moved in on the carefully prepared lairs of the 62nd Army's regular snipers, banged off a few shots, and gave away the whereabouts of these positions – which became German artillery targets. The army council considered limiting the issue of sniper rifles to new volunteers. Faced with this prospect, Chuikov made a crucial intervention: he decided to encourage the new movement instead and incorporated it into the structure of the 62nd Army.

Mereshko said:

> Chuikov's support for the sniper movement was vital. Another commander might have banned it. But Chuikov saw its psychological potential to demoralize the enemy, saying famously: 'It will make every German feel he is living under the barrel of a gun.' He

believed it could enormously lift the morale of our soldiers. He carried the army council with him – and towards the end of October they decided to create sniper detachments in every division and regiment. It became our official policy.

Chuikov himself wrote:

We paid particular attention to the development of a snipers' movement amongst our troops. The Army Military Council supported this move. Our army newspaper published daily figures of the number of the enemy killed by our snipers, and published photographs of outstandingly accurate marksmen.

He added: 'I met many of the well-known snipers. I talked to them, helped them as far as I could and frequently consulted them.' He gave his impressions of Zaitsev, and a fellow sniper, Viktor Medvedev:

I was struck by their modesty, the leisurely way they moved, their particularly calm temperament, the attentive way they looked at things – they could look at the same object for along time without blinking. They had strong hands: when they shook hands with you they had a grip like a vice. The snipers went out 'hunting' early in the morning to previously selected and prepared places, carefully camouflaged themselves, and waited patiently for targets to appear. They knew that the slightest negligence or haste would lead to certain death.

Chuikov believed in these men, and he trusted them. Zaitsev was struck by the effect this had – and expressed a timeless truth about the relationship between a general and his troops:

Trust is the source of a soldier's inspiration and faith is the mother of his courage. For the commander, faith and trust are the keys to a soldier's heart – to that hidden cache of energy that a combatant may not realize he has inside himself.

Leading snipers now trained others in their craft. The first group formed within the army was not Vasily Zaitsev's 'leverets', but the 'apprentices' of another sniper ace, Anatoly Chekhov. On 30 October the combat journal of the 13th Guards Division noted proudly:

The sniper movement has now become militarily significant. The initiator of the movement within our division, Sergeant Chekhov, has already trained nine more snipers – one of his pupils, Red Army soldier Zolovsky, killed 22 Fascist within a few days.

But it was sniper Vasily Zaitsev who received most publicity. He was the first sniper to get over a hundred kills. The combat journal of the 284th Division trumpeted a new title: 'Honourable sniper – private of the first rank Vasily Zaitsev welcomed the anniversary of the October Revolution by destroying 130 Fascists.'

Hunting the Enemy

Sniping in the ruined city was incredibly dangerous because it was conducted in close proximity to the Germans. Kalentiev warned that a shooting distance of 25 metres would probably reveal a sniper's position – but sometimes it was just not possible to get further away. When Mikhail Mamekov began sniping in the Red October Factory the Germans were just 30 metres from him. 'At night we crept forward, and found spots for ourselves in attics, near the windows.' Here, the use of camouflage and decoys was essential – it was a battle of wits, and it was extremely risky to remain in one location too long. The 13th Guards sniper Stephan Vernigora had a golden rule: 'One position is never enough.' Mamekov stressed that each of his group had reserve firing positions – 'if we thought that we had been spotted at one location we could move unnoticed to another'.

Nevertheless, it was hard to stay vigilant. Fatigue could set in, and a sniper could remain too long in his lair. After a number of kills the Germans would try and flush the marksman out with artillery or mortar fire. Even if the sniper survived, he was likely to be hurt by falling bricks or masonry. Zaitsev described one such incident:

> It was my own fault – I got tired of creeping around from place to place, decided to stay where I was, and took about ten shots from there. The Germans replied with a mortar. I was showered in masonry and both my legs were left stuck in a pile of bricks.

Zaitsev painfully extricated himself. This was an inevitable hazard of the sniper's trade, and interestingly, Kalentiev suffered a similar injury to both legs, which he described in his second letter to his parents in early November.

But whatever its risks, sniping raised the morale of Red Army soldiers. Men enjoyed reading about the exploits of snipers in different divisions – their tallies, the techniques and tricks they used – and it fostered a spirit of unity and pride. Devising new ways of killing the enemy was a source of particular fascination. Zaitsev tried attaching a sniper scope to an anti-tank rifle, hoping he could put a round through the gun slit of an enemy bunker. Initially, the experience was a frustrating failure – the quality of the ammunition was unpredictable and no two rounds came close to the same target. But Zaitsev and his team of apprentices persisted with the experiment – and finally their efforts were crowned with success. 'Sniper Morozov managed to send an enemy bunker up in flames using an anti-tank rifle', the combat journal of the 284th Division announced delightedly.

The Communist Version of the Battle

Soviet propaganda subsequently played up the role of Vasily Zaitsev, as it had done with Pavlov. Both were members of the Komsomol, the Communist youth league, the party organization for teenagers and young adults. Stalingrad would subsequently be portrayed as a victory of communist zeal, with enthusiastic Komsomol members leading the way in house fighting, storm groups and the snipers movement. But in truth only a small proportion of Stalingrad's army were communists: just over 10 per cent of the officers and only about 3 per cent of the men.

Stalin himself recognized that communism alone would not be sufficient to defeat the Germans. Significantly, on 9 October 1942 he actually reduced the role of communist supervision within the Red Army hierarchy, downgrading the authority of the political officer – the commissar – who was previously required to approve the decisions of military commanders.

In Stalingrad, the NKVD took soundings over soldiers' responses to these changes. Most were pleased it had taken place. 'All military men support this decision', said one officer, 'there must only be one chain of command within the army.' A soldier's response was more forthright: 'I don't see the need for commissars at Stalingrad – they do nothing for us here – they have no military training.' Towards the end of the battle Sergei Zacharov, a tough street fighter with Batyuk's division, was asked by Chuikov to run instruction courses for the political officers within the army:

> I met with Chuikov several times a week. He wanted the courses to
> be like a smithy, to transform political officers into real soldiers. And

he was frank with me, saying simply 'No one is going to listen to those guys until they learn how to fight properly.'

'Sniperism' was not forged by a political ideology, however powerful. It arose viscerally, from a shared hatred of the foe. As Mark Slavin, a fighter in the Red October Factory, recalled:

> I never heard anyone yell 'For Stalin!' as they went into the attack. But I did find a burning desire to kill Fascists, and the sniper movement grew out of this. The majority of our soldiers may not have been well-educated, but they had such strong anger. In the summer of 1942 the Germans had humiliated us, and humiliated our country. Now we wanted revenge.

Zaitsev's Duel

In December1942, towards the end of the battle, Zaitsev was interviewed by Red Army reporters about his career as a sniper. He took this opportunity to pay tribute to Kalentiev: 'The sniper Kalentiev taught me. I went around with him for three days, closely observing his actions, and seeing how he worked with a sniper rifle. Then I went out and set up a stakeout myself.'

Nearly thirty year later, Zaitsev's memoirs *Notes of a Sniper* came out. The book had a huge impact, inspiring one of the most popular novels about the battle, David Robbins's *War of the Rats*, and the well-known film *The Enemy at the Gates*. But the communist authorities had heavily edited the text. Zaitsev became the initiator of the sniping movement, but within it Kalentiev was permitted a cameo appearance. Zaitsev must have been reluctant to disown his mentor entirely. So in the revised version of events, Zaitsev set up his sniping school, and its recruits were meeting one evening when a distinguished newcomer appeared:

> One of our number, a newcomer to Stalingrad named Sasha Kalentiev, was the most talented sniper amongst us. We treated him with the utmost respect, as we knew he was a graduate of the Moscow Sniper School and that he had a deep understanding of the rules of shooting with a sniper's rifle and telescopic lens. Once he opened up his knapsack, tossed out bullets, a grenade, and a dirty rag, and pulled forth a tiny folder in a leather cover. He opened up

the folder and read aloud a passage, which I immediately copied into
my notebook.

It is interesting to witness Kalentiev's metamorphosis from an illiterate
peasant hunter, with a few shooting lessons under his belt, to a formidable
instructor from the Moscow Sniper School. Strikingly, it echoes another transformation made in the same memoirs, when Zaitsev's German opponent in the
famous duel becomes the head of Berlin's Sniper School.

In his 1942 Red Army interview Zaitsev made no mention of such an eminent
protagonist. But he did describe an encounter with a German sniper. Some
enemy machine gunners were established on the Mamaev Kurgan and two
snipers from Zaitsev's group were sent to pick them off. They returned badly
wounded. A German sniper was believed to be positioned on the hill, and
Zaitsev and two more snipers were sent to flush him out:

> We hid ourselves in a trench. As soon as I lifted up a helmet, the
> Fritz hit it and the helmet fell. I realized that I was dealing with a
> skilled German sniper. We needed to find out where he was located.
> It was very difficult thing to do, because if anyone peeped out, the
> Fritz would kill him. We needed to deceive him – to find a way of
> outwitting him.
>
> I hunted him for about five hours. Finally, I figured out a method:
> I took a mitten off my hand, put it on a piece of wood and thrust it
> out of a trench. The German shot at it. I took the piece of wood
> down and looked where the mitten was pierced. By the position of
> the bullet-hole I established where the German was shooting from.

Zaitsev then waited and watched. Finally he saw his opponent. Some Russian
infantry were approaching, and the enemy sniper raised himself a little to look
at them, momentarily losing contact with his rifle. This gave Zaitsev his chance:
'I jumped out of the trench, stood up straight and shouldered the rifle. He did
not expect such audacity and was taken aback. He reached for his gun but I was
the first to fire.'

In this earlier account Zaitsev does not mention the identity of his assailant.
But he does say that a duel with a skilled opponent is the ultimate test of a
soldier's perseverance. In Zaitsev's memoirs, his teacher Kalentiev – recast as
a graduate of the Moscow Sniper School – makes much the same point:

> Every time he enters a duel, a sniper feels as if he is standing,
> balanced, on the edge of a sheer precipice. In order to hold out, and

not fall into the abyss below, three things are essential: courage, training and unshakeable presence of mind. The victor of a duel will be the one first able to conquer himself.

To embark upon a career as a sniper took deep reserves of courage. The Germans were constantly on the watch for these marksmen and one lapse of concentration could be fatal. But the 62nd Army's home-grown sniper movement had disconcerted the enemy. As in the battle as a whole, the psychological balance between the opposing forces was beginning to shift.

Chapter Nine

The Turning Point

In early October 1942 the German and Russian forces at Stalingrad readied themselves for the biggest clash of the battle. Hitler was urgently pressing the 6th Army to finish the job, and capture the whole of the city. It was becoming a matter of personal prestige for him that Stalingrad was taken. A new deadline was set for 14 October. 'Many such deadlines had already been announced, without achieving the desired result', Mereshko said, 'but this one was the most threatening. It would be the worst day for us in the entire battle.'

Chuikov confessed to Vasily Grossman: 'The [international] press was mocking Hitler [about his failure to take Stalingrad], and we were terrified. We were sitting there, knowing, feeling, realizing that Hitler had now sent his main force against us.' He later recollected simply: 'Those of us who had already been through a great deal will remember this enemy attack all our lives.' The 14th, and the two days which followed it, represented the critical point of the struggle.

The official version of the period 14–17 October is that Stalingrad's defence remained resolute in the face of devastating enemy pressure. Chuikov himself is at pains to say that, despite the terrible fighting and the proximity of the Germans to his HQ, 'we had no thought of withdrawing'. For personal and political reasons this became the accepted truth. Yet the reality – as on the earlier critical day of 14 September – was far darker. Only by understanding this darkness can we make real sense of the battle.

'These three days were utterly exceptional – even by Stalingrad's standards', said Mereshko. 'Only on 17 October did things get back to normal.' And Chuikov himself made a telling comment. 'After surviving those vital few days', he said 'we knew that our army would remain on the right bank of the Volga.' Chuikov was hinting at a crisis for the defenders, although he chose not to disclose the details of it. For the first time, it is now possible to reveal what really happened.

In his preparations for the biggest German attack on the city, Paulus persisted with a methodical approach. As a vital preliminary to the assault, he set about reducing the Orlovka salient – the gateway for a major attack on Stalingrad's northernmost bastion, the Tractor Factory.

Defending the Orlovka Salient

The defence of the Orlovka salient remains a largely unnoticed episode of the Stalingrad battle – it does not even get a mention in Antony Beevor's book. But holding the salient was of far greater military significance to the defenders than many of the oft-repeated episodes of city fighting. It is a story of remarkable resilience and heroism.

The Orlovka salient formed a 'nose', a promontory of land jutting out from the Russian position in Stalingrad and protruding 5 miles into German lines south-west of the suburb of Spartanovka, held by Gorokhov's group. The salient was only 2 miles wide, and surrounded on three sides by German divisions. But it played a vital role in Stalingrad's defence. In August 1942 it had delayed an assault on the city. In September, it prevented the Germans from committing all their forces to the attack. For as long as the Russians held Orlovka, there remained a risk that the armies of the neighbouring Stalingrad Front might break through the Germans' northern land corridor to the Volga and link up with these isolated units. As historian John Erickson put it: 'This was the salient the Stalingrad Front had tried to reach all September – if the left wing of their forces and the Chuikov's right ever connected the whole German flank would be imperilled.'

Chuikov understood how vital the salient was, and resolved to cling on to it, come what may, seeing that it 'hung like a sword of Damocles over the head of the main enemy group'. Its defenders also protected the river gullies of the Mechetka and Orlovka, which flowed into the Volga north of the Stalingrad Tractor Factory, thus blocking a tempting avenue for German infiltration and attack.

Chuikov placed the defence of Orlovka under the authority of Gorokhov's group and fed in supplies and reinforcements. The salient was held by Colonel Andryushenko's 115th Brigade and Vladimir Turov was now a battalion commander in this small Russian force. The latter emphasized:

> These were very different fighting conditions. We were not sheltering in the ruined city landscape, but out in the open, with scant cover for our soldiers – there was a complete lack of bunkers or concrete emplacements – and we had to seek protection from the might of German air power in any natural features we could find, such as ravines or gullies. But our task was crucial – to divert the enemy from launching a full-scale assault on northern Stalingrad.

The fighting at Orlovka was savage. Turov recalled one particularly horrifying episode in mid–September 1942:

> I saw a man running towards me, covered in mud and blood and without his gun. He was gulping, trying to speak, but the only sounds coming out were strange animal noises. He came closer and I recognized him. It was Senior Lieutenant Alexandrov – our oldest combatant – over 50 years old. He had been a teacher before the war and had insisted on joining up – he had wanted to do something for his country.

Turov continued:

> Slowly, Alexandrov began to find words again. At first, he just kept saying 'The Germans are here! The Germans are here!' It made no sense. But slowly, his story emerged. German infantry stormed his position in a surprise attack and a desperate hand-to-hand fight broke out. Alexandrov had never fought like that in his life. But when a young, tough German officer leapt into his trench – just a few feet away – and bayoneted a nurse standing next to him, it jolted him into a frenzied response. He clawed and tore at the German, knocking him off balance, and then sunk his teeth into his neck, severing the artery. Alexandrov was left splattered in blood. In a deep state of shock, he wandered off, utterly disorientated. He had temporarily lost the power of speech.

German pressure was relentless. Every day, their aviation and artillery struck hard at the Russian defences, then their tanks and infantry rolled into action. 'Our forces were dwindling away', Turov remembered.

> We got reinforcements, but never enough. Once Chuikov sent me another 400 soldiers, but when I put them along my front line, there were still gaps of 20–30 metres between my troops. We only had twenty heavy machine guns between us and three anti-tank guns. I was close to our observation post when the Germans launched their next attack. I saw a mass of tanks, and infantry following behind. I didn't think we could hold out – my battalion simply wasn't strong enough. But I realized my soldiers were feeling the same thing – and were watching my reaction intently.
>
> I have never felt the responsibilities of command so keenly. I had

Shell and bullet holes in a telegraph pole opposite the central Railway Station – preserved as a memorial to the fighting there.

The bullet-pocked walls of the 'Nail Factory' in central Stalingrad.

This statue of Vasily Chuikov, the commander of the 62nd Army, fittingly stands defiant on the Volga embankment. It was made by his son Alexander.

The Mill – the stronghold seized by the 13th Guards on 14 September 1942 and held throughout the battle.

Above and left: Relics of the 13th Guards' last defence line on the Volga embankment.

The Mamaev Kurgan – showing the Mother Victory statue and the modern church.

A monument to the fighting: the 'ruined walls' on the Mamaev Kurgan. The tableau shows soldiers swearing an oath before a military standard. Inscribed underneath are the words: 'There is no land for us beyond the Volga'.

This building – in the workers' settlement of the Tractor factory – was used for defence by the 37th Guards on 14 October 1942. The repairs to the brickwork in the centre show where the gun emplacement was situated.

The forecourt of the Tractor Factory, where units of the 112th Division made their last desperate stand on 14 October.

The 'Gully of Death' – which ran down to the Volga between the Red October and Barrikady Factories. In late October and November 1942 German snipers held the key vantage points overlooking the gully.

A Stalingrad time capsule: the steel processing laboratory in the Red October Factory, preserved exactly as it was during the battle.

The plaque honours the men of the 253rd (Tarachansky) Regiment of the 45th Division, who defended the laboratory.

The ruined command post of Lyudnikov's 138th Division, behind the Barrikady factory.

This tank turret, mounted on a pedestal (one of seventeen throughout the city) marks the last defence line of Stalingrad's defenders.

Red Army weaponry on display at the Volgograd Defence Museum.

The HQ of the 64th Army at Beketovka – where Paulus formally surrendered to General Shumilov.

The author and Colonel-General Mereshko at the Museum of the Great Patriotic War, Moscow.

been rolling a cigarette. Now the Germans were advancing, but I had a sudden, powerful realization – I must not show the slightest sign of panic or haste. So I paused, quite deliberately took a few moments to finish my cigarette, and then lit it. In that moment, I regained the resolve to withstand the enemy – and my men felt it too. I spoke quietly but with real conviction: 'Prepare for tank attack – spread the word, right and left.' All around me I heard a sea of voices passing my command on – becoming louder and more determined, like a wave of pride passing down the line. Hope had returned to us. It was like a voice, saying: 'We can do it!'

As the Germans approached we opened up on them with everything we had. The first tank burst into flames, the second wheeled to the side, but was also hit. We hadn't the ammunition to keep up an intense barrage for long but the enemy was disconcerted, and began to pull back. Somehow, we had managed to survive another day.

The exposed position of the Orlovka salient made it hard to get supplies and reinforcements through to the troops. On 19 September Gorokhov ordered Evgeny Kurapatov to set out from Spartanovka with a relief convoy for the beleaguered defenders. Kurapatov recalled:

Gorokhov was worried that we would not be able to hold Orlovka, but we had so little to give those guys. My division – the 196th – was stationed in Spartanovka, but we were reduced to a couple of hundred men, and we only had one supply vehicle left. Nevertheless, Gorokhov wanted to help them, to get food and ammunition through, and to evacuate the wounded. As we set out, German aircraft spotted us and began circling our column. They started a 'merry-go-round' of bombing, one plane coming in after another. I didn't think we would survive another hour. But all of us just had one thought – we didn't want to let our comrades down. We would take shelter, pushed forward a bit, then take shelter again. We suffered terrible casualties on that slow, interrupted journey but we refused to give up. I think we finally reached Orlovka through sheer will power.

Conditions in the salient were atrocious. 'We never had enough food for our men', Turov said.

When I heard a rumour that field kitchens had at last arrived in Orlovka I went to investigate. It was a five kilometre walk to the settlement from our frontline positions and I was struck by the fact that there were no blocking detachments in place anywhere – there was nothing to stop people running off. Chronic shortage of supplies had caused some Red Army units to desert their posts – but our guys stayed and fought.

For Turov, the will to resist came from a new spirit of leadership within the army.

When Chuikov took command a guiding principle spread amongst us: there should no longer be a divide between commanders and ordinary soldiers. As a result, we shared our food together, and slept in the same trenches and dug outs. Battalion and even regimental commanders stayed in the line and fought with their men. Our rule became: every man is equal to another. It changed the mood amongst our soldiers. Once, when my men were overrun by the enemy, and small groups were fighting on in encirclement, Andryushenko personally came with reinforcements and restored the situation. He fought his way through and rescued us. Actions like this created an atmosphere of extraordinary trust – and in return, no one wanted to let their commanders down.

A simple yet powerful idea took root amongst Orlovka's defenders. 'We felt a moral obligation to stay and fight', said Turov. 'We were not forced to do this. The Germans were daunting opponents – and their army was exceptionally disciplined and well-trained. But they were occupying our land.'

The resolve to stand firm against the enemy was cemented in one, defining moment. 'To be honest, at first we were uncomfortable with the recruits we had received from Central Asia', Turov continued.

We did not feel we could rely on them in the stress of combat. It was no fault of their own, but they were poorly trained and spoke little Russian. I had some Tartars in my battalion. They were just teenagers – and they seemed even younger than that. I didn't know what to do with them. Once I saw them sharing their bread together – it was so touching, they were like little children. But we were up against the Germans!

Then something remarkable happened. 'I was with Andryushenko when a young kid from Kazakhstan came to make his report', Turov recalled.

> He was a teenager who could only speak a few words of Russian. He was an anti-tank gunner but his gun now lay smashed and the rest of the unit had been killed. Badly wounded, with both his legs broken, he had nevertheless crawled to the command post. He struggled to find the correct words, gesturing to us with his hands, but there was no mistaking the pride in his voice – even in the terrible state he was in. He managed to tell us that he had destroyed three German tanks. Then he died, right in front of us.
>
> For a few moments there was an absolute silence. Men were so moved they were left stunned, and unable to speak. But within a few hours our whole defending force knew about that kid from Kazakhstan. Our Russian fighters now put aside their prejudices. Every soldier amongst us wanted to honour his memory. It was as if a silent, shared promise had manifested itself: we would not let the Germans through.

Paulus brought overwhelming force to bear in a bid to finally crush the Orlovka salient. He surrounded the defenders with several German divisions. On 1 October the remnants of Andryushenko's brigade were completely encircled. The position was utterly hopeless. There were only 500 soldiers left – and they were desperately short of ammunition. But these men fought on for another week, tying down a strong enemy group of Panzers and infantry at a vital moment of the battle.

Mereshko paid tribute to the surrounded force:

> The Fascists attacked Andryushenko from the north, west and south. They had a huge advantage in tanks and infantry – and almost total air superiority. The fighting was particularly bloody. Paulus launched his assault on 29 September, expecting to destroy the salient quickly and then deploy his forces against the Tractor Factory. If he had done so – before we were able to bring reinforcements in – I don't think our line could have held. But that small group of defenders in Orlovka managed to resist for nearly ten days, preventing the enemy from reaching the Tractor Factory until 7 October. By then, we had a fresh division – Zholudev's 37th Guards – in place to meet them. At this critical juncture, the heroism of Andryushenko's brigade saved the rest of us.

A few of Andryushenko's fighters finally broke out of encirclement and got back to Spartanovka. Overwhelming German force had failed – against all probability – to bring about the expected result.

The Balance of Forces

The bravery of Andryushenko and his men bought Chuikov precious time. 'Paulus paid dearly for his plan to destroy the salient in one blow', the 62nd Army's commander commented with grim satisfaction. Nevertheless, on 3 October 1942 the Soviet newspaper *Red Star* warned:

> The enemy is bringing up more reinforcements to Stalingrad and his pressure is increasing daily. The most decisive stage in the battle has been reached. Our men must hold out until the end; for there is nowhere left to retreat.

The motto at the head of the paper was a quotation from the Russian general Alexander Suvorov: 'In war, do what the enemy regards as impossible.'

The tough fighting on both sides raised awareness amongst the soldiers of what was at stake. On 10 October First Lieutenant K H Schumacher wrote back to Germany, commiserating with the widow of a recently killed soldier from his battalion:

> Here before Stalingrad the fighting has become especially hard. But we are all convinced of the necessity of this fight and we all know there is no freedom for our people as long as Bolshevism is not buried into the ground.

On 12 October Red Army artilleryman Nikolai Danilov wrote to his sweetheart, Maria:

> The fighting here is much fiercer than before. But I think that the complete defeat of the Germans will be in this place . . . Everyday we are draining the life force of the enemy. Yesterday I walked along the frontline, trying to figure out how things are going. I have wonderful guys with me – they fight so bravely. We all want to hold on to this city of Stalingrad – it is so special to us.

The Germans were now paying Stalingrad's defenders a grim compliment. Their earlier efforts to take the city had failed. The initial assault on 14

September had been frustrated. Further attacks, in greater strength, on 22 and 27 September, had pushed the Russians back, but had not been decisive. Over the following days, they had been faced by a determination and will to resist that they had not anticipated. So now they would throw all their power against it. Hans Mirocinszki, a soldier in the 6th Army's 295th Division, said revealingly: 'For the first time the Russians commanded our respect. Their position in September had appeared hopeless – but they had really pulled themselves together.'

In broader strategic terms, the Germans were now forced to take a considerable risk. By pulling so many of their troops out of the flanking positions on the Don and Kalmyk steppe they left themselves vulnerable to counter-attack. The most able Wehrmacht commander, Manstein, highlighted the dangers of their position – they were relying too much on the weaker armies of their allies:

> The principal striking force of Army group B – 4th Panzer and 6th Armies – was now tied down in the fighting in and around Stalingrad. The job of protecting the deep northern flank of this group along the Don was left to the 3rd Romanian Army, one Italian and one Hungarian army. Hitler must have known that even behind the Don the allied armies could not stand up to strong Soviet attack. The same was true of the 4th Romanian Army, which he had entrusted with the task of guarding the open right flank of the 4th Panzer Army [to the south].

Time was now of the essence. As Manstein emphasized, an attempt to take Stalingrad in a set battle – with such weak, overextended flanks – was 'only admissible on a very short-term basis'. Paulus had to finish things off fast – and then pull his Panzer divisions back as a mobile reserve. All now hinged on whether the defenders could continue to hold out.

Paulus began to deploy his troops for his greatest assault yet on the city. Chuikov reckoned he would be faced with nine German divisions, with a total strength of over 90,000 men, supported by over 2,000 guns and mortars, and more than 300 tanks. His own army had been reinforced at the beginning of October. General Guriev's 39th Guards had moved behind Smekhotvorov's shattered 193rd Division in the Red October Factory, Gurtiev's 308th Division had moved into the Barrikady Factory and Zholudev's 37th Guards now occupied the Tractor Factory. But these divisions had been depleted by the fighting in the first week of October – leaving Chuikov unsure whether he had enough men to withstand a new onslaught.

The overall strength of the 62nd Army at this critical juncture is usually given at around 50,000 men and 80 tanks, giving the Germans close to a 2:1 advantage in combat infantry and 4:1 in tanks. In reality, the position of the defenders was much worse. 'The numbers given for the strength of our army at this stage of the battle are misleadingly inflated', said Mereshko. 'When Paulus made his biggest attack on us, in the middle of October, he had between five and six times as many infantry and twelve times as many tanks.'

Many of the 'new' divisions reaching Chuikov were undermanned. Guriev's 39th Guards reached Stalingrad on 1 October with only 3,800 men, the third of the size of a full division, and Gurtiev's 308th had even fewer soldiers. The forces of the army's 23rd Armoured Brigade – recorded as eighty-one tanks – had in fact dwindled down to thirteen operable tanks and a further eight which could be hulled down and used as firing points. When a reinforcement brigade – the 84th – was ferried across the Volga it was found that all its heavy tanks, including its T-34s, were too large for the river barges and had to be left on the far side of the bank. And then there was German air superiority – which Chuikov aptly described as the enemy's 'unbeatable trump card in attack'.

More forces should have been made available to the 62nd Army. The Stalingrad Front was carefully husbanding divisions and supplies for a hoped-for counter-offensive later in November. But, as Chuikov repeatedly stressed in private conversation, 'If the Germans were able, at this stage, to break through and push the city's defenders into the Volga, there would be no counter-offensive. The psychological effect of losing Stalingrad would be catastrophic.'

Military historian Stephen Walsh, in his *Stalingrad: The Infernal Cauldron*, gave a powerful summary of the situation:

> On 14 October 1942 Hitler halted all German operations elsewhere on the eastern front. Stalingrad was now the objective by which success or failure in the 1942 campaign was to be judged . . . Paulus knew he had to break the will of Chuikov's army, while Hitler believed – because he had to – that defeat at Stalingrad would destroy the spirit of the Soviet Union. The 6th Army was about to make a supreme effort, one that would take it and Chuikov's 62nd Army to the limits of human endurance.

Zholudev's Redoubt

General Viktor Zholudev's 37th Guards held a special place in the Russian defence line. They were a tough division of paratroopers, confident, immaculately kitted out and possessing a remarkable *esprit de corps*. Mereshko said:

> Visiting Zholudev's HQ in the Tractor Factory was an extraordinary experience. Nothing was ever easy at Stalingrad – but it was incredibly difficult to reach that spot: it was like a redoubt, right on the very edge of our defences. Zholudev was a charismatic commander. He was relatively young for a general – about 35 years old – a tall guy, slim, handsome and very brave. He was always calm – and really commanded his men's respect. His soldiers stood out – neat, well-presented, wearing their paratrooper's knives on their belts. I remember Zholudev's had a black, inlaid handle. His division made a big impression straightaway. We realized these soldiers would be really important to us.

The 37th Guards showed urgency and focus from the start. When troops of its 109th Regiment reached Stalingrad, late on the evening of 3 October, they were ahead of schedule. Chuikov, Krylov and Gurov came down to the Volga embankment to watch them landing. Amidst the rush of activity, one of the battalion commanders, Captain Tkachenko, looked up in irritation. 'What are you guys hanging around for – what do you need?' One of the group responded immediately: 'I am Commander Chuikov. Which division are you – 37th Guards?' 'Yes, yes, 37th Paratroopers', Tkachenko replied, still resenting the interruption. Chuikov, Krylov and Gurov exchanged glances, and burst out laughing. 'Paratroopers – is that how you got here so fast – have you been flown in by plane?' Gurov joked. Tkachenko stood on his dignity. 'We did fly, but on our feet, marching fast to repulse the enemy.' Gurov stepped up to him. 'Good lads', he said warmly, 'good lads', and shook the captain's hand.

For a few minutes the commander of the 62nd Army watched the boats being unloaded on the shoreline. Then Chuikov drew Tkachenko aside. 'Why do you have so little infantry?' he asked with concern. 'Don't worry, Comrade Commander', Tkachenko said, 'we have loaded the boats with ammunition and supplies – the infantry are crossing the pontoon bridge.' The 37th Guards were using the alternative Volga ferry point – known as the 62nd crossing – which had its landing stage behind the Red October Factory. It was supplemented by a pontoon bridge which ran across the river at Zaitsevski Island. After the

Germans put the central crossing out of action it was the 62nd Army's last surviving lifeline to the eastern bank of the Volga. Chuikov stood for a moment in silence, evidently impressed. Then he smiled: 'Keep moving fast. I won't distract you any more Captain – you guys are doing great. Reinforce the defence position in the workers' settlement of the Tractor Factory.'

Vignettes like this tell us a lot about the way the 62nd Army was working. As has already been described, the day before the army command had nearly been incinerated when their HQ, situated by oil tanks behind the Red October Factory, was engulfed in a sea of flames. The Germans had spotted the command post and launched a bombing raid against it, blowing up the oil tanks – which were still half full of fuel. Chuikov said simply:

> Surrounded by fire, we stayed where we were and continued administering the army. The fire lasted several days, but we had no emergency command post – all our units, including the sappers, were out fighting; we decided, therefore, to carry on working in dug outs, trenches and shell-holes, under fire. We did not sleep.

This was absolute hell. Stalingrad Front desperately radioed through, trying to find out whether there was still an HQ in existence in the city. 'Where are you?', they kept asking. Chuikov and Krylov responded simultaneously: 'We're where the most flames and smoke are.' In the midst of this chaos, they were still administering the army, meeting with the newly arrived 37th Guards, issuing instructions and joking with the soldiers.

Soon, General Zholudev had established the 37th Guards divisional command post in the workers' settlement of the Tractor Factory. It was dangerously close to the German lines – and Chuikov and Krylov tried to persuade him to move his HQ nearer the Volga embankment. Zholudev refused. He wanted to stay close to his men.

Much now hinged on Zholudev. Alexander Rakitsky recalled:

> He was a smart guy with natural authority and his officers tried to emulate him. He never shouted or swore at people – but if something wasn't right he was always direct and would deal with it straightaway. He had a little mannerism of beckoning the culprit over and saying in a low voice 'This is wrong – we need to discuss it.' He never humiliated people in front of others – and our soldiers respected him for that – but he didn't tolerate anything less than the best. His style was restrained but incredibly powerful.

The 37th Guards were soon in action against the enemy. On 7 October – the day the Orlovka salient finally fell – they beat back a German assault on the Tractor Factory. A combination of resolute defending and accurate supporting artillery fire from the eastern bank of the Volga disrupted the enemy offensive. Factory chimneys were used as hide-outs for artillery spotters. Katyusha rockets, mounted on trucks, were brought up close to the frontline and fired at German assembly areas. One strike completely destroyed a whole battalion. Mark Ivanikin, a colonel in the 79th Katyusha regiment, described how it happened:

> Every divisional and regimental commander wanted a Katyusha unit – they were very popular with the troops. It was really dramatic seeing the rockets go off – and it lifted morale. But in October we didn't have many Katyushas in the city, and they were notoriously inaccurate. On 7 October our reconnaissance pinpointed a German battalion, waiting to go into the attack against the Tractor Factory. Our worry was that we would miss it completely. We had five separate Katyusha units aiming at it from different locations on our frontline – and fortunately one of our salvoes landed in the right place.

The following night Chuikov visited the division's HQ. Rakitsky recalled the moment:

> He wanted us to straighten out our frontline and seize some key strongholds. He encouraged us in our use of storm groups and traded tips about grenade fighting. Above all, he wanted to explain to us the idea of active defence. I can still remember what he told us: 'The enemy is trying to seize the workers' settlements and get down to the Volga between the Tractor Factory and the Barrikady, split the 62nd Army and destroy us piecemeal. Your task is to stop the Germans getting to the Volga, using methods of active defence – keep on with your counter-attacks. Make the enemy bleed. I wish you success.'

Here we see the different approaches of the two sides: the Germans were persisting with their encirclement tactics, wanting to break the enemy force into pieces, then isolate and destroy them; the Russians were adopting a more flexible response, relying on counter-attacks in small groups, trying to wear down the attackers. But although Paulus's plan was predictable, it would be carried out with enormous power. 'We knew what Paulus intended to do', Mereshko emphasized. 'The balance of forces was very disadvantageous to us. We had hoped for more reinforcements and ammunition. As things stood, we were genuinely unsure whether we had the strength to hold on.' For a few days there was an uneasy lull in Stalingrad. On 12 October Chuikov returned to Zholudev's command post, clearly worried.

Rakitsky continued:

> There was real tension in the air when Chuikov returned. He told Zholudev that according to the latest reconnaissance information Paulus was ready to throw everything into the assault: the Germans were determined to storm Stalingrad without further delay. Their main blow would be directed against the Tractor Factory. If they broke through they would roll up our front, striking south along the Volga embankment. A very strong shock group was being created for this purpose, consisting of five divisions. About 30,000 fresh German troops were arriving in Stalingrad for the offensive. Chuikov told us the blow was being prepared for 14 October. Then our commander paused, looked around at us, and spoke simply and from the heart: 'I don't have any reserves left. I've given you every-thing I can. Use engineering detachments to strengthen your defences. Your lines have to stand.'

That evening Chuikov did indeed send the 37th Guards everything he could spare. He ordered a regrouping along the whole line, dangerously weakening other sectors, to give Zholudev some sort of fighting chance. On the left flank of Zholudev's division he added one regiment (the 90th) from Gorishny's 95th Division; on the right, another (the 117th) from Guriev's 39th. Both were seriously under-strength. Scraping the barrel, the army council allowed workers' detachments from the factories to be incorporated as regular 62nd Army formations in a last-ditch effort to swell numbers. But these units were no match for German infantry and tanks.

Rakitsky remembered the flurry of preparations.

> For the next two days we worked non-stop. We all realized this was the decisive moment. Zholudev, on Chuikov's advice, pushed our frontline as close to the enemy as possible. We were laying mines, stockpiling explosives, knocking holes in buildings for our anti-tank guns. Barricades were put up on every street – with obstructions to delay the advance of tanks. All our artillery was readied to fire point blank, in close quarters fighting. And everywhere, special dug outs

were springing up. We nicknamed them 'swallow's nests' – the dug out was about 2 metres deep, and a metre wide at the top, and half a metre at the bottom. There were a couple of steps at the side. The whole idea was to enable our soldiers to jump in and out quickly – to give them some form of shelter from the expected German bombardment.

The Onslaught

Mereshko remembered:

> On the morning of 14 October it was no longer possible to see the sun, only a sad brown circlet, peeping through the clouds. Spumes of earth, fire and smoke rose up around us. It was not possible to hear the sound of individual shooting anymore – there was just a rolling, thunderous wall of noise. Sitting in one's trench – in the midst of this uproar – you felt that no one could be left alive, either around you or behind you, that everything was being consumed in this terrible bombardment.

First the enemy's aircraft bombed the Russian positions – in sortie after sortie – then their artillery and mortars found their range. 'It was a sunny day', Chuikov recalled, 'but the smoke and dust cut visibility down to a hundred yards. Our dug outs shook and caved in like a house of cards.'

This would be the battle's ultimate testing ground. John Erickson described the day's awesome beginning:

> That assault, bringing with it the most stupendous surge of fighting which Stalingrad would ever see, opened at 8.00 a.m. on Monday, 14 October 1942: five German divisions, three infantry and two Panzer, 300 tanks with mighty air support, moved off in one great wall of steel and fire to overrun the factory districts, to break through to the Volga in strength and to blot out the Soviet 62nd Army once and for all.

Rakitsky said:

> I remember the atmosphere in the divisional HQ. Our preparations had been going on all through the night. Soldiers were gathering

different types of grenades, piling up Molotov cocktails, and sharpening their knives. Zholudev spoke to us: 'We've pushed up our frontline close to the enemy – about 150 metres from their positions. But this is going to be very hot – we have to get even closer. We have prepared advance positions – about 50 metres from the Germans. When the bombardment starts I am going to order our regiments forward again. At that distance they won't bomb or shell us for fear of hitting their own troops. We have to protect our guys.'

This was Chuikov's tactical innovation – to get his troops as close to the Germans as possible. 'Our principle was to put our claws in the throat of the enemy', said Mereshko, 'and hold them close to us. That way we could stay alive.' But when the bombing started, the Germans employed improved tactics of their own, upping the ante. Their planes now undertook precision bombing of Russian targets with deadly power and accuracy. Major Hozzel, commander of the Stukas – the feared German dive bombers – described their new approach:

We had to do precision bombing to avoid danger to our troops entrenched too close to the target area. We could not risk making a dive-bombing attack from 4,000 metres because of the wide area of [bomb] dispersion. We had to fly a slant range attack, releasing the bombs directly over the roofs. We had to push the bombs into the target like loaves of bread into the oven, with one plane succeeding the other.

The Germans employed special, heavy bombs fitted with tank-busting heads and delayed action fuses, to penetrate roofs of buildings or bunkers. Hozzel described their impact: 'As on a string of pearls, one plane followed the others within an interval of a few seconds, throwing the bombs on the oblong target area divided amongst us. Not one missed its target.'

These new tactics proved very effective. Mereshko said:

The German bombing in the factories was absolutely devastating. Everything more than 100 metres from the frontline was blasted to smithereens. It brought terrible chaos to our positions – bricks, girders, pieces of locomotive track were littered everywhere.

After one and a half hours of terrible bombardment the German tanks and infantry prepared to move forward. 'Shortly before 8.00 a.m. we got a phone call from Army HQ', Rakitsky remembered. 'It was Mereshko on the line. He warned us that the enemy were massing close to our positions, and an attack was imminent.'

In the midst of this horror, there was an extraordinary determination to resist the enemy. 'Rocks were exploding because of the heat of the bombardment', Rakitsky continued.

> Iron was melting. Fire and death were all around us. The Germans didn't believe anyone could survive. But when the enemy advanced, our men clambered out of their dug outs and shelters, throwing Molotov cocktails and shooting from their 'swallow's nests'.

It was a remarkable moment. Communication along the frontline was down – telephone cable had disintegrated and radio transmitters did not work because of constant shaking from explosions. But quite spontaneously, everyone who remained alive fought back ferociously. 'It seemed as if our defences had been destroyed', Mereshko added, 'but the moment their tanks and infantry moved forward, every stone, every ruin and every gully came alive. The terrible fight for the Tractor Factory had started.'

Hozzel was shocked – his bombers had pulverized the Russian lines, yet the advancing German infantry was confronted by 'fierce counter-attacks as though nothing had happened; as if we had dropped toy torpedoes instead of bombs'. The first assault was beaten off.

The Germans regrouped, and then, shortly before 10.00 a.m., they attacked again. Heavy artillery was brought in. 'They were pushing, pushing, constantly probing our lines for weaknesses', Rakitsky remembered. Then the break-through came. Command points were overrun and infantry trenches rolled over by tanks. German machine ginners infiltrated behind the Russian positions. The force of their attack was simply too great. Regimental command posts were surrounded by the enemy. Whole units continued to fight on in encirclement.

Military historians have seen the assault of 14 October simply in terms of crude, battering-ram tactics. But the Germans had prepared a deadly finesse, targeting the key divisional command posts of the defenders, and their Army HQ, behind the frontline. This was made possible by accurate interception of Russian radio signals. Here the Germans were far ahead of their opponents in training and expertise. The 6th Army's chief signals officer, Colonel Wilhelm Arnold, had a well-equipped intercept group. 'We used high-powered receivers to search for the frequencies of the Russian transmitters', Arnold said. 'Once found, we could monitor the command channels of their army.'

Mereshko said:

We were reluctant to use radio communication for any length of time. The Germans were able track the location of our transmitters – and then direct artillery and aircraft strikes against them. But on 14 October we had no choice. The telephone cable had melted in the heat of the bombardment and the intensity of the fighting meant it was virtually impossible for communication officers to move along the line.

The defenders had prepared a back-up system to maintain contact with their scattered forces. 'The telephone link with our units has gone down', the 62nd Army war diary noted, 'so we have switched to radio.' An emergency radio service had been brought into action in the late morning, operated from the eastern side of the Volga. 'We sent our orders out by this radio', said Chuikov, 'and it retransmitted them across the Volga to the units on the western bank.' The Germans had anticipated such a moment. 'This was the first time in the battle that the enemy used one ton bombs against us', said Mereshko. 'They intended to direct them against our most important command posts.'

Shortly after midday the enemy struck. The HQ of Colonel Gurtiev's 308th Division in the Barrikady Factory came under intense, accurate fire from a German heavy, multi-barrelled mortar. The bunker completely collapsed. Thirteen or fourteen of the HQ staff were killed; Gurtiev was rescued. At 12.30 p.m. dive-bombers attacked Zholudev's command post by the stadium of the Tractor Factory.

Rakitsky described what happened:

> Our divisional command post was incredibly well-protected. It was in a narrow gully, and could only be reached through a deeply cut trench, which ran into a tunnel, 20 metres deep, that our engineers had dug. Everything was there – our communications room, my own operations department, and lower down, Zholudev's command post. It was well-camouflaged against aerial reconnaissance. But suddenly, shortly after our telephone communication went, and we had switched to radio, Stuka dive-bombers came straight for us in a precision attack. My last memory was of seeing this large bomb bouncing off the side of the gully – and then a deafening explosion.

Rakitsky was buried by the force of the blast.

After the shock, and the concussion, I came to. Fortunately, I had been wearing a helmet at the time. I had a spade close by – so did the other guy with me – and we began working our way to the surface. I could hear the sounds of digging on the other side and in half an hour we were pulled out. But Zholudev had been buried much deeper. There was a mountain of earth over his bunker. There were five of them down there and we heard sounds indicating that they were still alive. So someone found a long piece of piping and we hammered it through to get air to them. Then everyone started digging.

When Chuikov heard that Zholudev had been buried alive he sent a group from HQ staff to help in the rescue. Mereshko was one of them. 'Chuikov sent everybody he could to help – including all his security staff', he remembered. 'The Germans were already bombing our Army HQ. There was no one left to protect him if their machine gunners broke through.'

After five days and nights of hell under the burning oil refineries, Chuikov had managed to find an alternative HQ, further north, behind the Barrikady Factory. It was protected by the Volga embankment – but German artillery and bombers were now finding their range. At 1.10 p.m. the 62nd Army war diary noted: 'Two bunkers in the army command post have collapsed. One officer is stuck in a mound of earth with his legs in the air – we can dig him out.' Chuikov recalled the grim picture: 'Regimental command and observation posts were being blown up by shells and bombs. Thirty men had been killed at our Army command post. The Army HQ guard was unable to dig people out of destroyed dug outs.' The 62nd Army's ability to command and control was disintegrating. And at that moment of crisis, Chuikov sent his remaining HQ guard to the help of Zholudev.

Alexander Chuikov spoke of this terrible time:

My father would recall harrowing episodes from that day with a kind of gallows humour. The tension was virtually unbearable. On one occasion, a one ton bomb fell near his bunker. The explosion was of such force that it knocked him unconscious. When he came too, he was temporarily unable to see. He sensed he was partially buried in earth, and could smell smoke everywhere. His first thought was 'I am alive!' His second was 'Somewhere nearby there is a bottle of vodka.' He began to feel around for it. Suddenly, he heard a voice. 'What are you looking for?' It was Krylov. 'Oh, just something.' 'You are looking for the vodka', Krylov persisted. 'Well . . . yes.' 'Don't bother', his chief of staff replied, 'I've just finished it.'

Shortly after 3.00 p.m. Zholudev, his commissar, Scherbina, and the divison's political officer were hauled out. Rakitsky remembered:

> It was amazing to see them come out alive. I knew Scherbina quite well – and asked him how it had been. Scherbina had a great sense of humour and he always tried to keep people's spirits up. But it was quite a challenge for him down there, half-buried and surrounded by rubble. Zholudev had begun to lose heart. 'I never expected to die like this', he said, 'buried in my own bunker.' Scherbina tried to rally his spirits. 'It's not the time for burial – we will keep on fighting.' The rejoinder fell flat. Then Scherbina had a happy stroke of inspiration. He rounded on the hapless political officer. 'You should be happy. We've been trying to avoid your fucking lectures for the last two weeks. Now you've got a captive audience.' We all burst out laughing. 'And at that moment', Scherbina said, 'we decided we mustn't suffocate – we resolved to hold on. And we began to sing:
>
> > It's a lovely thing, my brothers,
> > To live the life we've had.
> > And when our general's with us
> > There's no reason to be sad.'
>
> It was the sound of singing that made us realize they were still alive down there.

The moment of exhilaration, as Zholudev and his comrades were retrieved from the collapsed bunker, was short-lived. Rakitsky continued:

> I had been talking to Scherbina for a few minutes when we heard the rattle of machine gun fire. A couple of Germans appeared on the top of the gully. The enemy was coming to finish us off. There was pandemonium – with the wounded crawling behind bushes for shelter, and guys scrabbling up the side of the gully to deal with the intruders. We heard a warning shout: 'More of them are coming!' Zholudev – still partially concussed – called me over. 'Rakitsky', he said, 'take Sutyerin [the chief of staff], form up an assault group, and deal with this. You have to wipe them out.'

It was 3.25 p.m. A small force was gathered from divisional staff and the Army HQ security guard. 'We got to the top of the gully just in time', said Rakitsky.

The Germans were only 30 metres away. There were three groups of them – about twenty in the centre, five each on the flanks. Sutyerin quickly commanded us 'Shoot on the move – forward Guards!' We concentrated all our fire on the flanks – then rushed the centre group, colliding with them at speed. I remember Sutyerin, next to me, grabbing a rifle from a soldier, bayoneting a German, and throwing him over his back. There was a ferocious fight, but we managed to finish them off.

Sutyerin had been badly wounded. 'He was carried back to the gully and our medical staff tried to save him', Rakitsky remembered, 'but it was no use. As he lay dying, it was as if he had been transported somewhere else. "Comrades", he said in a quiet voice, "I wish you happiness."'

There was no longer any effective co-ordination of the defence. After Zholudev was buried, and his communication equipment knocked out, Army HQ attempted to reach the scattered units of his division – but it was a near hopeless task. One phone line was briefly reconnected, allowing Chuikov to make contact with one of the surrounded regiments. It had lost its commander – but it was still fighting on. Chuikov reached the officer now in charge. The army commander spoke slowly, carefully emphasizing his words. He knew there were no reserves left and he could not offer any help. But he wanted to reach out to his men. His simple message of encouragement was not forgotten: 'You held their attack. You commanded the regiment through hellish, unheard-of conditions. Thank you, my friend. I embrace you. And I wish you luck.'

Those soldiers not surrounded now fell back towards the forecourt of the Tractor Works. They had not received any orders to do so – it was a purely instinctive response. Men of the 112th Division, fighting alongside Zholudev's Guards, reassembled in front of the Factory. 'We had a few anti-tank guns left', Alexander Fortov remembered. 'We knew there was no defence line inside the Tractor Factory and the Germans would try and break through with their tanks. They had to be stopped. So we positioned our artillery right up by the factory gates.'

Soon, others joined Fortov and a last terrible stand was made. 'Our division had been reinforced', continued Fortov, 'and we were up to nearly 2,000 men, which I suppose was a luxury by Stalingrad standards, but most of those guys died outside the Tractor Factory.'

We beat off the first assault. There is one moment that I always remember. We had a little kid with us, an orphan called Vanya – we nicknamed him 'Stalingrad Gavroche' because he reminded us of Victor Hugo's street-wise urchin. Vanya did reconnaissance work for us and helped carry ammunition. In the lull in the fighting he came up to our commander, Lieutenant Ochkin, and innocently presented him with something that had caught his eye, amidst the debris of battle. It was a shiny wing mirror. It must have broken off a German tank and Vanya found it strangely beautiful. Ochkin absent-mindedly put it in his breast pocket. Our little kid died in the next attack. Ochkin was hit – but the piece of steel he was carrying deflected the bullet. That little gift saved our commander's life.

At 4.20 p.m. German tanks and machine gunners broke into the Tractor Factory.

The Council of War

The remnants of Zholudev's HQ staff regrouped around the gully. Pieces of equipment had been retrieved from some of the bunkers, and a telephone connection with Army HQ was restored. Rakitsky said:

I was sitting next to Zholudev when Chuikov got through. I remember the relief in his voice. 'How are you guys?' he asked. He and Zholudev talked for a few minutes. 'Come and report to me', Chuikov said. 'Let me check the situation first – then I'll come over', Zholudev replied. But checking the situation was no longer a straightforward task. We had no idea what was happening to our men.

'At first we got no answer from any of our regiments,' Rakitsky continued.

We had a captured German radio transmitter as one of our trophies. We now used it, moving across different frequencies, trying to make contact. I sat next to Zholudev with a map, to mark up their positions – if we could find them. We were searching for anybody – battalions, even companies – still holding out. We dispensed with coded messages, simply asking 'Where are you? Where are you?' over and over again. And then we began to get responses. The first was from the 109th Regiment. The regimental command post had been forced back to a building known as the

'Professors' House.' They were completely surrounded and the Germans had brought up tanks – everyone was fighting there. Then the 118th Regiment came in: 'We are encircled in the Bread Factory. The regimental commander is fighting in the frontline with his men.' We heard that the 114th was still fighting somewhere near the Silicate Factory. Again, the Germans had surrounded them.

The 37th Guards had suffered appalling losses. The enemy had been able to punch through their lines and there were no reserves left to plug the gaps. One weak regiment – the 524th – had been waiting in a back-up defence line; it was now engaged in hand-to-hand combat in the streets of the workers' settlement. At 5.00 p.m. a desperate counter-attack was launched from the direction of the Tractor Factory stadium to link up with these men. Only eighty soldiers could be found for it – and were unable to make any progress: they were quickly bombed and machine gunned by German planes. Enemy tanks and infantry were now inside the Tractor Factory. Zholudev's units were broken and isolated – but they still kept fighting.

Early that evening Zholudev and Rakitsky made their way to the Army HQ. Bombing and shelling continued remorselessly as they moved along the Volga. They found Chuikov housed in a makeshift dug out. Zholudev was called in; Rakitsky stood by the door – which was a simple, tarpaulin flap. He could see and hear everything – and was thus a witness to the most important army council meeting of the entire battle.

'Chuikov was sitting at a small desk', Rakitsky remembered.

> Krylov and Gurov were standing on either side of him. Chuikov called Zholudev in and asked him to report on the situation. Zholudev spread out the map, and pointed to the different locations of our troops. 'I have checked what I can', he concluded. 'Our soldiers are trained to fight in encirclement. They will continue to resist. Our rule remains – not a step back!' Chuikov looked up at him: 'What about the Tractor Factory?' he asked. 'Have the Germans got it or not?'

The Tractor Factory was divided into two parts – an upper and lower level. The Germans had smashed the desperate resistance by the factory gates, then rushed the upper level. 'The enemy are inside it', Zholudev responded. 'Fighting is still going on.' But there were just a few small Russian units inside the factory – a handful of men from the 524th Regiment, a small NKVD group, and an under-strength workers' battalion. The Germans had pushed over a hundred tanks in, followed by their infantry, and their force was driving forward, supported by low-level Stuka bombing. It was clear that they would reach the Volga and split the 62nd Army in two.

Zholudev finished his report and there was silence for a few moments. His soldiers had fought with astonishing bravery – but the odds against them were simply too great. The 37th Division had been overwhelmed by the might of the German onslaught. Yet still its men were resisting. 'You could almost touch the emotion in the room', Rakitsky recalled.

> Then Gurov could no longer contain himself. Deeply moved, he came over and hugged Zholudev. 'Good guys, good guys', he kept repeating. 'One division against five – you know the whole army is talking about it.' Suddenly, Chuikov rose from the table. He pushed Krylov and Gurov to one side, and embraced Zholudev. 'I really believed in your division', he said. 'I knew you would be great.'

Then news came through confirming what everybody had feared. The 62nd Army war diary recorded bluntly: 'The enemy has reached the Volga near the Tractor Factory. The army front is split.' Everyone gathered around the map of the city. 'What do you think the Germans will do next?' Chuikov asked. Zholudev pointed at the suburb of Spartanovka. 'I think they will send some of their force north, along the Volga – they know our guys are weak in numbers there. They will hope to wipe out Gorokhov's group. But they will push the majority of their troops south, to break through into the Barrikady Factory.' Chuikov listened attentively. 'I imagine they will use two Panzer divisions – the 16th and 24th – supported by the infantry of the 305th. They will try to finish us off.'

Chuikov glanced at Zholudev. 'You are right – good thinking', he said. 'We have to stop them getting into the Barrikady.' He turned to Krylov. 'Can we form up a defence line anywhere?' Krylov studied the map closely, and then pointed to a railway siding between the two factories. 'If the Germans continue their attack tonight there will be no time to dig trenches', he said. 'We could pull a line of railway carriages across and try to gather some troops around it. That's all we can do.'

These makeshift measures would not withstand a major German offensive. At 9.00 p.m. there was a sudden crescendo of noise. An artillery barrage began, followed by bombing. The enemy was resuming his assault. Chuikov looked round at everybody. 'Do you think they will bring a new division in?' Paulus had a fresh division, the 79th, which he had not yet committed to the attack. The 62nd Army had nothing left to stop it with.

'Suddenly, we felt total despair', Rakitsky remembered.

> We couldn't see how we could hold on anymore. Most of our surviving 37th Guards were in encirclement. We had a small composite battalion fighting the Germans in the lower Tractor Factory. That was it. There were no reserves. And our whole line was under intense pressure – if we tried to withdraw anybody, it would buckle, and the enemy would break through somewhere else. The most Chuikov and Krylov had at their disposal was a small, under-strength battalion of marines. It was hopeless.

Chuikov turned to Zholudev. 'I ask you', he said simply, 'please, please try to create some form of defence line. Don't let them get into the Barrikady. I will send you everything I can.' Something struck Rakitsky about this appeal. 'Chuikov was now using the personal form of "you"', he recalled. 'It was as if he was no longer speaking as an army commander, but as a brother, and a friend.' Zholudev moved towards the door. 'I will take a machine gun and go and organize it myself', he replied. He even managed a joke. 'I'm a tall guy', he added, 'so naturally people will gather around me.' Chuikov looked surprised, then he stepped forward and hugged and kissed Zholudev. 'I believe you', he said, laughing. 'Amidst all our despondency', recalled Rakitsky, 'it was a wonderful moment.'

But after Zholudev and Rakitsky left, things deteriorated further. 'We heard bad news about our regiments', Rakitsky said.

> We had hoped that some of these guys might have been able to break out of encirclement, under the cover of darkness, and join with us. But they were on the point of being overwhelmed by the enemy. And apparently the marine battalion was not responding to the orders of Army HQ. We couldn't get a defence line together.

The 62nd Army war diary recorded a last, fleeting contact made with Zholudev's regiments, shortly after 9.00 p.m. The 118th was making a stand in a school building. It was fighting twelve enemy tanks and several companies of infantry and only twenty of its people were left. The Germans had broken into the command post of the 109th and its HQ staff was engaged in hand-to hand combat. The 114th could no longer be found. The diary concluded: 'The bombing has not stopped at nightfall. The enemy is introducing new forces and developing his offensive to the south. Our frontline and rear positions are under continuous bombing and artillery bombardment.'

There was now a crisis of command – which has remained hidden in all accounts of the battle. It was an axiom of Stalingrad's defence that Chuikov stayed on the western bank of the Volga: the presence of his HQ there was vital proof that the army would stand and resist. As veteran Anatoly Kozlov put it: 'It was forbidden to cross the Volga without permission because staying on the western bank became symbolic of a will to defend the city. To cross to the far bank meant to surrender.'

This point was so sensitive that on one occasion Chuikov even refused to cross the river – with his HQ smouldering under the burning oil containers – for a much needed bath and change of clothes: 'The temptation was very great, but I refused', Chuikov said. 'What would the soldiers think, seeing the army commander going across to the eastern bank at such a difficult moment?'

But now the cumulative strain may have told. 'We were living by the hour, by the minute', Chuikov told Vasily Grossman. He was struggling to communicate with his army and co-ordinate its defence in truly desperate conditions. Chuikov confided in Grossman about the sheer powerlessness he felt as a commander when signal cables were broken by shellfire and runners were cut down, and the frustration and fear which followed:

> It was the most oppressive sensation. There's firing and thunder all around. You send off a liaison officer to find out what's happening, and he gets killed. That's when you shake all over with tension . . . The most terrible times were when you sat there like an idiot, and the battle was boiling all around you, but there was nothing you could do.

At 9.40 p.m. Chuikov sent an urgent communication to the Stalingrad Front. Its remarkable contents can now be revealed:

> The army is cut in two. Our HQ is 800 metres from the enemy. Control of the fighting is only being maintained through the radio transmitter on the left [eastern] bank of the river. The telephone cables keep being cut. Our communications are breaking up. I am asking your permission to move to the emergency command post on the left [eastern] bank tonight, otherwise command [of the army] is impossible.

The request was refused, point blank: 'Resolution of the chief of staff of the HQ of the Front: the commander of the Front orders the 62nd Army's command post to remain on the western [right] bank of the Volga.'

Later that evening Chuikov received a phone call from Khrushchev. Khrushchev and Yeremenko had, of course, appointed Chuikov on the strict condition that he would defend the city or die in the attempt. Khrushchev had phoned the Army HQ once before, at another critical point in the battle, on the evening of 27 September. Now, on 14 October, according to Chuikov's account, there was a discussion about the threatening German position in the Tractor Factory – after which Khrushchev stressed once again the strategic and political importance of Stalingrad, emphasizing that it must be held at all costs. Chuikov spoke of chronic shortages in ammunition, 'and complained about the difficulty in administering the army, as telephone lines were going up in flames and radio equipment was being destroyed, together with the command posts'.

In Chuikov's written memoir, the telephone conversation ended in agreement. Khrushchev accepted that Chuikov did not have the resources to recapture the German-occupied part of the Tractor Factory, and promised to deliver more ammunition to the defenders. Interestingly, Chuikov cited the phone call as evidence that Stavka – the Soviet High Command – was worried about the Russian position in the city. Khrushchev's call was portrayed as a fact-finding mission in response to the concerns of his superiors.

Now it appears that Chuikov's dramatic request to the Stalingrad Front – asking that his HQ be transferred to the eastern bank of the Volga – was a more likely explanation for Khrushchev's phone call. The conversation may have gone in a rather different direction than that officially recorded. Given Chuikov's volatile temperament, and the amount of stress he was under, it is easy to imagine a frank exchange of views, with Khrushchev repeatedly emphasizing that the army command must stay in the city, and Chuikov emphatically repeating that rapidly deteriorating conditions made it impossible to command the army unless the HQ moved to the far bank.

At 1.00 a.m. on 15 October, the 62nd Army war diary recorded the issue of Military Order Number 205. Combat orders gave instructions to the various divisions of the army and they took a consistent form. They were always issued on the authority of the army council – Chuikov (as the 62nd Army's commander), Krylov (his chief of staff) and Gurov (the commissar). This procedure was absolutely standard. However, Order 205 was not issued on the authority of Chuikov, Krylov and Gurov, but quite exceptionally, on that of Krylov and two of his operational staff, Yeliseyev and Zalizyuk.

This was one of the most important army commands of the entire battle. It set out arrangements for a defence line to be created south of the Tractor Factory, along the railway line, and specified the individual units which would be put in place to guard it. It put all divisional commanders on full alert, ready to repulse a major German assault by 5.00 a.m. It is inconceivable that such instructions would not be released under Chuikov's authority, had he remained in command of the army.

Order 205 may well point to a remarkable, undisclosed sequence of events in which, following the phone conversation, Khrushchev and Yeremenko decided to dismiss Chuikov as commander of the 62nd Army, and replaced him with Krylov. Such a decision would mirror the fate of Chuikov's predecessor, Lopatin – who was also removed from his command during the battle by the Stalingrad Front, for attempting an unauthorized withdrawal on the grounds of military expediency (on 6 September 1942) – and again, was replaced by Krylov.

We will probably never know the full story of 14 October 1942. But at the end of the worst day in the battle of Stalingrad, with the defenders facing an all-out German assault, this new evidence strongly suggests that their inspirational commander was briefly sacked from his post.

The Day of Decision

On the morning of 15 October the Germans resumed their attack. They had three objectives: to maintain their pressure against Gorokhov's group in Spartanovka, to clear out the remainder of the Tractor Factory, and most importantly, to develop their offensive southwards, along the Volga, towards the Barrikady. Paulus was now in Stalingrad, meeting with his divisional chiefs, and personally supervising the assault.

Once again that morning, Chuikov was leading the 62nd Army. Accepting the likelihood of his dismissed only a few hours earlier, this seems an extraordinary volte-face. It may have been that Khrushchev and Yeremenko reconsidered matters in the cold light of day, and decided that the crisis point of the battle was not the best time to remove the defending commander. But another and more dramatic explanation also exists. Their decision may have been countermanded by Stalin's High Command.

On 13 October, the day before the great German offensive, Stalin was seized with alarm about the situation in Stalingrad. He took the view, rightly as it turned out, that continued resistance in the city was vital for the planned Soviet counter-offensive to stand a real chance of success. Crucially, he believed that Yeremenko was at fault for not giving Chuikov enough support, and for failing to provide him with the necessary reinforcements. John Erickson gives us the vital background:

> On this occasion he [Stalin] vented his rage on Yeremenko, whom he considered not to be properly discharging his duties; instead of giving Chuikov all the help he could, Yeremenko was holding on the eastern bank troops Stalin had specifically assigned for the defence of the city. Stalin instructed Vasilevsky to order Yeremenko 'in the name of the Stavka' [the Soviet High Command] to go in person to Chuikov's HQ, to investigate the position – the 'true position', observed at first hand – and to weigh up what help Chuikov needed to defend those parts of Stalingrad still held by Soviet troops.

Erickson adds that Yeremenko, 'prodded by Stalin', finally agreed to make this personal inspection on 15 October, although – because of the intensity of the German bombing and shelling – he did not actually cross the Volga until the night of the 16th. Vasilevsky made a revealing aside to the writer Konstantin Simonov, who was in Stalingrad at this time – one that was supportive of Chuikov and highly critical of Yeremenko:

> In that very difficult time for our defence, when Chuikov was literally clinging on to the edge – and Stalin had decided it was vital that Yeremenko personally visit Chuikov – Yeremenko spent two days trying to 'neglect' that order.

If Stalin's intervention led to the dismissal being rescinded – and Khrushchev had then to inform 62nd Army HQ of this – Chuikov's written account of their phone conversation, and their supposed 'mutual agreement', may have dealt very diplomatically indeed with an event which would have caused mayhem had it become known. Chuikov may have been understating the true nature of events to a remarkable degree with his comment: 'It was clear from the conversation that Stavka was worried about the position in the city, and was obviously asking the Front Council, and Nikita Khrushchev in particular, to clarify the situation.'

In the mean time, the position of the 62nd Army looked increasingly precarious. Fresh German forces had been introduced, and their attacks were developing along the Volga. The defence line protecting the Army HQ was extremely shaky. Rakitsky was candid about the attempt to move the marines of the 92nd Brigade – one of the army's weakest units – into position to protect the Barrikady, set out in Order 205:

We found out that the commander of the Brigade had refused to obey the order. He had to be arrested – and a political officer, Nikitin, brought in to replace him – before the marines finally moved into position. We didn't hold out much hope that these guys would stop the Germans.

Chuikov now made a second request to transfer his HQ to the eastern bank of the Volga. It is instructive to compare this with the version of events given in his memoirs of the battle. First, let us consider the 'official' version:

On October 15th the enemy threw fresh forces into the battle, and continued to press his attack northward and southward along the Volga . . . The northern group, under the command of Colonel Gorokhov, was fighting in encirclement against the enemy's superior numbers . . . Zholudev's division [the 37th], which had taken the main brunt of the attack, was split into several sections, fighting as separate garrisons in the Tractor settlement, and in the vicinity of Minusinskaya Street. Gorishny's division [the 95th] had also suffered heavy losses . . . The enemy, moving southward, was threatening to emerge in the rear of Gorishny's division and reach the Army command post. Enemy tommy-gunners infiltrated through breaches between our units. The Army HQ guard went into action.

Chuikov makes clear the fragility of his position:

During these hours of fighting Paulus did not have a single fresh battalion he could throw in to make a dash across the three hundred yards left to reach the Army command post. Only three hundred yards, but we had no thought of withdrawing . . .

Then, another request to the Stalingrad Front is alluded to:

I asked the Front command for permission to send several sections of the Army HQ to the emergency command post on the left bank, on condition that the entire Military Council stayed in the city. We wanted to be able to administer the 62nd Army from the left bank, in case the Army command post was destroyed. 'We will not give permission', was the answer I received.

It is now possible to reveal the actual content of Chuikov's second request to the Stalingrad Front, on 15 October 1942, and also the response to it:

> The enemy, introducing new forces of infantry and tanks, is approaching the northern group of Gorokhov. At the same time, the Germans are developing their blow to the south, reaching Minusinsk. The 37th and 95th Divisions total 200 people and are not able to prevent the enemy moving to the south and getting to the HQ of the army and the rear of the 308th Division. The situation has worsened. It is impossible to stay at our command post any more. Allow transfer of command post to the left [eastern] bank – there is nowhere else to go.
>
> Resolution of Front Commander Yeremenko to Comrade Chuikov: Request denied. The commander's HQ must stay in Stalingrad. Undertake measures to transport reinforcements – the 138th Division – to support the troops fighting on the right [western] bank of the Volga. This is to be done on the night of 15 October.

A fresh division – Lyudnikov's 138th – had now been made available for Stalingrad's defence. This was a tacit recognition that Yeremenko had been at fault in not providing Chuikov with more men before the German offensive. But only one regiment was in a fit state to cross the Volga on the night of 15 October. The rest would reach the city twenty-fours later. Their arrival coincided with Yeremenko's belated visit to 62nd Army's HQ. In the mean time, Chuikov still had to hold on.

It is fascinating to compare Chuikov's memoir against the harsh reality of actual events. It would have been very painful for him to acknowledge publicly that, however briefly and understandably, he had lost his belief that the defence would hold. All military memoirs were heavily edited and rewritten in the Soviet period – and it could never be openly admitted that Stalingrad might have fallen to the enemy. But within his family, and amongst fellow veterans, Chuikov was honest about the desperation he and his remaining HQ staff now felt. 'We all expected to die', Mereshko said simply.

HQ had now lost touch with the rest of the army. 'There was no longer any system of organized defence', Mereshko continued. The 62nd Army war diary recorded bleakly: 'Command post now under direct shelling and bombing. Many killed and injured. Our army's losses are unknown – they cannot be counted.' Late on the afternoon of 15 October Chuikov called over his younger brother, Feodor, who was serving on the HQ staff. Stalingrad's commander had now resolved to die defending the city:

'The next twenty-four hours will be critical', Chuikov began, in a semi-official tone. He stopped, and for a moment, the two men looked at each other. Then his voice changed, and he spoke differently, brother to brother. 'Feodor, one of us has to get out of here alive. When the Germans break through I will take my machine gun and make a last stand at the Volga's edge. I'm not going to surrender to them – I will die fighting. I will never leave this city.'

There was a pause. Chuikov rummaged around for something, and then brought out a sealed envelope. 'Could you get this to Valentina', he said (Chuikov's wife, Valentina, lived in Kuibyshev). 'It's a letter to say goodbye to her.' There was another pause. 'Feodor', he added. 'When you cross the river, wait. The Germans have to strike us hard before the reinforcements get through. Look out and see whether we are still here tomorrow morning. If we are, come back to us, and destroy this letter.' It was a desperate moment. But Chuikov suddenly smiled, and looked at Feodor keenly: 'If we are still here tomorrow morning, consider that we are winning.'

A line of bunkers and trenches was dug in a last-ditch attempt to delay the German advance. The intelligence officer of the advancing 24th Panzer Division reported that most of the enemy troops manning this position consisted of men from rear area services without sufficient training.

Artillery spotter Mikhail Rabinovich was summoned to Chuikov's HQ early that evening. His battery, on Zaitsevski Island, was famed for its accuracy – one of its first successes had been to destroy a German mortar position on the Mamaev Kurgan. Chuikov greeted him at the entrance and got straight to the point: 'We are expecting German infantry to penetrate our position and overrun our HQ.' Rabinovich stood speechless. Chuikov guided him into the bunker. 'I have prepared a place for you. You have a radio operator. Make contact with your battery, give them our co-ordinates, and put them on alert. When the Germans reach us call in an artillery strike on our command post. Correct the fire – everything here must be destroyed.'

Rabinovich was struck by Chuikov's eerie calmness. That evening, with some sort of communication link restored, messages started to come in from the army's scattered divisions and regiments. 'It is likely that they made these approaches to find out whether the 62nd Army command still existed', said Chuikov. 'We gave a short, clear-cut answer: "Fight with everything you've got, but stay put!"'

The Germans did not break through. On the morning of 16 October, Mikhail Rabinovich went back to his observation post in the Red October Factory, Feodor Chuikov returned to Army HQ, and his brother's farewell letter to his wife Valentina was destroyed. The first regiment of Lyudnikov's Division took up its defence positions north of the Barrikady Factory.

There is No Land for us Beyond the Volga

Many slogans were employed by the 62nd Army. 'Not a step back!' and 'Every man a fortress' were two of the most famous. But one slogan occupied a special place in the hearts of Stalingrad's defenders: 'There is no land for us beyond the Volga.' To connect with its remarkable power, we need to recall the extraordinary circumstances which gave birth to it.

On the morning of 16 October Vasily Zaitsev made his way to Chuikov's HQ. Zaitsev had not yet begun his career as a sniper; he was receiving a medal for his bravery in the city fighting. Here is Zaitsev's account of what followed:

> I remember my encounter with our army commander, General Vasily Chuikov. The commander had invited several of us to his bunker to receive awards. Chuikov regarded us. He was a short, dark man with wavy hair and a very intense gaze. He spoke that morning with surprising calm: 'By defending Stalingrad, we are tying the enemy hand and foot. The outcome of this war, and the fate of millions of Soviet citizens – our fathers, mothers, wives and children – depends upon our determination to fight here to the bitter end.' He placed in my palm a medal that read, 'For valour'.
>
> 'Our resolve to fight amidst the ruins of Stalingrad under the policy "Not a Step Back" is fulfilling a mandate of the people', the commander continued. 'How could we ever look our fellow countrymen in the eyes, if we retreat?'
>
> I felt the general was directing his question to me. He knew that I had been born in the Urals, and my family – grandfather, father and mother, as well as many of my comrades – were there now. No, there was no way I could face them, my eyes filled with shame and disgrace, if we were to give up Stalingrad. I answered the general, 'We have nowhere to retreat. For us, there is no land beyond the Volga.' For some reason, these words appealed to Chuikov.

Glimpsing Chuikov's own struggle with despair, we can understand more fully why this soldier's simple declaration of faith held such resonance for his commander. Chuikov had given everything he had to his army. He had created a tactical system of fighting to blunt the German advance and encouraged an atmosphere of equality and pride within the defenders. Above all, he had determined to trust the ordinary soldiers – and to try and restore their sense of hope and self-belief. In the crisis of 14–15 October, he had come to the end of his inner resources – and, briefly, had nothing left to fall back upon. But now, the soldiers of his army helped to renew his faith.

'We talked about those critical days a lot', said Mereshko.

> We felt that, somehow, the Germans had missed an opportunity to take Stalingrad. But the performance of our own fighters at this difficult time was remarkable. No organized system of defence for the city had existed in those few days. Only individual soldiers – or groups of soldiers – had continued to fight, cut off from their fellows. It was as if everyone – the wounded, the half-alive – stayed in their trenches, and carried on resisting. We reckoned that sometimes only small groups of soldiers, holed up in the ruins, prevented the Germans from making a final breakthrough, and getting their tanks round our position. These few guys – on their own initiative – gave our army the chance to hold its ground.

This was the force behind Chuikov's maxim: 'Every soldier is his own commander.' It was never truer than in Zholudev's fight in the ruins of the Tractor Factory. 'On 15 October we didn't have enough men to set up a defence line', said Rakitsky.

> But we used Chuikov's system of active defence in an attempt to throw the Germans off balance. The enemy liked to advance methodically, clearing each separate map grid of our fighters. So we resolved to mess up his neat little system. We used the warren of underground tunnels beneath the factory, and sent small groups of fighters, sometimes just two or three, behind the German frontline to create confusion, hoping this might slow their advance. We left it to the men's initiative and ingenuity. They responded magnificently – on one occasion, groups of our fighters popped up in seven different locations, all previously held by the enemy.

Chuikov and his fighters had found a deep reservoir of strength. As Ilya Ehrenberg wrote in the newspaper *Red Star*:

> If someone tells you that only a miracle can save Stalingrad, we will answer: the enemy still does not know what a Russian is capable of

when he is defending his own earth, his own land. Soldier – the earth beneath your feet is holy – don't give it up! Don't let the German onto it. At Stalingrad we are defending our Mother Russia. Kiss the earth. Swallow a pinch of the earth. Swear by the earth – by our immense country: for Stalingrad, for the Volga, for Russia!

In the searing fire of battle – as Stalingrad's defenders teetered on the edge of the abyss – these words were forged into a powerful truth.

It was on 16 October 1942, when Chuikov and his men had been pushed to the very limits of human endurance, that he made an appeal to his army. 'His simple message was transmitted by all means possible', said Mereshko. 'Our commander had found his faith – and it touched everyone: "Soldiers and officers of the 62nd Army – there is no land for us beyond the Volga."'

'At that moment, we resolved to stand to the death in Stalingrad', Mereshko continued. 'We were no longer fighting simply for a city, but for the Russian earth itself. Every scrap of land, every bush, stream and tree, became precious to us.'

The army loved the fact that this was a slogan coined by a soldier and publicized by a commander. 'It passed from unit to unit by word of mouth', said Sergei Zacharov, who was in the same division as Zaitsev – Batyuk's 284th. 'The message went along our soldiers' grapevine: "Have you heard what Zaitsev said – guys, there is no land for us beyond the Volga." Chuikov took Zaitsev's words, and fashioned them into an article of faith.'

The fighting of 16 October took on new ferocity. There was a fresh determination not to let the enemy through. Flamethrower units were brought in – and hulled-down tanks were put along the defence line. 'At that moment, our tank commander, Weinrub, showed exceptional ingenuity and bravery', said Mereshko. 'He worked wonders with the limited resources he had.' The Germans were beaten back from the Barrikady. That night the rest of Lyudnikov's Division crossed over and took up its positions, blocking the German advance south along the Volga. The 62nd Army had survived.

'We now had two defence systems', said Mark Ivanikin, 'our trenches, bunkers and dug outs – and the belief we felt in our hearts. The land had become sacred to us – and we would fight for every metre of it.'

Vasily Chuikov caught the extraordinary transformation which had taken place within himself and his army:

> As a former commander of the 62nd Army, I say that the enemy would have seized Stalingrad only on one condition – if all its

defenders had been killed. No Stalingrad defender would ever have crossed to the left bank of the Volga river. We swore to fight to the last drop of blood. And only death could relieve us of that oath. We acted not only from the strategic situation, and the necessity to hold the city by all means. We obeyed a call of our hearts.

'There is no land for us beyond the Volga!' was not merely a slogan – it was a sacred conviction.

Chapter Ten

An Army of Mass Heroism

After a vicious fight for the Tractor Factory, the Germans managed to capture the whole of the complex. They then regrouped and pushed southwards, towards the Barrikady. Lyudnikov's 138th Division was holding the section behind the factory, running down towards the Volga, Gurtiev's 308th Division occupied the workers' settlement and factory building. They now bore the brunt of the German assault.

In the Main Line of Attack

The journalist Vasily Grossman evoked the life and death of this division in a famous article, 'In the Main Line of Attack'. In a memorable passage he described Gurtiev's troops moving into position, ready to withstand the enemy offensive:

> The dark towering bulk of the workshops, the wet glistening rails already touched with spots of rust, the chaos of shattered goods trucks, the piles of steel girders scattered in confusion over a yard as spacious as a city square, the heaps of coal and reddish slag, the mighty smoke stacks pierced in many places by German shells . . . The division was ordered to stand fast in front of this plant. Behind it flowed the dark, icy water of the Volga.

The Germans had assembled a mighty arsenal to devastate this small area: flamethrowing tanks, six-barrelled mortars, armadas of dive-bombers, splinter bombs and thermite shells. They worked on a simple principle: it would not be possible for human beings to stand the strain of such an onslaught.

As Chuikov rightly said, if cowardice is contagious, so is courage. The remarkable resilience of Rodimtsev's 13th Guards, pressed back towards the Volga embankment, and Zholudev's 37th in the Tractor Factory, was becoming a mass phenomenon. The Germans still believed that when a division could no longer maintain its communications, and its units were isolated and surrounded, it would lose its will to resist. This has been proved true in battle many times. But, as Vasily Grossman related, it was no longer true in Stalingrad:

> The Germans succeeded in breaking through to the plant's grounds; their tanks roared beneath the walls of the workshops; they split up the defences and cut off the divisional and regimental command posts from the forward position. Deprived of direction, the division must surely lose its capacity for resistance and the command post, having come within direct reach of the enemy's blows, must be destroyed. But, astonishingly, every trench, every pillbox, every rifle-pit and every ruin turned into a stronghold, with its own system of command and communications. Sergeants and privates took the place of disabled officers and skilfully and efficiently repulsed the attacks. Commanders and staff officers turned their HQs into fortresses and themselves beat off attacks like ordinary privates.

Military censorship prevented Grossman from going into specific detail, but using the combat journal of the 308th Division and new eye-witness testimony, it is now possible to reconstruct the events he was describing. On 17 October the Germans successfully managed to encircle two regiments in the Barrikady workers' settlement. The division's combat journal noted: 'The enemy have cut off the regimental command posts from the troops. The surrounded units are engaged in really tough fighting. During the night, neither soldiers nor officers left their positions – they were destroying the Fascists, not caring about their own lives.' But by 18 October most of these men were dead. The Germans now broke into the Barrikady Factory in overwhelming force. A composite battalion of several hundred workers and some NKVD personnel was flung into their path, but in a few hours it had been reduced to just five survivors. The enemy concentrated its forces for a last push to take the factory.

German strategy for 19 October was to commence with a savage bombardment, both to devastate the area and to terrify any remaining survivors to a point where further resistance was impossible. The tactic might best be described as 'shock and awe', and the expectation was that, in its aftermath, the factory could be rapidly overrun. Instead, a battered regiment of defenders leapt from their dug outs and shelters and counter-attacked. Startled, the Germans fell back. Grossman's words about these men have become justly famous, and they are inscribed in a memorial to all Stalingrad's defenders on the Mamaev Kurgan:

A hail of bullets lashed their faces, but they pressed on and on. A superstitious dread began to grip the enemy. Were these fighters human beings, could they be mere mortals?

Yes, we were all mortals. And very few of us survived the battle. But we all fulfilled our sacred duty to the Motherland.

Following their planned capture of the Barrikady, the Germans intended to strike at the junction point of Smekhotvorov's and Lyudnikov's Divisions, and to infiltrate the Russian defence line. But the Russians surged forward, recaptured three factory workshops from the enemy, advancing about a kilometre, and completely disrupted the momentum of the German assault. Grossman remarked: 'Only here in Stalingrad, do men know what a kilometre means. It means one thousand metres, 100,000 centimetres.' Every piece of ground was being fought over.

Such a rally seems genuinely near-miraculous. How had it been accomplished? On the previous night of 18 October, with the Germans gathering their forces for an all-out assault, the divisional commander, Gurtiev, and Chuikov himself, turned up at the frontline command post. Konstantin Kazarin, a company commander in the 339th Regiment, remembered seeing them there as he came to make his report. 'Chuikov was standing there, in a simple black coat, with two bodyguards. In this hell, our commanders were with us!'

Kazarin gave his situation report and Gurtiev asked him about the condition of his machine gun company, the mood of the men and how much ammunition they had. Kazarin continued:

> We really respected Colonel Leonti Gurtiev. He always paid attention to people, he knew his officers' strengths and weaknesses – and his great skill lay in the way he delegated responsibilities: everyone had a job to do and knew what it was. But it was hard to be upbeat in my report – there wasn't much of a command structure left – most of the regiment had already been killed, and the rest of us were at the end of our tether.

Then Chuikov spoke. 'First, he gave me a soldier's tip', Kazarin recalled.

> I had been talking about how impersonal the fighting was: we were only too aware of the Germans' technological superiority – their precision bombing and shelling, their tank attacks – and it was wearing down our men. He said: 'Try and get your heavy machine guns into a position where you can see the enemy, see the casualties you are

inflicting on them. Elevate your gun positions. The mood of your guys will change when you can actually see you are killing them.'

Then Chuikov talked about his own philosophy as a commander:

'I always try and put myself in the mind of the enemy – I try to imagine what he is thinking and feeling, and what he is least expecting. Right now, he is ready to push you from your last defence lines. The last thing he is anticipating is a counter-attack. It may seem impossible to you, with the state your men are in. But I have found, again and again, when soldiers are beginning to despair, that a counter-attack can really restore morale.'

Chuikov looked directly at Kazarin.

'Give the fucking Fascists a taste of their own medicine. Remember, however powerful they seem to you, they are afraid of man-to-man fighting. If you feel your men cannot hold on, remind them what those bandits have done to us – and then give them this task.' Chuikov clenched his fist with a sudden, extraordinary fierceness: 'We'll show those bastards!'

Kazarin continued:

I went back to my regiment and told them that our commander was with us, and shared with them what he had said. The effect was electrifying. Immediately, several guys volunteered to do a reconnaissance of the enemy positions. We worked out a plan of attack for the following morning.

At 4.00 a.m. on 19 October the men of the 339th Regiment charged. The Germans were completely taken by surprise. Three factory workshops were recaptured – numbers 3, 21 and 26. Before the Germans retreated they set light to sections of the factory with inflammables, but the Russians continued to advance through the flames. Kazarin's company set up their machine guns in workshop number 3.

'I remembered the tip Chuikov had given me', Kazarin continued.

So we clambered up through the ruins, and got our machine guns higher, on the second and third floors of the building. And he was right: now we could see the Germans as we were killing them. The enemy threw tanks and infantry against us – and my men cheered as we drove them back. On one occasion a tank came up and fired at us at point-blank range, but he was unable to reach us. He could not elevate his gun high enough to hit our emplacement, which was protected by a really thick section of brick wall.

Late that afternoon the Germans brought up heavy artillery and blasted the walls under Kazarin's machine gun nest. He tumbled down into the rubble, but was able to crawl back to the Russian positions.

The men of the 339th Regiment were not able to hold their reclaimed ground for long. At 5.00 p.m. German tanks and machine gunners converged on their position. Most of the brave force was wiped out – leaving only a few survivors, who managed to retreat that night. But from a psychological point of view, their remarkable counter-attack represented an iconic moment in the battle.

Their heroism bought the Red Army precious time. The enemy had expected to push through the Barrikady on 19 October, but it took them another four days to subdue the 308th Division. Almost everyone stood their ground and fought. On 23 October, with most of the division wiped out, its training battalion fought a last desperate rearguard action, repelling ten German attacks before being surrounded. Only three trainees and one officer survived.

This is the story behind 'In the Main Line of Attack'. 'Heroism had become part of the life, the style, and manner of this division and its men', Grossman wrote. This heroism arose out of a fundamental shift in the relationship between the army's commanders and its soldiers. When Russian officers offered their men a hand of friendship and trust, they reciprocated with unswerving loyalty and courage. The war journalist Alexander Werth rightly said of the bravery Grossman commemorated: 'No doubt, there were moments of animal fear and despair which at the time he could not mention; but if such feelings had ever predominated, the results would not have been what they were.'

Camaraderie

Grossman described an exceptional comradeship binding the defenders of the Barrikady, and the psychological change brought about when men put others before themselves. 'In an army, bad habits start at the top, and then contaminate everybody', said Mereshko. 'We have a saying "a fish rots head downwards." But the same is true in reverse. Men judge their leaders by the way they act, not what they say. This was especially true at Stalingrad.'

'You could see it in the little things', said Kazarin.

> As an officer I got extra rations, so I would take the food down and share it with my men. My gesture was really appreciated. Once, I brought some salted herring. I was struck by the painstaking way that my soldiers divided that fish – counting for exactly the number of people they had. In the midst of all the horror and chaos, it was such loving care and attention to detail.

Out of myriad moments like these arose real comradeship in battle. One of the Soviet Union's greatest soldiers, Konstantin Rokossovsky, visited the 62nd Army in Stalingrad and said of its defenders:

> The fighting in the city was in a class by itself and required great courage, and stamina, enterprise and initiative on the part of both men and commanders, and, above all, a firm feeling of comradeship, up to and including self-sacrifice. Suvorov's behest, 'Die if need be, but rescue your comrade', was a law here. Thanks to this, and nothing else, they had succeeded in holding the thin strip of land along the Volga.

A spirit of camaraderie amongst the Red Army defenders blossomed as the fighting reached its climax. It began with a remarkable gesture by General Stephan Guriev, commander of the 39th Guards Division, as remembered by Mereshko:

> The arrival of Guriev's troops in the Red October Factory at the beginning of October marked an important psychological moment. In truth, up to that time our army looked terrible. Of course, there was constant fighting during September. But we had grown accustomed to looking shabby and dishevelled – we were just hanging on from day to day. Then Guriev's fighters appeared in their 'Siberian uniform', with their white greatcoats – and these tough soldiers remained distinctive, keeping themselves neat and tidy, and bothering to shave and wash, even in the midst of horrific fighting. Zholudev's division was the same. It woke up the rest of us – men began to take trouble over their appearance again.

So, at the beginning of October, Red Army soldiers once again began to wash and shave, and as far as it was possible, wear clean uniforms. Such little details can reveal a great deal about the morale of an army. Towards the end of October, German soldiers stopped doing so.

The journalist Alexander Werth recalled a conversation with Lieutenant Lutsenko – who had recently been fighting in one of the Guards Divisions in Stalingrad – about the conditions in the city in early November 1942:

> All of us have observed one very odd difference between ourselves and the Germans. Nearly every morning we shave; the Germans are all unshaved and untidy. In our dug-outs, we have odd pieces of soft furniture, bunks, and even the occasional musical instrument . . . Hot food is carried to the front line, usually two or three hundred metres away; and every week – no matter how heavy the fighting – every soldier goes to the bath-house, and also gets a set of clean underwear. But the Germans – they don't wash and they don't shave, and it makes a big difference.

Guriev started the ball rolling. 'He became our master of ceremonies', said Mereshko.

> Shortly after arriving at Stalingrad he invited all the neighbouring divisional commanders over for a meal. Guriev had his own cook with him – and his speciality was Siberian dumplings. The invitation was received with disbelief. Generals and colonels, overwhelmed by the stress of the fighting, now found themselves being invited to a social event, and the request was brusquely dismissed: 'In the midst of all this chaos, these guys are sitting around cooking dumplings. Forget it – we have more important things to worry about.' But Guriev persisted. And despite all their grumblings, everyone struggled through the night-time city and showed up at his bunker. Something changed within the army after that meal.

Guriev encouraged everyone to take trouble over their bunkers and dug outs. 'He started a little competition amongst us', continued Mereshko.

> He acquired some wonderful doors for his dug out. I don't know where he got them from – possibly from some administrative building – but they were oak, very strong and impressive looking.

And Guriev began to joke 'Well – however tough the fighting, we have the best dug out in the army.' No one had really cared about how their dug outs looked, but that changed. Not to be outdone, Batyuk found some even more magnificent oak doors for the 284th Division's bunker. Suddenly, everybody was doing it. And when Guriev's doors were destroyed in an explosion – and he was very upset about that – a special army communiqué was sent out lamenting the damage.

Vasily Grossman caught this change, and the banter which accompanied it:

There was probably nowhere in the world where the construction of living quarters was taken more seriously than in Stalingrad . . . When you were talking about someone, you always mentioned the quality of his bunker: 'Batyuk's doing some fine work on Mamaev Kurgan with his mortars. He's got a fine bunker by the way – a huge oak door, just like the Senate building. Yes, he's certainly got a head on his shoulders.' While of another man it might be said: 'Well, what do you know, he was forced to retreat during the night. He had no liaison with his units and he lost a key position . . . As for his command post, it was visible from the air. And he had a soldier's cape by way of a door, to keep out the flies, I suppose. An empty-headed fellow – I heard his wife left him before the war.'

'Those are General Guriev's words', said Mereshko, 'and this was the way he chatted to people.' However much his division had suffered during the day's combat, Guriev would ring round other commanders at night, finding out how people were, and gossiping with them. He was a tough and resolute fighter, the kind of man, Chuikov observed, 'whom the enemy would not find easy to budge', and he trained his subordinates in the same spirit, but he also created a mood of togetherness in adversity. Chuikov remembered that 'Guriev did not leave his command post even with German tommy gunners at the entrance.' Mereshko and other HQ staff had to rush in as last-ditch reinforcements to rescue this much-loved commander. 'Enemy soldiers were throwing grenades into his communication trench when we got through to him', Mereshko remembered. 'But we were not going to lose our Siberian dumplings!'

Vasily Grossman gave a wonderful sketch of Stephan Guriev:

No one else had so few men as he did – between six and eight in each company. And no one else was so cut off from the rear – when they sent him reinforcements, a third of them would arrive wounded. No one, except perhaps Gorokhov, had to put up with that.

And yet he never let it overwhelm him. In the late evening he would take off his jacket and wipe the sweat from his red face, and the social niceties would begin:

> In the same harsh voice he would offer you vodka, shout orders down the telephone line to his battalion commanders, abuse the cook for failing to grill the dumplings correctly, and ring his neighbour, Batyuk, to ask if they were playing dominoes on the Mamaev Kurgan.

Guriev was proud of his fellow commanders. 'We've certainly got some good men here', he would say.

> They're a fine lot. Batyuk's certainly got a head on his shoulders. And General Zholudev at the Tractor Factory's an old friend of mine. And then there's Colonel Gurtiev at the Barrikady – only he's a monk, he never drinks vodka at all. That really is a mistake.

Everyone knew how tough the fighting was in Guriev's sector. 'When he took the trouble to ring round every night, others were struck by that, and began to respond', said Mereshko.

> Our men were being pushed back towards the Volga. The river was full of sturgeon, and because of the force of the bombardment, the dead fish would float up to the surface. Before, this was just depressing for us. But now, Guriev received a return invitation from a fellow commander: 'So, you have a chef who cooks Siberian dumplings very well. We have a particularly fine recipe for sturgeon. Join us to-night at 10.00 p.m.'

The banter was infectious. Stalingrad's divisional commanders connected with each other – and then began to reach out in times of need. Zholudev and Leonti Gurtiev - the commander of the 308th Division – were neighbours in the terrible battle for the Tractor Factory. Gurtiev, under pressure from the Germans himself, was unable to send any reinforcements to Zholudev's aid, but wanted to offer moral support: 'Gurtiev telephoned Zholudev and said: "Courage, I can't help. Stand firm!" When Zholudev was ordered to move to the left bank [i.e. withdraw from the battle] he said to Gurtiev: "Stand firm, old man! Courage!" and they both laughed.'

Mereshko continued:

> Regimental commanders now joined in. One would boast: 'I'm sitting 200 metres from the Germans, perched on the edge of the Volga, so we have a steam bath in our dug out, but no birch twigs!' Another would reply: 'Well I am sitting in an oven that used to make steel [the Martin furnaces in the Red October Factory] – so I need that bath, I look Afro-Caribbean.' A third would chip in: 'You guys are living the easy life. I am stuck in a piece of industrial piping. It is so draughty in here that even the 100 grams [the Vodka ration] doesn't help.'

Then the men followed suit. Delighted by their commanders' humour they began to invent a mock-serious slang for Stalingrad's deadly weaponry: they jokingly referred to the German six-barrel mortar as 'goofy', the dive-bombers with their sirens as 'fiddlers' or 'musicians', the different grenades they used as 'sausages' and 'pineapples'. Chuikov employed a rough, colloquial turn of phrase to connect with his men – an enemy artillery bombardment became a 'hot-milk delivery', and the commander's tough reception for someone who did not properly hold his lines a 'Russian egg-flip' – but it developed into a common language for the entire army.

Remarkably, this slang was also used to relay orders. The use of radio code was cumbersome and difficult, and many operators were not properly trained, so code names and instructions now identified divisional and regimental commanders by the type of wood they used for their dug out doors, and mischievously promised the enemy some Russian hospitality. On 11 November 1942 the deputy commander of the 45th division, Bakanov, warned regimental commander Serkov of an impending German assault in the Red October factory: '"Maple, maple", this is "Oak, oak". Von Schwerin [the German commander of the 79th Division] wishes to drink from the river. Please accommodate guests.' Serkov replied: 'Don't worry "oak", I'll accommodate them – but they'd better not count on Volga water. It's extremely cold these days – they might get a sore throat.'

'With all the problems we had', said Mereshko, 'and by late October we were in a truly desperate situation – this shared humour made all the difference. It brought humanity back into Stalingrad, and made the army feel whole again.'

Rituals

Rituals became part of the 62nd Army's way of life. The most important was the oath not to surrender Stalingrad, with its indomitable slogan 'There is no land for us beyond the Volga'. From 17 October 1942 new recruits swore this oath on reaching the small strip of land held by the defenders:

> The Germans have destroyed the avenues and brought down the factories of Stalingrad; but Stalingrad has remained invincible. Its burned-out houses, its ruins, its very stones are sacred to us. We swear to our last drop of blood, to our last breath, to our last heartbeat that we shall defend Stalingrad, and hold the enemy back from the Volga. We swear that we shall not disgrace the glory of Russian arms, and we shall fight to the end.

This pledge was incorporated in an 'Oath by the defenders of Stalingrad' addressed to Stalin on the anniversary of the October revolution, on 7 November 1942:

> We are writing to you at the height of the great battle, in the midst of the din of an unceasing cannonade and the roar of aircraft, and the red glow of fires. We are here, on the steep banks of the Volga, the great Russian river; and we are writing to you to say that our spirit is stronger than ever, that our will is as strong as steel, and that our arms are not wearied by striking the enemy. Our decision is to stand firm, to stand to the last man at the walls of Stalingrad.

Alexander Rakitsky recalled how the 'Oath by the defenders of Stalingrad' was drawn up.

> There was a big meeting of the army council in early November. We took our oath to defend Stalingrad – and our political officers then drafted some appropriate words around it. It was typed out and passed to Chuikov to sign first, as army commander. We planned to circulate it amongst the rest of the council, and get it signed by some of our soldiers, before dispatching it to Stalin. But Chuikov refused, and instead passed it up the table. 'Zholudev should sign first, not me. He held firm when I lost hope', he said simply.

But Chuikov had now recovered his faith. 'His resolve to defend Stalingrad or die spread amongst our defenders; everyone felt the force of Chuikov's will

– and his determination to fight to the death', said Mereshko. It encapsulated something greater, caught in the words of Ilya Ehrenberg: 'At Stalingrad we are defending our Mother Russia, we are defending our earth.' Anatoly Kozlov recalled that the oath 'involved swallowing a piece of Stalingrad's soil. By doing so, men swore to fulfil their mission under any circumstances – including giving up their lives.'

This ritual spawned a host of others. 'They were not supervised by commissars but came from the initiative of groups of combatants', Kozlov continued. 'Our soldiers created their own rituals during the battle.' Sometimes a group of men would swear over the body of a dead comrade to take revenge on the Germans. This ritual was particularly powerful for defenders, creating a mood of resolute defiance – something Vasily Grossman witnessed: 'It was as if the dead had passed on their strength to the survivors, and there were moments when ten resolute bayonets successfully held an area which had been defended by a battalion.'

This was the way the factory district was defended. 'It seemed unbelievable that anyone could continue to hold out', said Mereshko, 'but when a division of thousands was reduced to a couple of hundred soldiers, they would hold the ground for their dead friends.'

Mereshko stressed that many of the rituals arose from a solidarity felt with fellow soldiers. 'Life expectancy was so short', he said. 'Your life could be lost in a moment. You were living completely in the present. You never knew in the next few minutes whether you would be alive or dead.' One of these rituals was nicknamed 'Give me forty!' It involved sharing tobacco.

'Ammunition was our second most valuable commodity, along with vodka', said Mereshko.

> The most important was tobacco. We used newspaper to make a galley, put the tobacco in it, rolled it to form a tube, made a kink at the end and then smoked it as a pipe. Sharing was our rule. A soldier could make a request to anyone who was smoking, including officers: 'Give me forty!' The owner kept 60 per cent of the cigarette, the other got 40 per cent. When you received your share, you normally smoked it to the very end, until you burnt your mouth.

The most popular ritual was called: 'Swap without looking!'

> You could go up to anyone, touch your pocket, and say 'Swap without looking'. You were allowed to point to any pocket of the person you were exchanging with – trouser, tunic or greatcoat. The

swapping took place between fellow soldiers, and also soldiers and officers – and you had to agree to it. You might find you had swapped watches, you might lose your money and gain a cigarette butt, or you might pick up something really valuable, like a pistol.

Mereshko added:

It was like a kid's game, but it had a powerful underlying meaning. Conventionally valuable things no longer had any real significance at Stalingrad. Every moment a bomb or shell was exploding around us. Our lives were measured not in days and hours, but minutes and seconds. So nobody thought about whether they were 'winning' or 'losing' – you could lose all your wages and still laugh –it was the process itself which was of value. Death was all around – but something else was coming to life. We were pushed back to the Volga's edge – but the atmosphere amongst us was incredible.

A Village on the Volga

At the end of October 1942 the Red Army at Stalingrad was perched along a narrow strip of land, less than 200 metres from the Volga river. 'To get to the Barrikady or Red October Factories you had to go right along the Volga', Mereshko said.

This was where our wounded gathered for evacuation, where we received ammunition and food, and where our HQ was situated. And here – amidst an array of bunkers and dug outs that looked like swallow's nests on a river bank – were our soldiers, fixing clocks, sewing boots, and repairing and making all manner of items: in the midst of all the fighting, it was like a market.

At night, after the German offensive had died down, this market came to life. 'A few hundred metres from the frontline you could see the everyday life of our army', Mereshko continued.

Under the Volga embankment our soldiers knew the dug out where a good watchmaker or cobbler could be found, where a gramophone was located, where a knife could be sharpened. To bring down a German aircraft was not just a good 'trophy'. We recycled

everything. The plastic cover of the cockpit was especially prized –
you could make a cigarette holder from it, or a knife handle. A little
village had spread out along the Volga.

More than anything else, music restored the morale of soldiers exhausted by
the day's combat. Mereshko said:

> Retreating through the city, when apartments lay broken and aban-
> doned, everyone wanted to recover a gramophone record. Records
> were like gold to us. We didn't have many musical instruments to
> sing along to – we would have liked more accordions, but the
> Germans only had a limited supply, so they were difficult to
> capture. The gramophone was king at Stalingrad. And the most
> sought-after item in our Volga village was a gramophone needle –
> these were priceless. They had to be sharpened especially carefully.

Communal singing brought the Red Army back to life – and even the
Germans, whose lines were only a few hundred metres away, became curious.
'If you had a gramophone and a record of our favourite song, "Katyusha", you
might evade the enemy bombardment for a while', Mereshko added with a
smile.

> Sometimes there were brief breaks in the fighting. On one occasion
> the Germans, instead of shouting out their usual threat to drown us
> in the Volga – yelled something different: "Russ – play Katyusha!"
> It was hard to take this musical request seriously. But one Red Army
> soldier put the record on nonetheless, and many of our guys sang
> along to it. The shooting completely died down and the Germans
> just listened. Then, when the music was over, the bedlam started
> again.

The Loss of the 62nd Crossing

On 26 October 1942 the Russians' last lifeline to the far bank of the Volga – the
62nd Crossing – came under sustained enemy fire. The Germans, advancing
from the Barrikady into the Red October Factory, were just 400 metres away.
Seeing this, their soldiers burst out cheering. With this last river crossing out
of action, they were convinced the 62nd Army would be unable to hold out any
longer, and the battle would be over.

Instead, it spurred the defenders to a final, extraordinary effort. 'When we lost the 62nd Crossing, and neither the ferry nor the pontoon bridge could be used, it represented the supreme supply crisis for our army', said Mereshko.

> The Germans did not believe we could keep going any longer. But each of our divisions now organized its own 'crossing group' – and these brave men, supplied with small boats, made the hazardous journey across the river two or three times a night to bring in food and ammunition. Those small boats kept us going. When the enemy realized what we were doing they tried very hard to destroy them by aerial bombardment – but during the day we hid them, burying them under the sand by the Volga, and at night we dug them out again.

The Red Army's position looked desperate, but the defenders were determined to hang on. Teenagers, adopted by the army as 'sons of the regiment', were even swimming the river, pushing across rafts of supplies.

It was becoming extremely difficult to evacuate the wounded from the city. 'I remember one of our nurses – Vera Zavolovskaya – was carrying soldiers to the Volga embankment', said Konstantin Kazarin.

> When the Germans approached she was ordered to stop – it was simply too dangerous. But she stayed at the evacuation point, in the midst of the terrible bombing, caring for the wounded. Chuikov got to hear of this, and turned up himself: 'I ordered you to stop', he said, 'so why are you disobeying me?' She replied: 'Comrade Commander, our wounded are dying here – I want to help.' Chuikov looked at her for a while, and then stepped forward and embraced her. 'You are right', he said, 'We have to keep trying.'

Very little could be done. Mereshko recalled:

> We applied rudimentary first aid to those lying by the embankment', said Mereshko, 'but people had to wait for days and days – there were no longer the boats to take them across the Volga. We tied some to rafts of logs, and floated them down the river, hoping someone would help them, but most died by the bank of the river. We had no time to make crosses; we just dug large holes and buried them all.

But their suffering and appalling losses only increased the resolve of the defenders. A new Red Army practice was introduced when saluting the death of comrades: to fire the volley or salvo 'not in the air, but at the Germans'.

How Steel is Formed

The Red October Factory now witnessed the fiercest fighting. Mereshko noted:

> The battles there were particularly intense. The commander of one regiment had his HQ in a smelting furnace right on the frontline. He would step out to a 120mm gun, shoot, then pick up the phone and ask 'Did I aim correctly?' Soldiers, battalion and regimental commanders all mixed together, actively participating in the fighting.

On 23 October 1942, when the attack on the Red October Factory began, Paulus introduced his last remaining fresh division, the 79th Infantry. Timing is everything – and this decision seems deeply puzzling. Why not sooner? Days before, on 15 October, Chuikov had feared that the division would be brought forward, knowing that if it was, he would almost certainly be overrun. Instead Paulus held back, and the events of those few days had enormous impact on the self-belief and conviction of both sides.

Had Paulus thrown the new division into the battle raging for the Tractor Factory there is a high probability that victory would have been his in October 1942. Chuikov had known it. But German commander's cautious and methodical approach dictated that reserves should be held back and that these fresh troops should then be used to consolidate the position after the Tractor Factory and Barrikady had been reduced. Such a systematic way of thinking has its strengths. Here it resulted in delay until the moment of truth had already passed.

A German officer in the 79th, Lieutenant-Colonel Richard Wolf, made a powerful criticism of Paulus's thorough but over-regimented style of command:

> An independent change of plan, such as following through after reaching an objective, had been forbidden to the combat troops . . .
> I had spoken out against these restrictions. It was my opinion and experience that the momentum of an attack – if it was successful – should not be restrained by a fixed battle plan. If the enemy is

weak and withdraws he should not be given any time to reform again. Nothing strengthens the fighting morale of the Russians as much as when they are allowed a breather, which they see as a sign of weakness. This opinion was proven right in many battles with them.

Red Army's more flexible approach, particularly their use of storm groups, and the growing sniper movement, began to tell against their opponents. At the end of the month the fighting momentarily eased – and a last batch of reinforcements – Sokolov's 45th Division – arrived to reinforce the defence of the Red October Factory. By now the frontline cut right through the factory site, with groups of Germans maintaining a hold on parts of it while the Russians hung on grimly in others. There was to be no further falling back. Even when the Germans brought in specialist troops, battalions of engineers skilled in city combat, for a final assault on 11 November, the attack was beaten off.

Sokolov and his men held the line with the same spirit as the rest of Stalingrad's defenders. In the brief breaks between the fighting, the commander ate with his men, swapped jokes and even chopped wood with them. 'All of us were on the same level', remembered Mark Slavin.

> The commanders mingled with the soldiers. Everyone counted. We had no space to manoeuvre and the German bombardment was relentless – but we passed along instructions from dug out to dug out. I once found Sokolov behind a smelting furnace right on our frontline. I was singing a martial song, loudly and discordantly, trying to keep my spirits up – and he called out to me, laughing, asking for a proper concert recital that evening. We were determined to hold on to that narrow strip of land.

The Germans used psychological tactics, trying to break the will of the defenders. Leonid Pokhodnya, a company commander with the 45th, was struck by this:

> They would keep revving up their tank engines, then the sirens would start wailing and their planes would drop empty, perforated barrels on us, which made a terrible, ear-splitting noise. They were even dropping dead, rotting horses on us. And then the bombing and shelling started, the planes swooping down on us, at low level, as if they were on a conveyor belt.

In the midst of this hell, two nurses, Sima Merzalyakova and Olga Vlaseva, crawled out to rescue a wounded battalion commander. As they reached him, German machine gunners opened fire. They died sheltering him with their bodies. When Red Army soldiers reached them, they recovered Sima's kitbag and found a book inside it. It was Nikolai Ostrovsky's *How Steel is Formed* and several of the book's passages were underlined. One of them was:

> Learn how to carry on when conditions seem unbearable – when everything seems terrifying and hopeless. You can survive and grow strong by reaching out and helping others. The real terror is to lose your own sense of worth.

Another section was also underscored: 'The most precious thing you have is your life. It is given to you only once. And you need to leave it without being ashamed of who you are and what you stand for.' The hero of the book was a construction worker named Pavel Korchagin. He was working on a railway line, and struggling with terrible pain. Korchagin believed the real battle was inside oneself. When things became really hard, and it no longer seemed possible to go on, one had to draw sustenance from a higher cause. Korchagin's was a deeply felt love for the Motherland.

At the end of the book Sima had written:

> Olga and I have read this book through to the very last page. Now we feel that there are three of us – us two and Korchagin, who is helping us through these difficult times. We have decided to behave like Korchagin – and we'll make it.

Sima and Olga did not make it. But their book was passed from soldier to soldier as a talisman. A month later, it was found under the belt of a wounded man with scores of signatures and comments: 'Dear Sima and Olga – I am with you. And I will be trying to be like Korchagin too.' 'I'm with you! – I'm joining this line of fighters.' 'I make my oath to serve the Motherland – like Korchagin did.' That book went all the way to Berlin.

Chapter Eleven

The Victory Parade

On 19 November 1942 the Russians struck back at the attackers of Stalingrad. Their counter-attack was codenamed Operation Uranus. The first blow was directed against the northern flank of Army Group B on the river Don; the second, a day later, against the southern flank on the Kalmyk steppe. The Romanian armies, allies of the Germans who were guarding these positions, disintegrated in chaos. By 23 November, both pincers of the Soviet attack had closed behind the German position. The 6th Army was now trapped. Some of its divisions formed a new defence line on the steppe lands between the Volga and the Don, others remained inside the city.

General Feodor Smekhotvorov, commander of the 193rd Division, wrote:

> The enemy's attacks suddenly ceased in the middle of November. We realized that the Germans – in the city which they themselves had gutted – had lost not only hundreds of tanks and tens of thousands of men, but had also lost confidence in their own powers. When our counter-offensive began on the morning of 19 November, we realized that we had been right to stand and fight at Stalingrad, and that victory would be ours.

By 19 November the defending 62nd Army had been split into three groups, clinging to the edge of the Volga. Gorokhov's northern group was still holding out in Spartanovka; Lyudnikov's 138th Division was completely surrounded by Germans behind the Barrikady Factory. The main army group held a strip of land along the Volga, in some places less than 200 metres wide, from the Red October Factory to downtown Stalingrad. When news of the counter-offensive passed along the soldiers' grapevine the relief was extraordinary. 'We all clambered out of our dug outs to listen for the sounds of our counter-attack', remembered Mereshko. 'It wasn't possible – it was too far north, but two days later we all heard the southern one – it was an incredible feeling. We were no longer alone.'

When Chuikov's wife, Valentina, heard the news she sent him a postcard of congratulation. It was seen by others, and it so moved them they asked Chuikov if it could be made into a pamphlet for the army, symbolizing the heartfelt joy of every soldier's wife. The commander agreed:

> I congratulate you on the victory and wish you even greater successes. Get revenge for everything they've done, for the humiliation and the losses. Go forward – don't stop. Finish off these snakes. On behalf of our whole family I give thanks to you for victory – our mutual joy – and for what you've done. Don't worry about us – we are all healthy and well. The hardest, black days are already in the past. Take this heavy stone off your soul – breathe, move freely, and go forward to complete victory. Au revoir my darling.

Chuikov was now enjoying the luxury of being able to stay put in his command post. It was situated on the Volga embankment, between the Red October Factory and the Mamaev Kurgan. He had moved into it on 17 October and remained there until the end of the battle. Mereshko described it:

> Our last Army HQ was almost comfortable. It was protected by an angled communication trench at the entrance, to deflect any bomb blasts. The command post was dug deep into the Volga embankment. There was a passage way, then a meeting room, and then on the right, Chuikov's room, and on the left, Gurov's room. Then there was a small reception area and a room for the HQ staff. There was another passage way, lined with wood and hardboard, leading to Krylov's room, a communications office, and the operations department. At the back were two or three tiny rooms with bunk beds where you could go and get some sleep.
>
> There was some primitive furniture – tables and bunk beds – but the benches were made of earth. We had a little bath house – a sort of 'cave', about 2 metres deep – where you could make a fire and take off your clothes. You would have two large pots of hot water – one for yourself, one for your clothes. You would wipe yourself with a hot cloth, then wash and 'iron' your underwear with hot stones, to get rid of the lice.

On 31 December 1942 Army HQ had a special visit. Colonel Ivan Lyudnikov's division had finally managed to fight its way through the German lines and rejoin the main army group. Lyudnikov arrived to make his report.

Lyudnikov's Island

Lyudnikov's division had been surrounded by the Germans during their last major offensive, on 11 November. 'At that stage our army had been cut into pieces like a sausage', said Mereshko.

> We called the defensive position occupied by the 138th Division 'Lyudnikov's Island' because the Germans were in front of it, and to the right and left, and the Volga was behind it. It was a very symbolic name for us – they were holding a tiny strip of land, just 500 metres by 500 metres, and a few ruined buildings, and were desperately short of food and ammunition – yet they continued to resist.

Jonathan Bastable, in his *Voices from Stalingrad*, wrote:

> Lyudnikov's predicament was, in a sense, a microcosm of the battle of Stalingrad. The Russians were aware the 138th was fighting on, and their fight came to be seen as one of those symbolic encounters – like Pavlov's House and the Nail Factory – which defined the struggle for them, and typified the grim righteousness of their fight. And as with these other mini-conflicts, the soldiers supplied a name to this little battleground. It was dubbed 'Lyudnikov's Island', and as such it became part of the contemporary geography and future mythology of Stalingrad.

Georgi Ivanov was a platoon commander in the 138th:

> Our casualties were terrible – the Germans were pushing us back all the time. They were bombing us in relays of planes. We were clinging on behind the Barrikady Factory, with our command post right on the Volga embankment. The Germans dropped leaflets on us, showing a sketch of our position – which had now shrunk to a very small size – with their tanks all around, saying 'You are en-circled – surrender!' We were pushed up against the Volga, but we determined to make a stand there.

Their resistance was extraordinary. On 13 November the Germans broke through the defences but were beaten off in hand-to-hand fighting by Lyudnikov and his HQ staff. The following day, the remnants of the division ran out of supplies. They continued to fight using ammunition captured from the enemy. Lyudnikov ordered all NKVD blocking detachment and security staff into the frontline – everybody was fighting.

After the Soviet counter-attack vital supplies at last reached the beleaguered defenders, and they began to claw their way back to the rest of the army. Their strength was severely depleted and as a result progress was painfully slow. The 62nd Army was now so short of numbers that storm groups were used as its main method of fighting. On 18 December Lyudnikov reorganized his troops in an attempt to drive through the German lines and reach Gorishny's 95th Division. He created one large storm group, consisting of a storming party, consolidation and reserve groups. This became the classic formation for storm group fighting

Yet Russian resistance at Stalingrad cannot simply be explained by tactical formations, however important. On 31 December 1942, with communications finally restored, Lyudnikov journeyed to the army's HQ. A simple yet moving reception awaited him. Chuikov, Krylov and Gurov had gathered with all the divisional commanders. Chuikov invited Lyudnikov to the table, vodka was poured and a toast was proposed: 'To the valiant soldiers of the 138th Division'. Then Chuikov turned to him and said: 'Now tell us how you lived and fought.'

Lyudnikov had held out against impossible odds, 'with Germans breaking around his position like waves round a cliff', as his combat journal poetically put it, but on receiving this request all poetry drained away: 'I was surrounded by experienced commanders who would not bat an eyelid at anything', Lyudnikov related, somewhat daunted. 'I only told them that the 138th had harassed the enemy without respite, and for this reason we had not even noticed autumn fading into winter out there on our own. My story fell flat.' Chuikov gazed at him somewhat reproachfully, and then, looking round the room, began to smile: 'How easy they've had it out there!' he said.

Bullet-Proof Batyuk

In December 1942 the 62nd Army decided to straighten out its defence line, and employ storm groups to wrest small sections of the city back from the enemy. Rodimtsev's 13th recaptured the German strongholds along the Volga: the House of Railway Workers, the L-Shaped House and the House of Specialists. Sokolov's 45th fought its way through the Red October Factory. Batyuk's 284th began a slow reconquest of the Mamaev Kurgan.

The beleaguered German 6th Army was now suffering terribly. Its winter clothing was utterly inadequate and there was insufficient food, ammunition and fuel. Manstein attempted to break through to the surrounded army with a fresh Wehrmacht force, but he was driven back on 24 December 1942. The Germans in and around Stalingrad were being supplied by airlift, but resources were overstretched and less and less was reaching them. 10 January 1943 was a special day for the defenders. The surrounding Soviet armies now launched Operation Ring to smash the surrounded 6th Army in a battle of annihilation. The threat of encirclement and destruction, which had hung over the defenders of Stalingrad for so long, was now being visited on their opponents.

By 11 January 1943 two most powerful symbols of Stalingrad's resistance had been regained by the 62nd Army. The Red October Factory was completely cleared of Germans, and the red flag once again flew triumphantly from the summit of the Mamaev Kurgan. Colonel Nikolai Batyuk's 284th Division had hung onto the north-eastern slope of the Kurgan throughout most of the battle; now Batyuk led his men back to the summit.

Batyuk was especially loved within the army. A tough, no-nonsense commander, he demanded much from his men and even more from himself. 'Our soldiers nicknamed him "Bullet-proof Batyuk" because he seemed genuinely impervious to danger', said Sergei Zacharov. 'He was a remarkably courageous man, and, like Chuikov, had a really good instinct for city fighting.'

The combat journal of the 284th Division recorded on 11 January: 'Our commander and his staff have joined the frontline regiments, mixing with the fighters, helping them with practical advice and the fulfilling of their duties.' All these regiments – much reduced in numbers – were being reorganized as storm groups, and Batyuk now led them against the enemy. 'The commander of the division appeared on the battlefield, encouraging the assembled troops through his own brave leadership', the combat journal stated proudly. This was the real story of Stalingrad.

The German Surrender

Operation Ring soon reached a climax. Fresh Russian armies were advancing towards Stalingrad from the west, having broken the last German defences on the steppe. On 26 January 1943 these new forces met with the defenders of Stalingrad. At the beginning of September 1942 the Germans had isolated the 62nd Army, leaving it standing alone against the might of their onslaught; five terrible months later its isolation was over.

On 31 January 1943 Paulus surrendered to the Russians – not to the 62nd Army, whom he had confronted during most of the city fighting, but to its neighbour to the south, the 64th. This may seem to us a largely irrelevant detail, but it mattered a great deal to Stalingrad's defenders. They had borne the chief burden of the city's defence and now they felt robbed of their prize: 'Our soldiers were really unhappy Paulus did not surrender to Chuikov', Mereshko said.

> Paulus's last HQ was in the Univermag Department Store in central Stalingrad, and this was in our zone of influence – but we had pushed our forces further north, to combat the German strongholds in the Factory District. With the 64th Army moving up from the south, central Stalingrad became something of a no man's land between the two armies – and it was soldiers from the 64th who reached the 6th Army's HQ first.

On 2 February the remaining German forces in the north of the city were surrounded. Chuikov arrived in person to supervise a massive artillery bombardment of their position, and in a powerful symbolic act, helped load and fire one of the Russian guns. The enemy surrendered at midday – an act of capitulation which marked the end of the battle of Stalingrad.

Mereshko remembered:

> The sudden silence was overwhelming, and some of our soldiers, habituated to the constant din of fighting, couldn't stand it. The only time there was silence during the battle was just before an enemy attack. Men were shooting rifles, letting off grenades, just to relieve the tension.

That afternoon, a mass of demoralized German prisoners was marched down to the Volga. Mark Slavin witnessed the spectacle:

> We knew the enemy intended to hold a victory parade on the banks of the Volga when they captured the city. So great had their confidence been that – typically – quite detailed plans had been drawn up for this. So we decided to oblige them. We lined them up in proper military order and a large group of our soldiers gathered to watch. For a moment there was absolute silence.

Alexander Fortov remembered that moment:

> There were thousands of Germans out on the ice. And only about ten Russian soldiers were supervising them. We couldn't believe

that such a formidable fighting force had been reduced to this ragged band. They scarcely looked human any more.

The dishevelled German remnants were given the order 'March!' As the defeated army began to move, stumbling and slipping on the ice, there were a few jeers and whistles.

'Then', as Mark Slavin recalled,

all our soldiers began to sing. We sang the Russian songs which helped to sustain us when all seemed hopeless. I took out my notebook – I was intending to write a short piece for our divisional newspaper. But I couldn't describe the scene before me. Instead, I found myself writing one sentence, again and again: 'Glorious Stalingrad is free!'

Conclusion

The Mamaev Kurgan

Two months after their victory at Stalingrad, the remnants of the 62nd Army reformed as the 8th Guards Army. Under the command of Chuikov they continued to fight the Germans, driving them back towards Berlin. On 2 May 1945 they reached the Reichstag itself – symbol of Hitler's regime. 'We had missed out on the surrender of Paulus, so it was hugely important when our army received the surrender of Berlin', said Mereshko. He was present in the room when the Nazi capitulation took place.

Stalingrad was the proving ground for a remarkable army. The street-fighting tactics it developed and perfected are now studied throughout the world. But what the defenders achieved transcended straightforward explanation. By all accepted analysis of military probability, it was impossible for the Russians to have held the city. 'It was almost supernatural', said Mereshko, simply and directly.

'After the battle ended the guys in my company turned to the Bible', said Alexander Fortov. 'We began to read sections of the Old Testament to each other. We were all atheists and communists, but those passages really spoke to us. It was as if someone really understood what we had gone through.'

It has been estimated that by the second half of October 1942 more than 75 per cent of Stalingrad's defenders – the equivalent of nine divisions – were destroyed, yet still the survivors continued to resist. Richard Overy, in *Russia's War*, put it simply: 'How the Red Army survived defies military explanation'. As Geoffrey Roberts emphasized in *Victory at Stalingrad*: 'Beyond tactics, fire power and force ratios, was the role played by morale, psychology and the human spirit.'

At the heart of this story lies the power of inspirational leadership. 'Stalingrad was a smithy for commanders', said Mereshko, 'and many of those who distinguished themselves in the battle went on to lead armies in their own right.' Today many of those commanders are buried on the Mamaev Kurgan, the hill that dominated the battle for the city. Their leader, Vasily Chuikov, was the first to choose it for his resting place. On 27 July 1981, during his last illness, he made an alteration to his will, declaring:

248

I wish to be buried at the Mamaev Kurgan, where I organized my first command post. Where you can hear the roar of the Volga waves, the sound of gun shot and feel the agony of Stalingrad's ruins. Here lie buried many of the soldiers that I commanded. Warriors of the Soviet Union – follow the example of the defenders of Stalingrad, and victory will be yours.

Somehow, in the burning hell that was Stalingrad, Chuikov created an army able to withstand everything the Germans threw at it. Their remarkable story has struggled hard to come to life, caught between the propagandist clichés of the communist state – insinuating everybody at Stalingrad was heroic, and that the city would never have fallen to the enemy – and Western cynicism, which believes that Red Army heroism was only created at the barrel of a gun. Neither suffices. This terrible fight took Chuikov and his troops to the very limits of human endurance, and their testimony, now finally uncovered, possesses a universal significance and power.

Those soldiers reached beneath deep despair and self-doubt and found a near-impregnable strength and resilience. Their shared faith was forged in the fire of battle – and they stood their ground at the last defence line, 200 metres from the Volga, when there was nowhere else to go.

'I remember sorting through my father's papers after his death' said Alexander Chuikov.

I came across a small, hand-written prayer and immediately recognized his writing. The paper was old and creased, the ink faded. The scrap of paper would have been folded, and kept as a talisman. My father – a committed communist – never spoke about it. But I knew from other members of the family that he carried it with him during the war.

The prayer read as follows: 'O Powerful One! The one who can turn night into day, and rough soil into a garden of flowers. Make light everything that is hard for me – and help me.'

Alexander Chuikov looked at me, and then said: 'That is how we were defending Stalingrad.'

Mist Over the Volga

I am standing on a steep bank
The mist hangs over the Volga like thick smoke
And through this smoke, the dark green and blue river is
    looking at me.

My native land has been kind to me
But it is the beginning of the road that I remember
Here and now – vibrant and alive
The soldiers' fires are smoking
And even the mist becomes smoke.

Once I had it
I had that smoke
It soaked right through me
And I was full with it for the rest of my life.

And here I am, standing on this fragile bank
Standing as if I am curved in time
Through the mist, the green and blue river is looking at me.

*Mikhail Borisov (Quoted, with permission of the author, from
his anthology* The Image of the Motherland*)*

62nd Army Order of Battle
– 1 November 1942

Commander of 62nd Army: Lieutenant-General Vasily Chuikov
Chief of Staff: Major-General Nikolai Krylov

Rifle Divisions
13th Guards: General Alexander Rodimtsev
35th Guards: Colonel Dubyanski
37th Guards: General Viktor Zholudev
39th Guards: Major-General Stephan Guriev
45th: Lieutenant-Colonel Vasily Sokolov
95th: Colonel Vasily Gorishny
112th: Colonel Yermolkin
138th: Colonel Ivan Lyudnikov
193rd: General Feodor Smekhotvorov
284th: Colonel Nikolai Batyuk
308th: Colonel Leonti Gurtiev

Marine Infantry Brigade
92nd, incorporating remnants of 42nd: Commissar Nikitin (Colonel Tarasov abandoned brigade on 22 Sept., subsequently court-martialled; Major Samodai court-martialled for failing to form emergency defence line on night of 14 Oct.).

Gorokhov's 'Northern Group' – Special Brigades
115th: Colonel K M Andryushenko
124th: Colonel Seymon Gorokhov
149th: Lieutenant-Colonel V A Bolvinov (killed 2 Nov. 1942); Major I Durnev

Remnants of Tank Brigades: Lieutenant-Colonel M G Weinrub

List of Veterans

Red Army veteran testimony forms the engine room of this book. Such material has to be used with caution, as some eye-witness accounts are unreliable, and in certain cases purely imaginary. I have worked closely with veterans' associations to choose trustworthy witnesses, and whenever possible have checked salient details against the combat journals of their divisions. But there is no substitute for the personal experiences of these remarkable soldiers, and the list details those I have interviewed. I have concentrated largely on the 62nd Army in an effort to recreate the spirit of Stalingrad's defenders. Many of these veterans have given days of their time to this project, and allowed me access to rare written articles and unit histories. Working with these extraordinary men and women has been a life-enhancing experience. With each passing year there are less and less of them. I salute their courage.

BARYKIN, IVAN A battalion commander in the 154th Marine Brigade, he fought in the defence of the Aksai river in August 1942, and saw Chuikov making the first award of the recently revived Order of Alexander Nevsky.

BELITSKAYA, EVDOKIA A nurse in the 64th Army, she was twice commended by General Shumilov for her bravery. She witnessed the surrender of Paulus at the 64th Army HQ on 31 January 1943. Evdokia was one of a first-aid team of forty medical staff put on stand-by because of a fear that the Germans would launch a bombing strike on the HQ, to prevent the Red Army capturing Paulus alive.

BORCHEV, MIKHAIL Borchev commanded a Katyusha unit at Stalingrad at the age of 19. His older brother Ivan was on Chuikov's staff. Borchev's Katyushas, mounted on the backs of trucks, were used in the defence of the factories – and often less than 800 metres from the German front line. He rose rapidly up the ranks of the Red Army, becoming an expert in the use of rocket weaponry, finally retiring as a Major-General.

BORISOV, MIKHAIL Borisov commanded an artillery unit on the retreat from Kharkov, and later fought on the Don bridgehead. In 1943 he was made a Hero of the Soviet Union for his courage during the battle of Kursk. A war poet, Mikhail has kindly given me permission to quote from his anthology, *The Image of the Motherland*.

DALLAKIAN, GAMLET He served on the staff of the Stalingrad Front under Yeremenko – and was responsible for laying telephone cable to maintain communication with the 62nd Army. He was wounded in Stalingrad at the end of September 1942. He recuperated in hospital next to Viktor Nekrasov. The two men became close friends and Dallakian helped edit Nekrasov's novel, *Front-Line Stalingrad*. (Nekrasov was a company commander in Batyuk's 284th Division, and wrote the book about the extraordinary comradeship which existed amongst Stalingrad's defenders. Veterans regard *Front-Line Stalingrad* as the best evocation of the spirit of their army.)

FAUSTOVA, MARIA A radio operator in 131st Division (part of the ill-fated First Tank Army) during retreat from Don – her communications unit was incorporated into the 62nd Army on 12 September 1942. The following day the HQ's communications completely broke down and she witnessed Chuikov, in a state of absolute frustration, striking a NKVD officer. Maria is Secretary of the 62nd Army Veterans' Council and married to Stalingrad veteran Alexander Voronov.

FORTOV, ALEXANDER An artillery commander in the 112th Division, he fought on the steppe, the Mamaev Kurgan and then at the gates of the Tractor Factory, before being transferred to Gorokhov's command in Spartanovka. 'It was at Stalingrad that our soldiers discovered how to stand up to the enemy', Fortov said. 'Often, battalions or smaller units were encircled within the city, unable to receive any orders. The Germans expected resistance to collapse, but we appointed our own commanders and worked out what to do. One principle became a law for us: we would hold our ground.'

GOROKHOV, VASILY Gorokhov fought on the Mamaev Kurgan with Batyuk's 284th Division. 'The bombing was terrible', he recalled, 'and the hill was permanently shrouded in smoke. But we could all see the position of Chuikov's HQ – there was a huge pall of burning oil hanging above it. When we heard, to our amazement, that they were hanging on in there, our soldiers made a promise: we would not give up the Kurgan, whatever happened.'

GUREVITZ, LEONID A communications officer in 34th Regiment of 13th Guards Division, Gurevitz recalled the terrible vulnerability of telephone cable in the city fighting: 'When the enemy launched an attack our cable was chopped into pieces as quickly as if you were cutting noodles on the kitchen table.'

ISAIVEYNA, LYUBOV Isaiveyna was one of the nurses responsible for organizing the evacuation of the wounded from the 62nd Crossing in October

1942. She believed it was vital that the Army HQ remained in the thick of the fighting and, like so many others, spoke of 'a remarkable sense of equality' amongst Stalingrad's defenders.

IVANIKIN, MARK A colonel and commander of a Katyusha unit at Stalingrad.

IVANOV, GEORGI A junior lieutenant and platoon commander in the 344th Regiment of Lyudnikov's 138th Division. When Lyudnikov's troops were being pulverized by low-level bombing, Ivanov was one of those Red Army soldiers who adapted an anti-tank rifle, mounting it on a wheel, in an attempt to bring down enemy planes. Chuikov loved this kind of ingenuity but it was a truly desperate measure. 'The key was to anticipate when the pilot would reach the end of his dive', Ivanov said, 'then guess and shoot.'

KALMYKOVA, TAMARA A communications officer with the 64th Army to the south of Stalingrad, she was wounded in November 1942.

KAZARIN, KONSTANTIN A company commander in the 339th Regiment of Gurtiev's 308th Division, defending the Barrikady Factory in October 1942: 'The Germans brought up flamethrowing tanks and fired at point-blank range. Somehow, we kept on fighting.' For Kazarin, the power of the ordeal took months to assimilate: 'I remember at Bryansk, in August 1943, a house was on fire and a woman was screaming "My baby is inside!" Soldiers stood by, unable to react: the heat was simply too intense. But a group of us – veterans of the Barrikady – plunged into the flames and rescued that little girl. Afterwards, I looked around at my mates: our uniforms were still smoking and every one of us had burns. Only then did I realize – this was the spirit of Stalingrad.'

KISELYOV, VLADIMIR A company commander in the 39th Regiment of 13th Guards Division, he participated in the storming of the Mamaev Kurgan on 16 September 1942: 'So many years have passed, and it is still agonizing to remember it', Kiselyov said. 'We were pushing through a burning wall of fire – struggling to breathe in the constant smoke. Later, when I was wounded and taken to a military hospital, it took months to get rid of the black dirt of Stalingrad.'

KOZLOV, ANATOLY He fought in First Tank Army during retreat in summer of 1942, and was then transferred to 13th Guards during the city fighting. Anatoly is now Chairman of the Volgograd Veterans' Association.

KURAPATOV, EVGENY A lieutenant in the 196th Division of the 62nd Army, in charge of procuring supplies. He fought his way out of encirclement in August 1942, and was then stationed in downtown Stalingrad, before being transferred to Gorokhov's northern group in September. The division, reduced to a couple of hundred men, was subsequently withdrawn from the Front. Evgeny now heads the Veterans' Council of the 62nd Army.

MERESHKO, ANATOLY As a young, 20-year-old lieutenant, Mereshko led a company of cadets during the summer retreat of 1942, and subsequently was promoted to the HQ staff of the 62nd Army, becoming 'officer for special tasks', and working directly under Chuikov and Krylov. He fought all the way through to Berlin and witnessed the German surrender of the city on 2 May 1945. After the war he rose to become a Colonel-General and Deputy Commander of the Warsaw Pact. Anatoly Mereshko has travelled with me round Stalingrad's battle sites, and his remarkable testimony forms the narrative spine of the book.

MIKOYAN, STEPHAN Son of Politburo member Anastas Mikoyan, he grew up in the Kremlin compound with Stalin's children and went to flying school with Stalin's son, Vasily. Responsible for protection of Baku oilfields in summer of 1942, at the time of the German advance on Stalingrad he conducted secret aerial reconnaissance on the mobilization of the Turkish army and its incursions across the Soviet border, reporting directly to Molotov. Both Stalin and Molotov believed Turkey would enter the war as an ally of Germany if Stalingrad fell.

MIRZOYAN, SUREN Mirzoyan served as private with 33rd Guards Division of 62nd Army on the retreat to Stalingrad, and then joined the 13th Guards as a storm group fighter during the city battle. Suren still vividly recalls the savagery of hand-to-hand combat: 'After Stalingrad I am no longer afraid', he said simply.

POKHODYNA, LEONID A company commander in 253rd Regiment of 45th Guards Division, he fought in the Red October Factory and was wounded there in mid-January 1943. He said of the last desperate German assault on 11 November 1942: 'We were motivated by one simple thought – we would not let the enemy reach the Volga.'

POTANSKI, GEORGI A reconnaissance and artillery spotter from 13th Guards Division, Potanski is one of only two surviving members of Pavlov's House. He said of Pavlov: 'He was my fighting buddy – brave, straightforward and honest – but there were many others like him in our garrison who haven't entered the history books: it was the spirit of comradeship which made our force so strong.'

PSTYGO, IVAN A lieutenant in the Red Army's 8th Air Fleet, he was ordered by Rodimtsev to provide air cover for the daylight crossing on 14 September

1942. After the war, Pstygo became an air marshal and deputy commander of the Soviet Air Force.

RABINOVICH, MIKHAIL A commander of an artillery unit on Zaitsevski Island, he also became an artillery spotter with Smekhotvorov's 193rd Division in the fighting in the Red October settlement in early October 1942. On 15 October he was summoned to 62nd Army HQ and ordered by Chuikov to call in an artillery strike on the Army command post in the event of a German breakthrough.

RAKITSKY, ALEXANDER Rakitsky was head of special operations in the 37th Guards Division. He is the only surviving witness to the crucial army council meeting of 14 October 1942.

SCHYLAEV, IVAN Schylaev was an artillery commander in 39th Regiment of 13th Guards Division during the battle of Stalingrad, and subsequently became historian and founder of the 13th Guards Division Museum. He said of the September fighting: 'Its sheer ferocity was quite unbelievable – the German attacks were like endless waves crashing against us: smoke, dust, a constant roaring sound and a sun you could hardly see.'

SEREBRYAKOV, MIKHAIL A reconnaissance officer in the 57th Army, he fought his way into southern Stalingrad in January 1943, and witnessed the recapture of the grain elevator.

SHATRAVKO, FEODOR He was commander of the 21st tank battalion – a training battalion stationed in Stalingrad in August 1942. He was transferred to Gorokhov's 124th Brigade in Spartanovka at the beginning of September, and subsequently wounded in a tank battle at Latoshinka.

SLAVIN, MARK A 19-year-old private in Sokolov's 45th Division, he fought in Stalingrad from the beginning of November 1942 to the end of the battle. A regular contributor to the divisional newspaper, Slavin was particularly interested in the development of heroism amongst Red Army soldiers during the battle. He subsequently became a war journalist, travelling with Vasily Grossman.

SPIRIDINOV, VALENTIN Spiridinov commanded an anti-aircraft unit in Stalingrad during the German bombing raid of 23 August 1942, and was then transferred to the 1078th artillery regiment of 62nd Army. He witnessed the daylight crossing of the Volga by the leading detachments of the 13th Guards on 14 September.

TUROV, VLADIMIR Turov was a battalion commander in Andryushenko's 115th Brigade in the Orlovka salient.

VORONOV, ALEXANDER A commander of the 617th Artillery Regiment, incorporated into the 13th Guards Division. Alexander, and his wife Maria Faustova, later became close friends of General Alexander Rodimtsev.

ZACHAROV, SERGEI Zacharov was a company commander in the 1045th Regiment of Batyuk's 284th Division. A skilled storm group fighter, he perfected a technique – using explosives – to break through to the upper levels of a house when the enemy held the staircase. It subsequently became standard throughout the 62nd Army and brought him to the notice of Chuikov. Chuikov asked Zacharov to train political officers in street-fighting techniques, and the two men subsequently became friends.

ZOLOTOVTSEV, GEORGI A cartographer at the 13th Guards HQ, he witnessed the German flooding of the conduit pipe on 22 September 1942. In December he worked out a system of mapping enemy strongpoints which became standard amongst 62nd Army reconnaissance units when preparing storm group attacks.

Further Veteran Testimony

My work with veterans has been greatly assisted by Laurence Rees and his producer on *War of the Century*, Martina Balazova, who have kindly made available the full transcripts of their interviews for the series. In the case of Albert Burkovski, who was adopted as a 14-year-old 'son of the regiment' by the 13th Guards, I have drawn extensively on this material, as Burkovski was too ill to be interviewed fully. It has also been very helpful in the cases of Tamara Kalmykova, Valentina Krutova and Suren Mirzoyan, and as a useful frame of reference when working with Anatoly Mereshko.

Artem Drabkin, compiler of the important collection of Red Army veteran testimony 'I Remember', provided me with additional interview material on Georgi Potanski. My translator and interpreter Lena Yakovleva did the same with Alexei Voloshin, Leonid Gurevitz and Vladimir Kiselyov. Other useful pieces of testimony have been found on the Voice of Russia website (battle of Stalingrad): www.vor.ru/Stalingrad.

Russian Ministry of Defence Archive, Podolsk

I am grateful to Sergei Petrunin for his help obtaining the following:

> 62nd Army war diary
> Divisional combat journals: 13th Guards; 37th Guards; 42nd
>   Special Brigade; 112th Division; 138th Division; 284th
>   Division: 308th Division.
> Regimental combat journals: 883rd Regiment of 193rd Division.
> Combat maps and instructions: 13th Guards; 37th Guards, 39th
>   Guards; 45th Division; 95th Division; 112th Division; 284th
>   Division.

Corresponding German Material

I am grateful to Jason Mark for checking through the German 6th Army war diary and divisional records. On Zaitsev's sniper opponent Jason declares emphatically: 'German records of officer casualties do not show either a Koenig or a "SS Colonel Thorwald" – and the death of such a high-ranking officer would certainly have been noted.' Jason also confirms that the 79th Infantry Division, which on 14 October 1942 was standing by on the Don – ready to enter Stalingrad – was not ordered into the city by Paulus until 17 October. The German commander's characteristic hesitation let slip a tremendous opportunity to finish off the battle.

Notes

Introduction

The significance of Stalingrad as a turning point in history remains a subject of much academic discussion, but Vasily Grossman, who was there at the time, wrote powerfully in *Life and Fate*: 'Every epoch has its own capital city – a city that embodies its will and soul. For several months of the Second World War this city was Stalingrad. The thoughts and passions of humanity were centred on it.' The introduction, which attempts to convey the particular experience of Russia's 62nd Army during the battle, is drawn from veteran testimony, particularly Anatoly Mereshko, and Vasily Chuikov's personal papers, photographs and reminiscences – kindly made available by his son Alexander. I owe the quotation from Mao Tse-Tung to Albert Axell. Specific examples of heroism and cowardice are taken from Sergei Kozyakin, *Their Names Live in our Memory* (Moscow, 1995).

Chapter One

I owe to the Feldgrau website (www.feldgrau.net) a useful translation of Herbert Selle's original 1956 article 'The German Sixth Army on its Way to Catastrophe'. The horror of the retreat is conveyed in Viktor Nekrasov's *Front-Line Stalingrad*. Military details are taken from Anatoly Mereshko's article on 'The 62nd (8th Guards) Army', in *Soldiers of the Twentieth Century* (Moscow, 2003). Vital NKVD documents, letters of soldiers and other important material have been gathered in *Stalingrad Epoch: Documents Declassified by the Federal Security Service of the Russian Federation* (Moscow, 2000). I am grateful to Anatoly Kozlov for drawing this source to my attention and discussing it with me. Kozlov, along with many other veterans emphasizes the psychological effect of constant retreat, and the desperation felt by ordinary soldiers: 'People today cannot imagine what it was like. We all thought that we had been condemned to death. As we approached Stalingrad we believed there were three options open to us – to be killed, captured or go mad.' Further material is found in Alexander Fortov's 'Memories of an artillery unit commander', in

Recollections of the 149th Brigade (Tomsk, 2002). For an excellent discussion of Stalin's Order 227, see Geoffrey Roberts, *Victory at Stalingrad* (London, 2002).

Chapter Two

To get a sense of the city before, during and after the conflagration, see the excellent collection of photographs and commentary in: *Tsaritsyn – Stalingrad – Volgograd* (Volgograd, 2000). The suffering of the city and its population is a much neglected topic, which has now been thoroughly examined by Sean Kearney in his forthcoming book, *City of Tears*. The inadequacies of the city's defence system are made clear in Mereshko's '62nd (8th Guards) Army', by veteran testimony and the recently published material in *Stalingrad Epoch*. Gamlet Dallakian's descriptions of the mood of the Stalingrad Front command have been supplemented with his article 'The Communication System at Stalingrad', in B S Abalihin (ed.), *The Stalingrad Battle* (Volgograd, 1994) and his 2001 personal memoir.

Chapter Three

This portrait of the 62nd Army's extraordinary commander has benefited from the advice of Anatoly Mereshko and his article on Chuikov in *Soldiers of the Twentieth Century*, and the personal papers kindly made available by Alexander Chuikov, which have been used alongside Vasily Chuikov's written memoir, *The Beginning of the Road* (MacGibbon & Kee, 1963). I disagree with the assessment of Chuikov's military career made by Richard Woff in H shukman (ed.), *Stalin's Generals* (Weidenfeld and Nicolson, 1993), which wrongly puts him in command of the 9th Army from the start of the Finnish campaign. Antony Beevor's *Stalingrad* portrays Chuikov as a brutal general who needlessly threw away men's lives. In contrast, I have tried to put the veterans' view. Georgi Potanski emphasized: 'Chuikov was tough but we really respected him. Soldiers can always tell whether a punishment is fair or not, and when a commander makes bad decisions and wastes lives unnecessarily.' There is an excellent new edition of Chuikov's *Mission to China* (East Bridge, 2004) by David. P. Barrett.

Chapter Four

This chapter has been greatly assisted by Ivan Schylaev, who provided me with the invaluable testimony of NKVD officer Ivan Yerofeyev. Additional material has been provided by Alexander Chuikov, Natalia Rodimsteva and Anatoly Mereshko. Background detail is from the 62nd Army war diary and the combat journal of the 42nd Brigade. For Grossman's comments see *A Writer at War: Vasily Grossman with the Red Army 1941–1945*, ed.Antony Beevor and Luba Vinogradova (Harvill, 2005).

Chapter Five

Once again, Ivan Schylaev has guided the shape of this chapter, generously offering me material from his own researches, including a transcript of his interview with Anton Dragan. Further information has been drawn from the 13th Guards combat journal, Samchuk's divisional history (made available to me, in translation, by Jason Mark) and Mereshko's 'The 62nd (8th Guards) Army'. Natalia Rodimtseva has kindly put me in touch with other 13th Guards veterans.

Chapter Six

Georgi Potanski, one of the last surviving members of Pavlov's House, has spent many hours sharing with me the real experience of this remarkable house garrison. I am very grateful to Artem Drabkin of *The Russian Battlefield* website for putting me in touch with him. Ivan Schylaev and Natalia Rodimtseva have given me additional material.

Chapter Seven

The outline of this chapter is derived from the experience of Anatoly Mereshko, who discussed Panikakha's heroism with the 193rd Division's commander, General Feodor Smekhotvorov, at the time of the battle, and Smekhotvorov's own writings, kindly made available to me by Jason Mark. The crucial background material is provided by the 883rd Regiment's combat journal. Testimony from 193rd Division veterans is rare, but Viktor Kartashev's account of fighting in the Red October Factory can now be found in Jonathan Bastable's *Voices from Stalingrad*.

Chapter Eight

I owe the identification of Alexander Kalentiev, and access to his letters and other additional material, to the kindness of Svetlana Novikova, curator of the Museum of the 62nd Army, Leninstev, Moscow. The 'bank of revenge' is from Sergei Kozyakin's interviews with snipers, reproduced in *Their Names Live in our Memory*. Mereshko makes clear Chuikov's vital role in encouraging this mass movement. The relatively small proportion of Red Army soldiers who were members of the communist party is shown in David M. Glantz and Jonathan House, *When Titans Clashed. How the Red Army Stopped Hitler*. Zaitsev's original 1942 interview is in the 2003 edition of *Notes of a Sniper*. Additional details on the spread of 'sniperism' are taken from the combat journals of the 13th Guards and 284th Divisions.

Chapter Nine

The importance of the fighting in the Orlovka settlement is shown by the remarkable testimony of Vladimir Turov. Alexander Rakitsky has guided me through the attack on the Tractor Factory, and also drawn to my attention to additional material on the 37th Guards in his article, 'We Stood to the Death', in a new veteran compilation, *We Kept to our Oath* (Moscow, 2005). Additional material has been drawn from the 62nd Army war diary and the combat journal of the 37th Guards, and Jason Mark has sent me extracts from their divisional history. The devastating German bombing tactics are described in Joel Hayward, *Stopped at Stalingrad: The Luftwaffe and Hitler's Defeat in the East, 1942–43*. Alexander Fortov kindly took me round the site of the 112th Division's last stand. His testimony has been used alongside the 112th Division's combat journal. The recently printed transcripts of Chuikov's astonishing requests to Stalingrad Front on 14 and 15 October 1942 have been made available by Jason Mark. Vasily Chuikov's conversation with his brother Feodor has been relayed by Alexander Chuikov and Mikhail Rabinovich's testimony corroborates this desperate moment in Stalingrad's defence.

Chapter Ten

Most of Grossman's 'In the Line of the Main Attack' was published by Alexander Werth in his *The Year of Stalingrad* (Hamish Hamilton, 1946), but extracts from Grossman's notes for the article can now be found in *Writer at*

War: Vasily Grossman and the Red Army. Kazarin's testimony has been supplemented by material from the 308th Division's combat journal. The core of this chapter is inspired by reminiscences of army life provided by Anatoly Mereshko. Material on the defence of the Red October Factory is drawn from Sergei Kozyakin, *Their Names Live in our Memory*.

Chapter Eleven

I owe Valentina's postcard of congratulation to Alexander Chuikov. Lyudnikov describes his welcome reception in *Two Hundred Days of Fire*. The first major storm group successes were on 3 December 1942, when the House of Railway Workers and the L-Shaped House were finally recaptured from the Germans. 'We had to fight for every room', the 13th Guards combat journal noted bluntly. Some excellent testimony on the storming of the L-Shaped House has been gathered in Jonathan Bastable's *Voices from Stalingrad*. Further military details are from the combat journals of the 138th and 284th Divisions.

Conclusion

Material on Chuikov's last will and the talisman prayer has been provided by Alexander Chuikov. The last soldiers of the 62nd Army are now passing away. The visit of Mereshko, Kurapatov and other veterans to the Mamaev Kurgan on 2 February 2006 was featured in an article in *Evening Moscow*: 'Colonel-General Mereshko stepped towards the grave of Marshal Chuikov – buried on the Mamaev Kurgan in Volgograd – and bowed his head. His comrades-in-arms joined him, and for a moment there was silence. Then Mereshko spoke quietly: "Hello, Commander of the Army. Your fighters stand with you."'

Further Reading

Albert Axell, *Russia's Heroes* (Constable, 2001)

Jonathan Bastable, *Voices from Stalingrad* (David & Charles, 2006)

Antony Beevor, *Stalingrad* (Penguin, 1998)

Antony Beevor and Luba Vinogradova, *A Writer at War: Vasily Grossman with the Red Army, 1941–1945* (Harvill, 2005)

Vasily Chuikov, *The Beginning of the Road* (MacGibbon & Kee, 1963)

Alan Clark, *Barbarossa* (Cassell, 1965)

William Craig, *Enemy at the Gates* (Penguin, 1973)

John Erickson, *The Road to Stalingrad* (Weidenfeld & Nicolson, 1975)

Will Fowler, *Stalingrad: The Vital Seven Days* (Spellmont, 2005)

David M Glantz and Jonathan House, *When Titans Clashed: How the Red Army Stopped Hitler* (University of Kansas, 1995)

Vasily Grossman, *Life and Fate* (Harvill, 1980)

Joel Hayward, *Stopped at Stalingrad: The Luftwaffe and Hitler's Defeat in the East* (University of Kansas, 1998)

Eric von Manstein, *Lost Victories* (Zenith Press, 2004)

Jason D Mark, *Island of Fire* (Southwood Press, 2006)

Catherine Merridale, *Ivan's War: The Red Army 1939–45* (Faber & Faber, 2005)

Viktor Nekrasov, *Front-Line Stalingrad* (Fontana, 1964)

Richard Overy, *Russia's War* (Penguin, 1997)

Laurence Rees, *War of the Century* (BBC Worldwide, 1999)

Geoffrey Roberts, *Victory at Stalingrad* (Longman, 2002)

Two Hundred Days of Fire: Accounts by Participants and Witnesses of the Battle of Stalingrad (Moscow, Progress Publishers, 1970)

Stephen Walsh, *Stalingrad 1942–1943: The Infernal Cauldron* (Simon & Schuster, 2000)

Alexander Werth, *The Year of Stalingrad* (Hamish Hamilton, 1946)

Hans J Wijers, *Stalingrad: The Battle for the Factories* (Brummen, 2003)

Vasily Zaitsev, *Notes of a Sniper* (Press Inc., 2003)

Index